Young People, Faith & Mental Challenges

Finding Inner Peace by Blending Christian Faith and Mental Health in Everyday Life

By
Dr Francis Labinjo
NHS Consultant Psychiatrist
and Committed Christian

16 East Croft House, 86 Northolt Road,
Harrow, England, HA2 0ER,
United Kingdom

Copyright © 2025 Dr Francis Labinjo

ISBN (Paperback)
ISBN (Hardback)

All rights reserved

Cover Design by London Book Publisher

No part of this publication may be reproduced, stored in a retrieval system, copied in any form or by any means, electronic, mechanical, photocopying, recording or otherwise transmitted without written permission from the publisher.

You must not circulate this book in any format. Under no circumstances will any blame or legal responsibility be held against the publisher, or author, for any damages, reparation, or monetary loss due to the information contained within this book, either directly or indirectly.

For more information, visit: www.londonbookpublisher.co.uk

Faith is taking the first step even when you don't see the whole staircase.
– *Dr Martin Luther King Jr.*

Table of Contents

The Oxford Dictionary's Definition of Faith — 1

Introduction to Faith and Mental Health — 2

1 — 4
Dealing with Doubt

2 — 44
Faith Communities and Support Systems

3 — 50
Faith-Based Programs and Resources

4 — 88
Stress and Burnout

5 — 108
Anxiety and Depression

6 — 142
The Intricate Relationship Between Faith and Mental Health

7 — 158
Cultural and Spiritual Sensitivity

8 — 201
Future Directions

9 — 209
Mental Health Stigma

10	**233**
BLENDING MENTAL HEALTH PRACTICES WITH SPIRITUAL CARE	
11	**258**
NEURODIVERGENCE AND FAITH - ADHD, AUTISM	
12	**390**
SUICIDE	
FROM A CAREGIVER MOTHER	**471**
GLOSSARY	**474**
REFERENCES	**478**

The Oxford Dictionary's Definition of Faith

noun

[uncountable] trust in somebody's ability or knowledge; trust that somebody/something will do what has been promised

- *It could become the market leader if the company can retain its customers' faith.*
- Faith in somebody/something. *I have faith in you, and I know you'll do well.*
- *We've lost faith in the government's promises.*
- *Her friend's kindness has restored her faith in human nature.*
- *I wouldn't put too much faith in what she says.*
- *He has blind faith* (= unreasonable trust) *in doctors' ability to find a cure.*

Introduction to Faith and Mental Health

DEFINE THE INTERSECTION OF FAITH AND MENTAL HEALTH AND EXPLAIN WHY EXPLORING THIS CONNECTION IS IMPORTANT.

The Meaning of Faith

Religious faith typically includes belief in a higher power, deity, or sacred force that is often beyond human understanding.

1. **Trust and Commitment**: It encompasses trust in the teachings and tenets of a religion and a commitment to living according to those principles.

2. **Spiritual Experience**: Faith often involves personal spiritual experiences and feelings that reinforce belief and provide a sense of connection to the divine.

3. **Community and Tradition**: For many, religious faith is accompanied by participation in a community of believers and adherence to religious traditions and rituals.

4. **Moral and Ethical Guidance**: Faith can also guide individuals in making moral and ethical decisions, providing a framework for understanding right and wrong.

5. **Hope and Meaning**: It provides hope and meaning in life, offering answers to existential questions and a sense of purpose.

Religious faith does not require empirical proof or scientific validation, as it is often viewed as a deeply personal and subjective experience. It varies greatly among individuals and religious traditions, each with unique beliefs, practices, and interpretations.

Faith in the Bible

The Bible, particularly the New Testament, offers a rich discourse on the concept of faith. Here are some important aspects of faith according to the Bible:

1. **Faith as Belief and Trust**: Faith in the Bible often means complete trust and confidence in God and His promises. It is about believing in God's character and His word. *"Now faith is confidence in what we hope for and assurance about what we do not see." – Hebrews 11:1*

2. **Faith and Salvation**: Faith is central to salvation in Christian doctrine. Belief in Jesus Christ as Lord and Saviour is emphasised as the path to eternal life. *"For it is by grace you have been saved, through faith—and this is not from yourselves, it is the gift of God." – Ephesians 2:8*

3. **Faith and Works**: While faith is crucial, it is also often coupled with action. True faith results in deeds that reflect that belief. *"In the same way, faith by itself, if it is not accompanied by action, is dead." – James 2:17*

4. **Faith's Ability to Overcome**: The Bible presents faith as a powerful force that can overcome obstacles, doubts, and fears. It is through faith that believers can access God's power. *"Truly I tell you, if you have faith as small as a mustard seed, you can say to this mountain, 'Move from here to there,' and it will move. Nothing will be impossible for you." – Matthew 17:20*

5. **Faith as a Journey**: Faith is presented as a journey of growth and perseverance, requiring believers to trust God amidst trials and uncertainties. *"Consider it pure joy, my brothers and sisters, whenever you face trials of many kinds, because you know that the testing of your faith produces perseverance." – James 1:2–3*

1

DEALING WITH DOUBT

ADDRESSING THE CRISIS OF FAITH THAT CAN ACCOMPANY MENTAL HEALTH STRUGGLES

Mental Health

I have used the term *"mental health challenge"* as, in my professional opinion and experience, it is more empowering and less stigmatising to the person experiencing such difficulties. It normalises their experience and promotes the idea of resilience and support. Our language can influence how individuals perceive their mental health and whether they seek help, so choosing inclusive and supportive terminology is crucial.

The Author

I have practised my medical profession for over four decades and have continually strived to incorporate my Christian faith into my expertise as a psychiatrist. I must stress that my experiences are mostly personal, although some patients—whether Christian or Muslim—whose faith beliefs are strong, have either been directly assisted or signposted to faith-based support as part of an integrated, holistic approach.

I do not recommend replacing the advice or role of mental health professionals with faith alone. Incorporating faith is scriptural, as the expertise of professionals has been placed at our disposal by God. It is not an either-or situation, but a combined effort to restore wellness.

There have been times when I have had suicidal thoughts—some intense. Faith brought me through. I came close to completing a suicidal act after my divorce, at a train station. On another occasion, I attempted to strangle myself with my tie. I have spoken to dozens of patients whose suicidal actions were discovered purely by accident. When interviewed, most did not actually want to end their lives.

To the Reader

I invite you to explore a fascinating topic: the intersection of faith and mental health. It's about how spiritual beliefs and practices can support mental well-being in communities.

Faith can provide individuals with a strong sense of hope, purpose, and meaning—elements that are crucial for mental health. Many people find that their faith offers comfort during tough times, acting as a supportive framework when facing challenges. This emotional and spiritual support can be a valuable component of mental health resilience.

Incorporating faith-based perspectives can enhance therapeutic approaches. It helps in understanding diverse cultural backgrounds and respecting individual values. Faith communities often offer a sense of belonging and support, which can be vital for those feeling isolated or struggling.

Moreover, many religious communities engage in charitable activities and provide resources and services to those in need. These efforts significantly contribute to community mental health initiatives by offering additional support systems.

The key is open dialogue—collaboration between mental health professionals and faith leaders to create a holistic support system. This partnership can help break stigma, facilitate understanding, and promote collective well-being. It is also about time!

HISTORICAL PERSPECTIVES: HOW RELIGIOUS TRADITIONS HAVE APPROACHED MENTAL HEALTH

The Challenges of Writing This Book

As a faith-led psychiatrist, writing this book offers me unique insights, but there are both advantages and potential drawbacks I have had to consider.

My Unique Perspective: Combining faith and psychiatry provides me with a comprehensive approach to mental health, addressing both spiritual and psychological needs. I have been a born-again Christian for over two decades and a consultant psychiatrist for around the same period. I have constantly considered the role of faith in my clinical practice and explored how best to serve my patients. For eight years, I also served as the minister for care and social responsibility for my church—the New Testament Church of God, Brixton, South London.

Caveat: Individuals should consult healthcare providers to develop a comprehensive treatment plan that integrates faith where appropriate, alongside other treatment modalities. Balancing faith with medical treatment and professional counselling can lead to a more effective and sustained recovery.

Holistic Approach: Over the past 20 years, I have explored ways to integrate spiritual beliefs with mental health practices, offering a more rounded approach to healing and well-being. I am a member of the Spirituality and Psychiatry Special Interest Group (SIG) of the Royal College of Psychiatrists, which was established in 1999 to explore the role of spirituality in mental health. This group promotes integrating spiritual considerations into clinical practice and respects their importance for both patients and practitioners. Publications like *Spirituality and Psychiatry* provide foundational insights into this integration, advocating for spirituality as an essential aspect of psychiatric care.

While I do not position myself as an expert on spirituality, I recognise that all faiths share a belief in a Higher Entity, and I am careful not to present myself as all things to all people.

Accessible and Relatable: This work may resonate especially with Christian audiences seeking mental health guidance that aligns with their faith.

Promotes Understanding: I have tried to use rare opportunities to bridge the gap between religious communities and the mental health field, fostering greater understanding and collaboration. I remain attentive and open when my patients want to talk about their faith beliefs. I refer them to the hospital chaplain as appropriate. The NHS has highly trained chaplains of various faiths who see patients confidentially and can signpost them to the appropriate faith leaders.

Supportive Community: I see opportunities both in mental health and faith settings to create a supportive community where individuals feel comfortable discussing mental health within a faith-based context.

Encouraging Dialogue: We must initiate important conversations at the intersection of faith and mental health to reduce stigma and promote understanding.

Faith-Based Tools: Where appropriate and aligned with individual preferences, spiritual practices such as prayer and meditation can be offered as complementary tools for mental health support.

Challenges to Consider

1. **Narrow Appeal:** By primarily appealing to Christian readers, I may limit the book's reach to a broader audience. However, I am aware of my limitations and aim to emphasise what all faiths have in common, without claiming to represent all traditions. I have found it as easy to talk to a Muslim or Hindu patient as to a Christian one.

2. **Scientific Integrity:** I am certainly not prioritising religious beliefs over scientific evidence. This book includes references to nearly 600 research papers to provide a robust evidence base.

3. **Diverse Beliefs:** Christian teachings vary widely, making it difficult to address all perspectives in one volume.

4. **Avoiding Stigma:** Discussions about faith and mental health must be handled carefully to avoid reinforcing stigma or misconceptions. Individuals with mental health challenges often face prejudice. For example, not all mentally ill people are violent, yet the image of mentally disordered offenders can influence public perceptions. I often ask my patients: "Are all bad parents mentally ill?" After a pause, they answer no. I follow up with, "Then are all mentally ill people bad parents?" The link is tenuous, yet the judgment remains. It's tough enough for someone dealing with low self-esteem and being judged for an illness outside of their control.

5. **Perceived Exclusivity:** Non-Christian readers may feel excluded, but the topics discussed—self-image, gender and sexuality, or the mental health challenges of Generation Z—are relevant across all faiths.

The Rise of Generation Z and the Work of the Holy Spirit

The rise in church attendance among 18–24-year-olds is notable. Christian faith, like many religious traditions, is evolving as it intersects with Generation Z (those born approximately between 1997 and 2012).

- **Mental Health Awareness**: This generation is highly attuned to mental health issues. Churches that integrate mental health support into their teachings and community activities are better positioned to support younger members.

- **Digital Natives**: Having grown up with the internet and social media, Gen Z often explores faith through digital platforms. Online church services, faith-based apps, and social media influencers play a pivotal role in their spiritual journeys.

- **Community and Authenticity**: Gen Z values genuine community and authenticity. They prefer transparent and inclusive environments where open dialogue, questioning, and diverse perspectives are welcomed.

- **Social Justice and Activism**: Many Gen Z individuals intertwine their faith with action. They are driven by causes such as climate change, equality, and global justice. Churches and faith groups that engage in activism resonate deeply with them.

- **Diverse Worldviews**: Global connectivity exposes Gen Z to a variety of belief systems. While some retain traditional Christian values, others blend their faith with elements from different religions, leading to a personalised spirituality.

- **Scepticism and Secularity**: There is a growing trend towards scepticism and secular values. Some Gen Z individuals question traditional religious teachings, seeking understanding and evidence-based beliefs.

- **Visual and Interactive Learning**: Being highly visual learners, Gen Z engages more effectively with faith content that includes visuals, storytelling, and interactive elements such as videos, podcasts, and dynamic sermons.

- **Individualism**: Gen Z values individual expression and often seeks faith experiences that allow them to express their unique identities and beliefs.

In summary, the intersection of Christian faith and Generation Z is marked by adaptability, digital engagement, social activism, and a quest for authenticity and community. Faith communities that recognise and respond to these trends can create meaningful connections with this emerging generation.

Hyperfocus and Generation Z

- **Technological Immersion**: Growing up with digital devices, Gen Z has developed an acute ability to focus intensely on tasks, often using technology to enhance productivity. From designing graphics to coding apps, this hyperfocus enables them to channel their creativity and skills.

- **Mental Health Awareness**: With a broader understanding of neurodiversity and mental health, many Gen Z individuals recognise hyperfocus as part of conditions like ADHD. They harness it positively, using tools and techniques to manage and direct their attention effectively.

- **Educational Platforms**: They actively engage with online learning platforms, leveraging micro-credentials and digital courses to master new skills. Their focus on self-improvement is driven by an ever-evolving career landscape.

Faith and Spiritual Activism

Many Gen Z individuals incorporate faith into activism, aligning their spiritual or religious beliefs with social justice movements. They advocate for causes that resonate with their morals and values.

Intersection of Hyperfocus and Faith

- **Mindfulness and Meditation**: Gen Z often uses mindfulness and meditation practices, combining them with religious or spiritual rituals. This enhances hyperfocus by promoting mental clarity and balance.

- **Digital Faith Platforms**: The integration of faith and technology allows access to digital faith platforms, where they can participate in virtual spiritual gatherings, discussions, and study sessions.

- **Purposeful Living**: The pursuit of meaning is a common theme, with many Gen Z individuals striving to live purposeful lives. Their ability to focus intently enables them to align daily actions with long-term spiritual and personal goals.

Gen Z's approach to hyperfocus and faith reflects a generation that values growth, community, and purpose. They adapt to a changing world with resilience and creativity, crafting individualised paths that incorporate both technological advancements and deep-rooted spiritual connections.

Examples of Social Justice Initiatives Churches Can Support

- **Environmental Care**: Participate in initiatives like tree planting, recycling programmes, and community clean-up events. Advocate for sustainable practices and educate congregants on environmental stewardship.

- **Racial Equality**: Host workshops and discussions on racial justice and diversity. Partner with organisations that work towards racial equality, and support local or national movements fighting racial discrimination.

- **Mental Health Advocacy**: Organise mental health awareness campaigns, provide access to mental health resources, and offer counselling services. Encourage open conversations about mental health within the church community.

- **Homeless Outreach**: Support homeless shelters or create programmes that provide food, clothing, and resources to those experiencing homelessness. Engage in advocacy for affordable housing and social services.

- **Refugee Support**: Offer language classes, job training, and support networks for refugees and immigrants. Partner with organisations dedicated to refugee assistance and advocacy.

- **Voting and Civic Participation**: Encourage civic engagement by hosting voter registration drives and providing information on local, state, and national elections. Educate congregants about the importance of their voice in the democratic process.

- **Ending Human Trafficking**: Collaborate with groups fighting human trafficking by raising awareness, providing support to survivors, and advocating for stronger laws and policies.

- **Hunger and Food Security**: Support food banks, community gardens, or meal distribution programmes to combat hunger. Raise awareness about global and local food insecurity issues.

- **Educational Access**: Work towards educational equality by supporting underserved schools, offering tutoring programmes, and providing scholarships to students in need.

- **Health Care Access**: Advocate for equitable healthcare access, organise health fairs, or support clinics providing services to underserved populations.

- **Gender Equality**: Support initiatives that empower women and promote gender equality within the church and community. Engage in efforts to combat gender-based violence and discrimination.

- **LGBTQ+ Inclusion**: Foster an inclusive environment for LGBTQ+ individuals by promoting acceptance, providing support networks, and opposing discrimination.

By actively engaging in these social justice initiatives, churches can embody their values, address pressing societal issues, and demonstrate love and care for all members of their communities.

How Gen Z Uses Technology to Support Hyperfocus in Spirituality?

- **Meditation Apps and Tools**: Apps such as *Calm*, *Headspace*, or *Insight Timer* offer guided meditations, ambient sounds, and structured routines to help users attain focus during spiritual practices.

- **Virtual Communities and Social Media**: Platforms like Instagram, TikTok, or Discord host communities where Gen Z can share insights, learn, and stay accountable. Short, impactful content on these platforms supports a focused mindset on faith topics.

- **Online Classes and Webinars**: Online spiritual courses often feature interactive elements like quizzes and Q&A sessions, which help maintain focus and enhance learning.

- **Digital Journaling**: Apps like *Day One* or *Journey* enable Gen Z to keep digital journals for personal reflection, spiritual growth, and gratitude—structured in ways that support hyperfocus.

- **Virtual Reality (VR) Experiences**: Emerging VR technologies offer immersive spiritual experiences, such as VR church services or meditative environments, promoting a deep level of engagement.

- **Podcasts and Audiobooks**: A wide range of faith-based podcasts and audiobooks allow Gen Z to absorb spiritual content while commuting or multitasking, using audio to support sustained focus.

Conclusion

As a Christian psychiatrist, writing a book on faith and mental health offers valuable insights into the interplay between spiritual beliefs and psychological well-being. By addressing both the benefits and challenges, this work aims to serve as a meaningful resource for those interested in an integrated approach to mental health within a faith context. I have strived to balance faith-based perspectives with established psychiatric principles to ensure the book is both informative and inclusive.

This is what we know

- 60% say faith is an important factor in supporting their mental wellness.
- 57% would seek help from a faith leader for mental health concerns.
- 3 in 5 would seek mental health care if a faith leader recommended it.

"We know that research shows that people turn to their faith leaders in times of crisis. They also turn to the medical system. When the two are in sync, it makes for a better, more holistic treatment strategy."
— Rev. Jermine Alberty, M.Div., Executive Director of Pathways to Promise, US

Quoted from: *BJPsych Bull. 2021 Jun;45(3):170–174. doi: 10.1192/bjb.2020.34*

APA Foundation Releases New Guide for Faith Leaders on Mental Health

WASHINGTON, D.C. — A survey released by the American Psychiatric Association (APA) found that six in ten adults (60%) agree their faith or spirituality plays an important role in supporting mental wellness. However, among those belonging to a religious community, just half (52%) report their community discusses mental health openly and without stigma.

Some Facts

- Nearly 3 in 10 employees will experience a mental health issue in any given year.
- According to the Royal College of Psychiatrists 1 in 5 people recover completely.

- Only 24% of adults with long-term mental health conditions are in work.

- Just 40% of employers say they would hire someone with a mental illness.

- Research shows many of us learn about mental illness through the media.

Stigma and Discrimination in Media

Examples of harmful headlines:

- *The Sun*: "Bonkers Bruno locked up."

- *The Daily Mail*: "Knife maniac freed to kill. Mental Patient ran amok in the Park."

- *The Sun*: "Violent, Mad. So Docs set him Free."

The Unheard

A book by Dr Rageshri Dhairyawan explores the medical practice of silencing, based on her experiences as both a doctor and a patient.

"I know what it feels like to not be heard as a patient. Not being taken seriously in healthcare seems to be a nearly universal experience. Most people I've spoken to have a story—either about themselves or someone they know. We often talk about delivering healthcare, but for many, it doesn't feel like healthcare services care about them.

This is a book about who gets listened to—and who doesn't—in medicine, and how this leads to a culture of silencing that deepens health inequities. It also offers a prescription to close the gap for the most marginalised in society and, by doing so, improve healthcare for all."

— Dr Rageshri Dhairyawan

"Unheard is about who gets listened to and who doesn't in medicine and how this leads to a culture of silencing that exacerbates health inequities, on an individual and global scale. It's also about what we can do to make sure everyone's voice is equally heard and valued; a prescription to close the gap for the most marginalised in society and improve healthcare for all."

Medical Gaslighting

Medical gaslighting occurs when healthcare professionals dismiss or downplay a patient's symptoms or concerns, causing the patient to feel they're exaggerating or misinterpreting their health issues. This can happen unintentionally or intentionally, often leaving patients feeling invalidated, frustrated, or confused. It is particularly common among women, minorities, or individuals with chronic or mental health conditions.

What to do if you're experiencing it:

1. **Document symptoms**: Keep a detailed record, including frequency and triggers.

2. **Seek a second opinion**: Another provider may better validate your concerns.

3. **Bring an advocate**: A friend or family member can help voice your needs.

4. **Educate yourself**: Knowledge is empowering during consultations.

5. **Assert your needs**: Be clear about your concerns and request appropriate care.

Mental Wellbeing Self-Screening Tool

A tool to help ensure young people receive appropriate support and assistance.

Wellbeing or Wellness

Hey! What's popping? Let's dive into well-being and wellness—a cool way to live your best life. Imagine feeling fantastic every single day. Sound good?

1. **What is Wellbeing?**

    It's like having an epic balance of physical health, mental vibes, and emotional calm. Feeling good in your skin and your life.

2. **Why It Matters?**

   Wellbeing isn't just about eating salads or doing yoga. It's about feeling energised, staying positive, and enjoying life without constant "ugh" moments.

3. **Physical Fun:**
   - *Move It*: Dance-offs, skateboarding, or a walk with friends—whatever you enjoy!
   - *Eat Like a Champ*: Fuel your body with energy-giving food, and treat yourself occasionally.
   - *Rest and Recharge*: Sleep is your best mate—essential for mind and body recovery.

4. **Mind Magic:**
   - *Mindful Moments*: Breathe and chill—mini holidays for your brain.
   - *Gratitude Attitude*: Think of three awesome things from your day to shift focus from stress to success.

5. **Social Scene:**
   - *Connect with Cool Cats*: Spend time with people who lift you up.

6. *Share and Care*: Listening and talking helps ease the load.
   Digital Detox:
   - *Screen Breaks*: Step away from screens. Read, doodle, or go outside—creativity = happiness.
   - *Be Selective*: Follow uplifting content, not stuff that drags you down.

7. **Chase Your Passions:**

   Whether it's music, sport, gaming, or art—doing what you love gives a huge wellbeing boost.

8. **Ask for Help:**

   Feeling overwhelmed? Totally normal. Everyone needs a hand sometimes. Asking for support = strength.

Wellbeing is a journey—keep discovering what makes *you* feel amazing.

Catch up soon?

Mental Health and Wellbeing Screening Questionnaire

Section 1: General Wellbeing

1. On a scale of 1 to 10, how would you rate your overall wellbeing in the past month?

2. How often do you engage in activities that you enjoy?
   - Daily
   - Several times a week
   - Weekly
   - Rarely

3. Do you feel content with your current work or personal life balance?
   - Yes

- No
- Sometimes

Section 2: Mood and Emotions

1. Over the last two weeks, how often have you felt down, depressed, or hopeless?
   - Never
   - Occasionally
   - More than half the days
   - Nearly every day

2. How often have you experienced little interest or pleasure in doing things?

3. How frequently do you feel anxious or uneasy?

Section 3: Stress and Coping

1. How often do you feel overwhelmed by your responsibilities?

2. Do you find it hard to relax or unwind?

3. How often do you rely on alcohol, drugs, or other activities to help you cope with stress?

Section 4: Sleep and Appetite

1. How would you rate your sleep quality in the past month?
   - Poor
   - Fair
   - Good

- Excellent

2. Have you noticed any significant changes in appetite or weight in the past month?

Section 5: Social Connections

- Do you have a support system you can rely on (friends, family)?
  - Yes
  - No
- How often do you feel lonely or isolated?

Section 6: Thoughts and Behaviours

1. How often do you have thoughts that worry you excessively?
15. Have you ever thought about harming yourself or others?
   - If yes, please contact a mental health professional immediately.

Section 7: Seeking Help

1. Have you ever sought help from a mental health professional?

2. Are you interested in receiving more information or speaking with someone about mental health?

- Yes
- No (If no, please specify why)

Instructions:

- Please answer these questions honestly.
- Seek immediate help if you have thoughts of self-harm or harming others.

- The results of this questionnaire are not a substitute for professional diagnosis.

This questionnaire aims to identify areas where an individual may need support and guide them to appropriate resources.

Note your answers and take them to your faith leader, a mental health professional, or someone you trust.

What Should I Do If My Doctor Doesn't Take My Concerns Seriously?

If you feel that your doctor isn't taking your concerns seriously, consider the following steps:

1. **Document Your Concerns:** Write down your symptoms, concerns, and questions ahead of your appointment to ensure nothing is overlooked.

2. **Communicate Clearly:** Use specific language to explain how your symptoms are affecting your daily life.

3. **Ask for Clarification:** Don't hesitate to ask why the doctor doesn't see your concern as serious or why they're not recommending particular tests or treatments.

4. **Seek Understanding:** Request an explanation of the doctor's reasoning behind their diagnosis or treatment plan.

5. **Involve a Trusted Person:** Bring someone with you to help support your case and advocate alongside you.

6. **Request a Follow-Up:** If you feel your concerns weren't fully addressed, schedule another appointment to revisit the discussion.

7. **Consider a Second Opinion:** Another healthcare provider might offer a different perspective or explore other treatment options.

8. **Use Patient Advocacy Resources:** Many facilities have patient advocates who can help mediate between you and the healthcare provider.

9. **Provide Feedback:** Give constructive feedback to the clinic about your experience.

10. **Explore New Providers:** If necessary, seek a new doctor who better listens to and respects your concerns.

You deserve to feel heard and supported; advocating for yourself is a key part of your care journey.

Examples of How to Communicate Your Concerns

Here are some examples to help you communicate clearly with your doctor:

1. **Symptom Description:**
   - "I've been having severe headaches every morning for the past two weeks. They're intense and different from any I've had before. They're impacting my daily routine."

2. **Impact on Daily Life:**
   - "The ongoing nausea makes it hard to eat, and I've lost weight. I'm worried about how this is affecting my health."

3. **Request for Clarification:**
   - "Could you explain why further tests aren't being recommended at this stage?"

4. **Expressing Concerns About a Diagnosis:**
    - "I'm not sure the current medication is working. My symptoms remain unchanged. Can we explore other treatment options?"

5. **Requesting Further Action:**
    - "I'd feel more reassured if we could run a few more tests to rule out other causes."

6. **Asking About Alternatives:**
    - "Are there any alternatives to the treatment I'm currently on that might be more effective?"

7. **Follow-Up on Previous Discussions:**
    - "We talked about my fatigue last time, but there's been no improvement. What else can we do?"

8. **Pointing Out New Symptoms:**
    - "Since our last visit, I've noticed dizziness and a fast heart rate. These symptoms concern me."

9. **Expressing Worry:**
    - "I'm beginning to think this might be something more serious. Could we reassess my symptoms and next steps?"

Clear, polite, and assertive communication will help ensure your concerns are properly understood and addressed.

The Concept That Black People Are Better at Dealing with Pain

The belief that Black individuals have a higher pain tolerance is a harmful stereotype with no scientific basis. It has historical roots and continues to affect healthcare outcomes.

1. **Historical Context:**
    - This stereotype emerged during slavery to justify inhumane treatment and persists today in subtler forms.

2. **Impact on Healthcare:**
    - It leads to Black patients being under-treated for pain. Research shows healthcare providers often underestimate their pain levels.

3. **Individual Variability:**
    - Pain tolerance differs from person to person, influenced by psychological, cultural, and physiological factors — not race.

4. **Importance of Communication:**
    - Effective pain management depends on open dialogue between patient and doctor, free from stereotypes.

5. **Addressing Bias in Medicine:**
    - Medical education must include training to confront these biases and ensure all patients receive fair and adequate care.

Recognising and challenging these misconceptions is crucial for equitable healthcare. If you feel your pain is being dismissed, advocate for yourself and seek a provider who will listen and take your experiences seriously.

Don't Accept Being Ignored. Write a Complaint; Where's the Support?

If you feel healthcare professionals are ignoring you, it's important to advocate for yourself and ensure you receive the attention and care you deserve. Here are some steps you can take:

1. **Communicate Clearly**: Express your symptoms, concerns, and questions clearly. Be specific about what you're experiencing and the outcomes you hope to achieve.

2. **Ask Questions**: Don't hesitate to ask questions if something is unclear. Understanding your health and treatment plan is your right.

3. **Seek Support**: Bring a trusted friend or family member to appointments. They can provide support, help articulate your concerns, and ensure your issues are addressed.

4. **Request Documentation**: Keep records of your symptoms, tests, and treatments. Documenting can help track your health journey and provide evidence if something is overlooked.

5. **Get a Second Opinion**: If you feel your concerns are not being taken seriously, don't hesitate to seek a second opinion from another healthcare provider.

6. **Use Patient Advocacy Services**: Many healthcare systems have patient advocates who can help navigate the system, voice your concerns, and assist in securing the care you need.

7. **Give Feedback or Make a Complaint**: Use the feedback mechanisms available at healthcare facilities to report

incidents or express concerns. This can initiate improvements in service and care.

8. **Educate Yourself**: Understanding your health condition can empower you to have informed discussions with healthcare providers and challenge any decisions you're uncomfortable with.

9. **Know Your Rights**: Familiarise yourself with your rights as a patient, including the right to respectful care, access to information about your treatment, and the ability to refuse or seek alternative treatments.

10. **Adopt a Proactive Mindset**: Remember, you are a vital part of the healthcare team. Your experiences and feelings matter—you deserve to be heard and respected.

By being proactive and assertive, you can better navigate the healthcare system and work towards receiving the quality of care you merit.

What Should I Say to a Healthcare Professional Who Dismisses My Concerns?

If a healthcare professional dismisses your concerns, it's important to advocate for yourself calmly and assertively. Here are some things you might say:

1. **Express Your Feelings**: "I feel that my concerns are not being fully addressed, and I'd like to discuss them further."

2. **Clarify Your Needs**: "I need to understand why my symptoms are being dismissed and what evidence supports this decision."

3. **Request Additional Information**: "Can you explain why you believe this isn't a concern? I'd like to understand your perspective better."

4. **Ask About Alternatives**: "What other actions or steps can we take to ensure nothing is being overlooked?"

5. **Seek a Collaborative Approach**: "I believe understanding my health is a team effort. How can we work together to address my concerns?"

6. **Request Further Examination**: "I would appreciate it if you could consider further tests or a referral to a specialist."

7. **State the Impact**: "These symptoms are significantly affecting my daily life, and I'm concerned about underlying causes."

8. **Express Understanding**: "I understand that you see many patients, but my situation is unique and deserves a closer look."

9. **Reiterate Commitment**: "I'm committed to my health and believe a thorough evaluation is necessary. How can we ensure that happens?"

10. **Consider Escalation**: "If we can't reach an understanding, what would be the next step in seeking another opinion?"

By calmly and assertively voicing your concerns, you create an opportunity for the healthcare professional to reconsider their approach and provide the attention needed.

Are There Any Studies on Racial Bias in Healthcare?

Yes, numerous studies have examined racial bias in healthcare, highlighting how such biases can affect treatment and outcomes. Key findings include:

1. **Pain Management**: Research shows that racial bias can lead to disparities in pain assessment, with Black and Hispanic

patients often receiving less pain relief compared to white patients for similar conditions.

2. **Maternal and Infant Health**: Studies reveal that Black women in the U.S. are more likely to experience complications during pregnancy and childbirth, with significantly higher maternal mortality rates than white women. These disparities are linked to both socio-economic factors and differential care provision.

3. **Chronic Disease Management**: Racial bias can affect the management of conditions like diabetes and hypertension. Black patients may receive less aggressive treatment and fewer specialist referrals.

4. **Implicit Bias in Providers**: Many studies explore how unconscious attitudes among healthcare providers' influence decisions, often resulting in inequitable treatment and poorer outcomes for minority patients.

5. **Healthcare Access and Quality**: Structural racism can influence access to care, service quality, and health insurance coverage, worsening disparities.

Efforts to address these issues include:

- **Education and Training**: Encouraging healthcare providers to recognise and manage their biases.

- **Policy Reform**: Advocating for policies that promote equitable access and care.

- **Cultural Competency**: Enhancing systems so that care is respectful and culturally responsive.

Addressing these disparities is essential for ensuring equity in healthcare and improving outcomes for all communities.

Potential Drawbacks of Relying Solely on Faith for Mental Health

While faith can provide comfort, relying exclusively on it for mental health support may pose risks:

1. **Lack of Professional Guidance**: Faith may not offer the medical insight required to diagnose or treat mental illness. Professionals are trained to manage complex conditions.

2. **Delayed Treatment**: Sole reliance on spiritual support can delay essential clinical care, worsening symptoms.

3. **Stigma and Misunderstanding**: In some faith communities, mental health issues may be seen as weakness or lack of faith, discouraging individuals from seeking help.

4. **Detachment from Reality**: While faith brings hope, it can sometimes lead to denial of the actual problem, preventing effective coping.

5. **Guilt and Shame**: Individuals might feel personal or spiritual failure if faith doesn't resolve their struggles, leading to guilt.

6. **Lack of Scientific Support**: Faith-based interventions often lack empirical evidence to prove their effectiveness in treating clinical mental health disorders.

7. **Limited Coping Strategies**: Faith alone might not offer the range of tools provided in therapy, such as cognitive-behavioural techniques and structured stress management.

8. **Unmet Needs:** Sole reliance on faith might overlook other unmet psychological or social needs, such as trauma resolution, relationship counselling, or lifestyle changes that require a comprehensive approach.

9. **Dependency on Faith Leaders:** Individuals might become overly dependent on faith leaders for mental health advice, who may not be qualified to provide such guidance.

10. **Barrier to Open Communication:** The pressure to appear spiritually sound may create a barrier to openly communicating challenges and feelings, impacting the healing process.

In conclusion, faith can be a valuable part of an individual's support system. However, it is often most beneficial when integrated with professional mental health care and a broader, holistic approach to well-being. Combining faith with medical and psychological support provides a more robust framework for addressing mental health issues.

Stress Management:

High stress levels from school, work, and relationships are a major concern, leading to increased interest in stress-relief techniques.

CBT, Faith, and Early Intervention for People and Family Members Affected by Psychotic Illness

Cognitive Behavioural Therapy (CBT) and early intervention play crucial roles in supporting individuals and their families affected by psychotic illnesses. Psychotic disorders, which include conditions like schizophrenia, are characterised by disruptions in thinking, perception, emotional regulation, and behaviour, often leading to distressing symptoms such as hallucinations and delusions.

Cognitive Behavioural Therapy (CBT):

CBT is a well-established therapeutic approach that helps individuals understand and manage their thoughts, feelings, and behaviours. For those experiencing psychosis, CBT can be tailored to address specific symptoms, such as delusions and hallucinations. The therapy works by:

1. **Identifying and Challenging Maladaptive Beliefs:** CBT helps patients recognise distorted thoughts and develop healthier ways of thinking.

2. **Coping Strategies:** It provides strategies to manage stress and triggers, reducing the intensity and frequency of psychotic episodes.

3. **Increasing Functionality and Quality of Life:** By focusing on problem-solving skills and social functioning, CBT aids in improving overall quality of life.

Faith and Spirituality:

Integrating faith and spiritual practices can offer additional support to individuals and families dealing with psychotic illnesses. Spirituality can provide:

1. **Hope and Meaning:** For many, faith offers a framework for understanding life's challenges and finding meaning in their experiences.

2. **Community Support:** Faith communities can offer emotional support and a sense of belonging.

3. **Coping Mechanisms:** Spiritual practices, such as prayer or meditation, may serve as coping mechanisms during times of stress or crisis.

Early Intervention:

Early intervention is critical in managing psychotic illnesses effectively. Recognising and treating symptoms early can lead to better outcomes, as:

1. **Reduced Chronicity:** Early treatment can prevent symptoms from becoming entrenched and reduce the risk of chronic disability.
2. **Improved Prognosis:** Starting treatment early can help maintain educational and occupational performance, improving long-term recovery prospects.
3. **Family Involvement:** Early intervention often involves families, providing education and support to help them understand and manage the illness.

In conclusion, combining Cognitive Behavioural Therapy with a supportive faith-based approach and implementing early intervention strategies can significantly benefit individuals and families affected by psychotic illnesses. This holistic approach not only addresses the clinical aspects of the disorder but also nurtures the emotional and spiritual well-being of those affected.

Mobile Crisis Teams

Mobile crisis teams are specialised groups of mental health professionals who respond to individuals experiencing a mental health crisis in the community. These teams are designed to provide immediate, on-site support and intervention to stabilise the situation and connect individuals with appropriate resources and care. Here are more details on mobile crisis teams:

1. **Composition:** These teams typically include a combination of mental health professionals, such as clinical social workers, psychologists, psychiatrists, and psychiatric nurses.

Some teams may also include peer support specialists who have lived experience with mental health challenges.

2. **24/7 Availability:** To be effective, mobile crisis teams often operate around the clock, ensuring that individuals can receive help whenever a crisis occurs, regardless of the time of day.

3. **De-escalation and Assessment:** The primary goal of the team is to de-escalate the situation and assess the individual's mental health needs. They aim to provide immediate care to prevent harm to the individual or others.

4. **Collaboration with First Responders:** Mobile crisis teams often work in collaboration with law enforcement, EMS, and other first responders. They may accompany police officers to calls involving a mental health component or serve as the primary responders in such cases.

5. **Connection to Services:** After stabilising the situation, the team connects individuals to appropriate follow-up care and resources. This may include arranging for transportation to a mental health facility, scheduling appointments with mental health professionals, or referring individuals to community-based support services.

6. **Avoiding Hospitalisation and Incarceration:** By providing timely and effective intervention, mobile crisis teams can reduce the need for hospitalisation or incarceration, which are often the default responses to mental health crises.

7. **Cost-Effectiveness:** Although establishing and maintaining these teams requires investment, they can be cost-effective by reducing unnecessary hospital admissions and the criminal justice system's involvement.

8. **Community Engagement:** These teams often engage with the community through outreach and education efforts, working to raise awareness about mental health issues, reduce stigma, and encourage individuals to seek help before a crisis occurs.

Mobile crisis teams aim to provide compassionate, person-centred care during crises, fostering a more supportive community environment and minimising the disruptions often associated with mental health emergencies.

Examples of Successful Mobile Crisis Programmes:

Several successful mobile crisis programmes have been implemented in various regions. Here are a few examples:

1. **CAHOOTS (Crisis Assistance Helping Out On The Streets) – Eugene, Oregon:** Established in 1989, CAHOOTS is a community-based public safety programme. It dispatches a team consisting of a medic (usually a nurse) and a crisis worker with mental health experience to respond to non-violent crises. Operating 24/7, CAHOOTS handles a range of situations, including mental health crises, substance abuse issues, and homelessness-related incidents. It has served as a successful model for many other cities.

2. **STAR (Support Team Assisted Response) Programme – Denver, Colorado:** Launched in 2020, the STAR Programme involves mental health clinicians and paramedics who respond to non-violent calls related to mental health, poverty, homelessness, and substance abuse. The aim is to connect individuals with support services while reducing police involvement in non-criminal situations.

3. **MCIT (Mobile Crisis Intervention Teams) – Toronto, Canada:** A collaborative effort between the Toronto Police Service and mental health nurses from local hospitals, the

MCIT in Toronto focuses on de-escalating crisis situations and directly connecting individuals with mental health services. The teams work to ensure that those in crisis receive compassionate and appropriate care.

4. **Mental Health Crisis Intervention Units – Queensland, Australia:** In Queensland, these specialised units involve partnerships between the police and mental health practitioners who jointly respond to mental health crises. The approach emphasises early intervention and ongoing support, reducing the need for hospitalisation and providing community-based care.

5. **Project Respond – Portland, Oregon:** Project Respond offers immediate crisis intervention services throughout Multnomah County as part of the Cascadia Behavioural Healthcare system. The programme includes crisis counsellors who provide assessment, support, and referrals to individuals in crisis, helping to stabilise situations in a compassionate manner.

6. **Behavioural Health Response (BHR) – St. Louis, Missouri:** BHR offers a 24/7 crisis hotline and mobile outreach services. It serves the larger St. Louis region by providing rapid response and intervention for mental health emergencies. Their approach focuses on assessment, stabilisation, and connecting clients to necessary resources.

These programmes emphasise the importance of providing specialised, compassionate care for individuals experiencing mental health crises while reducing the reliance on law enforcement and emergency medical services for non-violent situations. They often rely on strong community partnerships and continuous evaluation to adapt and improve their services.

What professions are typically part of a mobile crisis team?

Mobile crisis teams usually comprise a multidisciplinary group of professionals who work together to address mental health crises. Some of the typical professions included are:

1. **Licensed Mental Health Counsellors**: Provide therapy, crisis intervention, and assessment.

2. **Clinical Social Workers**: Counsel, assess, and connect individuals to community resources.

3. **Psychiatric Nurses**: Offer medical assessments, administer medications, and provide education about mental health conditions.

4. **Psychiatrists or Psychiatric Nurse Practitioners**: These professionals may be involved in diagnosing and prescribing medications if necessary.

5. **Peer Support Specialists**: Individuals with lived experience in mental health issues, offering support and guidance from a personal perspective.

6. **Case Managers**: Coordinate care and ensure individuals receive appropriate services and follow-up.

7. **Behavioural Health Technicians**: Assist in de-escalating crisis situations and providing practical support.

8. **Substance Abuse Counsellors**: Focus on individuals facing both mental health and substance use challenges.

Having a diverse team allows mobile crisis units to address a wide range of issues and provide comprehensive support during a crisis. The team's composition might vary depending on the community's specific needs.

The Role of Faith in Early Intervention

CBT, Faith, and Early Intervention for People and Family Members Affected by Psychotic Illness

Quality Statement

Adults with psychosis or schizophrenia are offered cognitive behavioural therapy for psychosis (CBTp).

Rationale

CBTp, in conjunction with antipsychotic medication—or on its own if medication is declined—can improve outcomes such as psychotic symptoms. It should form part of a broad-based approach that combines different treatment options tailored to the needs of individual service users.

Quality Measures

The following measures can be used to assess the quality of care or service provision specified in the statement. They are examples of how the statement can be measured, adapted, and used flexibly.

Structure

Evidence of local arrangements to ensure that CBTp is available to adults with psychosis or schizophrenia.

Data source: Data can be collected from information recorded locally by healthcare professionals and provider organisations, for example care protocols.

Process

a) Proportion of adults with psychosis who receive CBTp.

- **Numerator** – the number in the denominator who receive CBTp.
- **Denominator** – the number of adults with psychosis. *Data source:* Data can be collected using the Royal College of Psychiatrists' National Audit of Schizophrenia: Audit of Practice Tool, questions 42 and 44.

b) Proportion of adults with schizophrenia who receive CBTp.

- **Numerator** – the number in the denominator who receive CBTp.
- **Denominator** – the number of adults with schizophrenia. *Data source:* Data can be collected using the Royal College of Psychiatrists' National Audit of Schizophrenia: Audit of Practice Tool, questions 42 and 44.

Outcome

Relapse rates of psychosis and schizophrenia in adults. *Data source:* Data can be collected from information recorded locally by healthcare professionals and provider organisations, for example from patient records.

What are some case studies showing successful integration of faith-based counselling in early intervention?

Early intervention services for preventive mental health focus on identifying and addressing mental health issues before they fully develop. These services are organised into three levels: primary, secondary, and tertiary prevention.

- **Primary prevention** aims to stop mental health problems before they start through strategies like mental health awareness programmes and psychoeducation.

- **Secondary prevention** targets individuals at higher risk, offering support groups and access to therapy.
- **Tertiary prevention** focuses on those already affected, aiming to reduce impairment and improve quality of life.

These interventions are effective in reducing the incidence and severity of mental disorders.

Early Intervention Services for Preventive Mental Health and the Critical Role of Faith

Early intervention services for preventive mental health can significantly benefit from the integration of faith-based approaches. Faith-based counselling provides holistic support by incorporating spiritual beliefs with psychological practices, which can enhance mental well-being by offering comfort, hope, and guidance. Faith can complement psychological interventions, providing a sense of purpose and community that supports mental health recovery.

Additionally, faith-informed therapies can be beneficial in clinical settings, though they require careful implementation to avoid biases. Including faith leaders in mental health promotion can address spiritual needs and improve outcomes, as religious belief often correlates with better mental health.

Integrating faith-based counselling into early intervention mental health services involves several key strategies:

1. **Personalised Faith Integration**: Therapists can incorporate clients' spiritual beliefs and practices, such as prayer or meditation, into their treatment plans. This approach respects individual preferences and enhances therapeutic outcomes by aligning with clients' values.

2. **Training for Faith Leaders**: Providing mental health training to faith leaders enables them to recognise mental

health issues and make appropriate referrals. This partnership can improve access to care and reduce stigma within religious communities.

3. **Community-Based Platforms**: Utilising church-based platforms allows trained clergy to deliver mental health interventions, increasing accessibility in underserved areas.

4. **Holistic Care**: Combining psychotherapy with spiritual guidance offers a comprehensive approach to mental health, addressing both emotional and spiritual needs.

Faith and Mental Health: A Journey of Healing

This book explores the deep connection between faith and mental well-being, offering practical insights, personal stories, and spiritual practices to promote mental health, while addressing common challenges and stigma within faith communities.

1. **Understanding Faith-Based Mental Health**: Explore the connection between faith and mental health, including how spiritual beliefs can influence mental wellness.

2. **Personal Stories of Transformation**: Share testimonies from individuals who have experienced healing through their faith, showcasing various journeys of mental health improvement.

3. **Practices for Spiritual and Mental Well-being**: Discuss practices such as prayer, meditation, scripture reading, and other faith-based activities that promote mental health.

4. **The Role of Community**: Highlight the importance of faith communities in providing support, encouragement, and accountability in mental health journeys.

5. **Faith and Resilience**: Explore how faith can build resilience and provide strength during times of mental health challenges.

6. **Addressing Stigma in Faith Communities**: Discuss the stigmas surrounding mental health in faith communities and how open dialogues can foster acceptance and support.

7. **Faith Leaders' Perspectives**: Include insights from faith leaders on supporting mental health within a spiritual framework.

8. **Integrating Professional Help with Faith**: Talk about the importance of seeking professional mental health help alongside faith-based approaches.

9. **Scriptural Insights on Mental Health**: Analyse scriptures or spiritual texts that speak to mental well-being, providing spiritual insights into modern mental health issues.

10. **Developing Spiritual Coping Mechanisms**: Offer techniques and strategies grounded in faith that can help individuals cope with mental health issues.

11. **Faith in Crisis**: Address how to maintain and grow one's faith during periods of mental health crises.

12. **Creating a Personalised Faith and Mental Health Plan**: Guide readers in developing a plan that integrates faith and mental health practices tailored to their individual needs.

2

FAITH COMMUNITIES AND SUPPORT SYSTEMS

ANALYSING THE ROLE OF RELIGIOUS COMMUNITIES IN PROVIDING SUPPORT AND RESOURCES FOR MENTAL HEALTH

Faith practices, such as prayer or meditation, can offer coping mechanisms that help individuals manage stress and anxiety. These practices can foster a sense of calm and resilience. Faith can provide a moral and ethical framework that guides behaviour and decision-making, potentially reducing anxiety about choices and actions.

On the flip side, for some, faith can be a source of stress, especially if there is a conflict between personal beliefs and religious teachings, or if there is pressure from within faith communities on issues such as sexuality, domestic violence, and divorce.

1. **Christian Churches**: These include denominations like Catholic, Protestant, Orthodox, Baptist, Methodist, Presbyterian, and Anglican communities. They gather in churches for worship, prayers, and community activities.

2. **Muslim Mosques**: Islamic communities gather in mosques for daily prayers, Friday congregational prayers (Jumu'ah), and religious education. They often participate in community service and charitable activities.

3. **Jewish Synagogues**: Jewish communities come together in synagogues for worship, Torah study, and community events. They observe religious holidays and engage in cultural activities.

4. **Hindu Temples**: Hindu faith communities meet in temples for worship (puja), rituals, and festivals. They also engage in spiritual teachings and community support activities.

5. **Buddhist Sanghas**: These communities gather in temples or meditation centres for meditation practice, teachings, and ceremonies. They emphasise mindfulness and compassion.

6. **Sikh Gurdwaras**: Sikh communities come together in gurdwaras for worship (Naam Japna), community meals (Langar), and social service (Seva).

7. **Pagan and Wiccan Circles**: These groups often meet in nature or private spaces for rituals, ceremonies, and celebrations of seasonal events.

8. **Baha'i Communities**: Baha'is gather in homes or community centres for prayer, study of the Baha'i writings, and service projects.

9. **Unitarian Universalist Congregations**: These inclusive communities focus on spiritual growth, social justice, and ethical living, welcoming people of various beliefs.

10. **Indigenous Spiritual Communities**: Many Indigenous peoples have spiritual communities based on traditional beliefs, often involving nature and ancestral practices.

Practise Your Faith

Faith-based practices that can support mental health:

1. **Prayer**: Engaging in regular prayer can be a source of comfort and connection, allowing individuals to express concerns, seek guidance, or find peace.

2. **Meditation**: Many faiths incorporate meditation, which can promote mindfulness, reduce stress, and enhance emotional well-being.

3. **Scripture Reading**: Studying religious texts can offer wisdom, encouragement, and a sense of connection to one's faith tradition.

4. **Community Worship**: Attending services or gatherings can foster a sense of community, belonging, and support.

5. **Sacred Music**: Listening to or participating in religious music can evoke feelings of joy, peace, and inspiration.

6. **Pilgrimage**: Travelling to sacred sites or participating in spiritual journeys can provide opportunities for reflection and renewal.

7. **Rituals and Ceremonies**: Engaging in meaningful rituals, such as lighting candles or observing holy days, can offer comfort and a sense of stability.

8. **Fasting**: Practised in some faiths, fasting can be a way to deepen spiritual focus and self-discipline.

9. **Acts of Service**: Many faiths emphasise helping others, which can enhance feelings of purpose and connection.

10. **Journaling**: Reflective writing from a spiritual perspective can help process emotions and experiences.

What the Quran Says

Faith in the Quran involves belief in things beyond human perception, such as God, angels, and the hereafter. *("Alif, Lam,*

Meem. *This is the Book about which there is no doubt, a guidance for those conscious of Allah - Who believe in the unseen..."* - Surah Al-Baqarah 2:1-3). The Quran outlines faith as a holistic concept, deeply interwoven with acts of worship, ethical conduct, and personal commitment to God's will.

Faith is characterised by total trust and reliance on God (Tawakkul). Believers are encouraged to depend on God in all matters. ("And when you have decided, then rely upon Allah. Indeed, Allah loves those who rely [upon Him]." - Surah Al-Imran 3:159).

Genuine faith is often linked with righteous actions. The Quran emphasises that belief should lead to moral behaviour and actions. ("Who believe and do righteous deeds - their Lord will guide them because of their faith..." - Surah Yunus 10:9).

True faith is more than just verbal acknowledgment; it involves sincerity and a complete devotion of the heart to God. ("The Bedouins say, 'We have believed.' Say, 'You have not [yet] believed; but say [instead], 'We have submitted,' for faith has not yet entered your hearts." - Surah Al-Hujurat 49:14).

The Quran assures believers that true faith brings tranquillity and peace to the heart. ("Those who have believed and whose hearts are assured by the remembrance of Allah. Unquestionably, by the remembrance of Allah hearts are assured." - Surah Ar-Ra'd 13:28).

What Judaism Says

In Judaism, faith, or "Emunah" in Hebrew, is an important but nuanced concept. Here are some key points regarding faith in Judaism:

1. **Faith as Trust**: Emunah is often translated as trust or faithfulness. It implies loyalty and confidence in God, aligning with the covenantal relationship between God and the Jewish people.

2. **Knowledge and Understanding**: Unlike blind faith, Jewish faith is often grounded in understanding and knowledge. Studying the Torah and Jewish texts is crucial to developing a deep, informed faith.

3. **Faith and Actions**: Judaism emphasises deeds over belief. While faith is important, the focus is on fulfilling commandments (mitzvot) and living a life aligned with Jewish law and ethics.

4. **Questioning and Faith**: Judaism encourages questioning and intellectual engagement as part of one's faith journey. This pursuit of understanding is seen as a way to deepen one's relationship with God.

5. **Covenantal Faith**: Faith in Judaism is relational, focusing on the covenant between God and the Jewish people. It includes a commitment to uphold God's laws and teachings.

6. **Faith Amidst Challenges**: Jewish history has been marked by trials and tribulations, and maintaining faith during difficult times is a recurring theme. Stories from the Bible, such as those of Job or Abraham, illustrate enduring faith despite hardships.

In summary, Judaism views faith as a combination of trust, knowledge, actions, and a personal relationship with God, emphasising study, moral living, and resilience.

LONELINESS AND ISOLATION

Faith can play a role in mental health, functioning in several ways, depending on individual beliefs and contexts. For many, faith can be a source of comfort and strength during difficult times. For others, it can provide a sense of purpose and meaning, which can be beneficial to mental well-being.

Being part of a faith-based community can offer social support and camaraderie, decreasing feelings of loneliness and isolation.

Loneliness isn't just an emotion; it's a complex scientific phenomenon! Scientists have found that our brains react to loneliness in similar ways as physical pain. Yup, it's that powerful!

When you're lonely, your brain's threat responses kick in, making loneliness feel like an alarm saying, "Hey, I need connection!" It's just your body trying to nudge you to reach out.

Feeling isolated can impact both mental and physical health. It's not just about feeling blue; prolonged loneliness can increase the risk of health issues, like heart disease or depression.

Ever felt super lonely after scrolling through social media? You're not alone! While social media connects us, it can also spark feelings of isolation. It's crucial to balance online interactions with real-life connections.

Studies show that having strong social bonds can actually boost brain health! Engaging in conversations and shared activities lights up the brain, keeping it active and happy.

Everyone feels lonely at times, and that's okay. Building meaningful connections can be as simple as joining clubs, volunteering, or even reaching out to a friend you haven't spoken to in a while.

Loneliness isn't limited to having people around. It's more about the quality of connections than the quantity. Even a single supportive friend can make a world of difference!

Understanding the science of loneliness can help reduce its stigma. Remember, reaching out, either to friends, family, or a community group, can be a significant first step toward feeling less isolated.

3

Faith-Based Programs and Resources

Providing Information on Programs, Workshops, and Retreats that Focus on Integrating Faith and Mental Health

Faith-Based Treatment and Therapy

By What Ways and Means?

Delivering a Christian faith-based community mental health service involves integrating spiritual care with mental health support to meet the holistic needs of individuals. Here are key steps to consider:

1. **Understanding the Need**:
    - Assess the community to understand specific mental health needs.
    - Consider cultural and religious factors that might influence mental health perceptions.

2. **Developing the Team**:
    - Recruit professionals who are both licensed in mental health services and familiar with Christian faith.
    - Include a mix of counsellors, social workers, volunteers, and clergy.

3. **Creating a Safe Environment**:
    - Ensure confidentiality and respect for all individuals.
    - Provide a space where clients feel safe discussing both mental health and spiritual issues.

4. **Integrating Faith-Based Approaches**:
    - Incorporate prayer, scripture, and religious rituals that align with mental health practices.
    - Use spiritual resources alongside traditional therapy methods to provide holistic care.

5. **Training and Education**:
    - Provide regular training for staff on both mental health best practices and spiritual care.
    - Educate staff about the integration of faith and psychology.

6. **Program Development**:
    - Develop specific programs that address different aspects of mental health, such as anxiety, depression, or grief.
    - Include support groups, workshops, and individual counselling sessions.

7. **Community Partnerships**:
    - Collaborate with local churches, healthcare providers, and other community organisations.
    - Build a network that supports referrals and community involvement.
8. **Accessibility**:
    - Make services affordable and accessible to all community members.
    - Consider offering telehealth services for remote support.
9. **Evaluation and Feedback**:
    - Regularly evaluate the effectiveness of your services through feedback and outcome assessments.
    - Use this information to improve programs and address any gaps.
10. **Outreach and Awareness**:
    - Conduct outreach activities to raise awareness about mental health and the services provided.
    - Utilise church bulletins, community events, and social media to share information.
11. **Legal and Ethical Considerations**:
    - Ensure compliance with legal standards for mental health services.
    - Uphold ethical practices in both counselling and spiritual guidance.

12. **Self-Care for Providers**:
    - Encourage self-care and spiritual renewal for staff to prevent burnout.
    - Offer resources and support for those providing care.

Social Media and Mental Health:

The influence of social media on self-esteem, anxiety, and depression is a hot topic. Many young people want to understand how online platforms affect their mental well-being.

Faith-Based Therapy

1. **Pastoral Counselling**: Many churches offer pastoral counselling services. These counsellors are often trained in both theology and psychology, providing faith-integrated therapy.

2. **Focus on the Family**: This organisation offers Christian counselling resources, including a network of therapists who incorporate faith into their practice.

3. **American Association of Christian Counsellors (AACC)**: AACC connects individuals with Christian counsellors and provides various resources for therapy grounded in Christian beliefs.

4. **Faithful Counselling**: An online therapy platform that connects individuals with licensed Christian counsellors for video, phone, or chat sessions.

5. **Catholic Charities Counselling**: Provides faith-based counselling services and supports people from all walks of life, integrating Catholic teachings.

6. **Jewish Family Services**: Offers counselling and mental health services that incorporate Jewish values and cultural understanding.

7. **Muslim Mental Health Directory**: Provides resources and a directory of counsellors who integrate Islamic principles into therapy.

8. **Spiritual Directors International**: Connects individuals with spiritual directors who can provide guidance and counselling rooted in spirituality.

9. **Books and Literature**: Books like *The Wounded Healer* by Henri Nouwen or *The Gifts of Imperfection* by Brené Brown provide spiritual perspectives on healing and mental health.

10. **Faith-Based Support Groups**: Support groups facilitated through religious organisations or faith communities provide communal support and shared values.

These resources can be a great starting point for anyone looking to integrate faith and spirituality into their mental health journey.

Designing a Christian Faith-Based Mental Health Service in Lambeth

Designing a Christian faith-based mental health service in Lambeth involves integrating spiritual care with mental health support to address the needs of the community. Here's a conceptual outline of how you could design such a service:

Mission and Vision

- **Mission**: To provide holistic mental health care rooted in Christian values, fostering healing and resilience through faith and professional support.

- **Vision**: A compassionate community where mental health is nurtured harmoniously with spiritual growth, empowering individuals to thrive.

Core Components

1. **Spiritual and Psychological Integration**
    - Develop programs that integrate Christian teachings with evidence-based psychological therapies.
    - Offer sessions that include prayer, meditation, and scripture study alongside cognitive behavioural therapy (CBT) or other modalities.

2. **Qualified Staff**
    - Employ licensed mental health professionals who are also trained in spiritual counselling.
    - Engage with pastors or clergy members who have an understanding of mental health issues.

3. **Community Engagement**
    - Run workshops and seminars on mental health awareness within churches and community centres.
    - Establish support groups that provide spiritual encouragement and peer support.

4. **Cultural Sensitivity**
    - Ensure services are tailored to the diverse cultural backgrounds represented in Lambeth.
    - Provide multilingual resources and translators if necessary.

Services Offered

- **Individual Counselling**: Personalised sessions focusing on mental health concerns with spiritual support as a backbone.
- **Group Therapy**: Facilitated group discussions incorporating Christian principles while addressing mental health topics.
- **Crisis Intervention**: Immediate support for mental health crises with spiritual guidance when appropriate.
- **Educational Programs**: Classes and workshops that educate on mental health from a faith-based perspective.

Facility Design

- Create a welcoming and serene environment that reflects Christian values, with quiet spaces for prayer and reflection.
- Use faith-based symbols and artwork to enhance the spiritual ambiance while being inclusive and open to all.

Partnerships

- Collaborate with local churches, Christian organisations, and healthcare providers to expand reach and resources.
- Engage with community leaders to promote the service and ensure it aligns with local needs.

Evaluation and Feedback

- Regular assessments are used to gauge the effectiveness of the services offered.
- Encourage feedback from service users to improve and adapt the service continuously.

Marketing and Outreach

- Develop materials that communicate the integration of faith and mental health support.

- Utilise social media, church bulletins, and community events to raise awareness.

Bringing Your Ideas of Spiritual Healing to the Community

Here are some strategies to consider:

1. **Community Workshops & Seminars**: Organise workshops and seminars focusing on the intersection of mental health and spirituality. Invite guest speakers to provide diverse perspectives and encourage community participation through discussions and activities.

2. **Mental Health and Spirituality Groups**: Establish support groups where people can share their experiences and learn about the role of spirituality in mental health. These groups can provide a safe space for individuals to explore spiritual practices that promote healing.

3. **Integrating Faith and Therapy**: Offer therapy sessions incorporating spiritual elements if the client is open to it. Tailor your approach to individual needs, respecting each person's spiritual journey.

4. **Writing and Publishing**: Write articles, blogs, or even books on the topic of spiritual healing in psychiatry. Share insights, case studies, and practical tools others can adopt in the field.

5. **Collaboration with Faith Communities**: Work with local churches and religious organisations to create initiatives that

address mental health from a spiritual perspective. This can involve co-hosting events or offering educational resources.

6. **Educational Content**: Create online courses, podcasts, or video series focusing on spiritual aspects of mental health. These resources can reach a broader audience beyond your immediate community.

7. **Inspirational Speaking**: Engage in public speaking at community events, conferences, and schools to share your perspective on the synergy between faith and psychiatric healing.

8. **Volunteer and Outreach Programs**: Get involved in community service projects or volunteer at facilities that align with your spiritual and professional values.

9. **Social Media Engagement**: Use platforms like Instagram, Facebook, or LinkedIn to share quotes, tips, and personal stories related to spiritual healing in psychiatry. Build an online community around these discussions.

10. **Patient Education Materials**: Provide clients with resources like brochures or handouts that explain the benefits of integrating faith and mental health practices.

Implementing Effective Outreach Strategies for Spiritual Healing

Building connections and fostering community engagement involves the following strategies:

1. **Partnerships with Local Organisations**: Collaborate with churches, spiritual centres, and community organisations that align with your mission. Co-host events and workshops to reach a wider audience.

2. **Workshops and Seminars**: Conduct free or low-cost workshops on topics related to spiritual healing. Offer practical tools and guidance, and encourage participants to share their experiences.

3. **Online Platforms and Social Media**: Use social media to share content like inspirational stories, spiritual insights, and healing practices. Host live sessions, webinars, or online groups to engage with a broader audience.

4. **Community Events**: Participate in or organise community fairs, health expos, or open houses where you can set up booths to provide information and resources on spiritual healing.

5. **Newsletters and Blogs**: Create newsletters or blogs that offer regular insights, tips, and updates on spiritual healing topics. Encourage readers to share with friends and family.

6. **Partnership with Healthcare Providers**: Collaborate with local healthcare providers to integrate spiritual healing into traditional healthcare settings. Provide materials and training on spiritual approaches to health.

7. **Testimonials and Case Studies**: Share testimonials and success stories from individuals who have benefited from spiritual healing. Use these stories to highlight the positive impact of your approach.

8. **Workshops for Practitioners**: Conduct training sessions for other healthcare providers or spiritual leaders to expand the reach of your methods through professionals who already work with your target audience.

9. **Community Service and Volunteering**: Engage in volunteer work, demonstrating your commitment to healing and helping others. This can enhance community trust and interest in your approach.

10. **Local Media Engagement**: Reach out to local newspapers, radio stations, or TV channels to share your knowledge on spiritual healing. Offer to write columns or participate in interviews.

11. **Interactive Activities**: Facilitate interactive events, such as meditation circles, yoga sessions, or prayer groups, where community members can experience spiritual healing first hand.

12. **Feedback and Adaptation**: Collect feedback from participants and community members to continuously improve and adapt your strategies to meet better the needs of those you serve.

Promoting Spiritual Healing on Social Media

To connect with and inspire your audience, use these effective strategies:

1. **Content Variety**: Share a mix of content formats such as inspirational quotes, videos, live sessions, blog links, and infographics. This diversity can keep your audience engaged and interested.

2. **Inspirational Quotes and Stories**: Post uplifting quotes or personal success stories related to spiritual healing. Encourage followers to share their own stories and experiences in the comments.

3. **Live Sessions and Webinars**: Host live Q&A sessions, meditation, or yoga classes. This interactive approach allows real-time engagement and fosters a sense of community.

4. **Community Building**: Create a private group or page for your followers to connect, share experiences, and support each other on their spiritual journeys.

5. **User-Generated Content**: Encourage your audience to share their spiritual healing practices, tag your page, or use a specific hashtag. This can increase your reach and build a community.

6. **Engagement and Interaction**: Regularly respond to comments, messages, and posts. Engaging with your audience on a personal level can build trust and loyalty.

7. **Collaborations and Influencer Partnerships**: Collaborate with other spiritual leaders or influencers whose audiences align with your message. This can help you reach new potential followers.

8. **Educational Posts**: Share valuable information on myths, benefits, and spiritual healing methods. Create informative posts that educate your audience about different spiritual healing techniques.

9. **Hashtag Strategy**: Use relevant hashtags to increase the discoverability of your posts. Research trending hashtags related to spirituality and healing and incorporate them into your content.

10. **Stories and Highlights**: Use Instagram or Facebook stories for quick, engaging updates. Save important content in highlights so new followers can easily access it.

11. **Giveaways and Challenges**: Host giveaways or challenges to encourage participation. For example, a gratitude challenge where followers share daily thankful moments can increase engagement.

12. **Consistency and Timing**: Post consistently to keep your presence visible. Use analytics to determine the best times to post when your audience is most active.

13. **Polls and Surveys**: Conduct polls or surveys to engage your audience and gather insights into what they want to learn or discuss.

14. **Aesthetic and Branding**: Maintain a consistent and visually appealing aesthetic that reflects your core values and message. This helps you build brand recognition.

By implementing these strategies, you can create an engaging and supportive online community that cultivates interest in spiritual healing and resonates with your audience's needs and aspirations.

Starting a Personal Blog or Engaging on Social Media as a Psychiatrist

Starting a personal blog or engaging on social media can be beneficial for a psychiatrist. Here are some points to consider:

1. **Audience Engagement**: Both platforms allow you to connect with a broader audience. You can share insights, debunk myths, and educate people about mental health.

2. **Professional Growth**: Sharing your knowledge can establish you as an expert in your field, potentially leading to speaking engagements, networking opportunities, and collaborations.

3. **Platform Choice**:
    - **Blog**: Ideal for long-form content, in-depth articles, and case studies. It allows for comprehensive exploration of topics and can be used as a portfolio of your expertise.
    - **Social Media**: Perfect for quick tips, updates, and more interactive engagement. Platforms like Twitter, Instagram, or LinkedIn allow for shorter content and direct interaction with your audience.

4. **Content Consideration**:
    - Maintain patient confidentiality at all times.
    - Focus on general advice and insights.
    - Share findings from current research, emerging trends, and personal professional experiences.
5. **Building Community**: Both platforms enable you to create a community around shared interests, allowing your audience to discuss and engage with mental health topics.

In conclusion, both blogging and social media offer distinct advantages, and the choice depends on your content style, audience engagement preference, and the type of information you wish to share.

Engaging and Relevant Topics to Cover in Your Psychiatry Blog

Here are some engaging and relevant topics you can cover in your psychiatry blog:

1. **Mental Health Tips**: Share practical advice on managing stress, anxiety, and depression.
2. **Common Psychiatric Disorders**: Provide insights on conditions like ADHD, bipolar disorder, and schizophrenia.
3. **Therapeutic Techniques**: Discuss therapies such as CBT, mindfulness, and EMDR, explaining how they work and who they benefit.
4. **Child and Adolescent Psychiatry**: Address the mental health challenges faced by younger demographics, offering guidance for parents.

5. **The Impact of Technology**: Explore how social media and smartphones affect mental health.

6. **Stigma and Mental Health**: Write about the societal challenges surrounding mental health disorders and ways to combat stigma.

7. **Patient Stories (Anonymous)**: With permission, share anonymised stories or general case studies to illustrate specific mental health issues.

8. **Latest Research and Trends**: Discuss the latest findings in psychiatry, new medications, and emerging treatment modalities.

9. **Self-Care and Wellness**: Offer advice on building resilience and finding work-life balance.

10. **Cultural Perspectives**: Explore how different cultures view and handle mental health issues.

11. **Medication Management**: Provide information on how various psychiatric medications work and considerations for their use.

12. **COVID-19 and Mental Health**: Discuss the ongoing impact of the pandemic on mental health and coping strategies.

13. **Interview Experts**: Feature interviews with colleagues or other mental health professionals to provide diverse perspectives.

14. **Mind-Body Connection**: Delve into how physical health influences mental well-being.

Start by choosing topics that you're passionate about and that cater to the interests or needs of your target audience.

Creating Mental Health Content: A Meaningful and Impactful Endeavour

Here are a few content ideas to help you on your journey:

1. **Personal Experiences**: Share your personal mental health journey, highlighting challenges and what you've learned along the way. This can foster a sense of connection with your audience.

2. **Educational Posts**: Explain common mental health issues like anxiety, depression, and stress in simple terms. Break down symptoms, causes, and possible treatments.

3. **Coping Strategies**: Offer practical tips and strategies for managing mental health on a day-to-day basis. Consider exercises, meditation techniques, or journal prompts.

4. **Interviews with Experts**: Collaborate with psychologists, therapists, or other mental health professionals to provide expert insights and advice.

5. **Self-Care and Wellbeing Tips**: Create content around self-care practices that promote mental well-being. This could include things like setting boundaries, prioritising sleep, or engaging in creative activities.

6. **Support and Encouragement**: Offer words of encouragement and support to your followers. Positive affirmations or motivational quotes can uplift your audience.

7. **Interactive Content**: Encourage engagement with polls, Q&A sessions, or live streams where you address mental health topics and answer audience questions.

8. **Book/Resource Recommendations**: Suggest books, podcasts, or online resources that provide valuable information on mental health.

9. **Awareness Campaigns**: Participate in awareness campaigns for World Mental Health Day or other related events to bring focus to mental health topics.

10. **Community Building**: Foster a supportive online community where people feel safe to share, discuss, and seek help.

ECHOES OF FAITH AMIDST MENTAL CHALLENGES

Letter from a Concerned Parent:

"Good morning Dr. Labinjo,

This is David's mum, Olivia. Thanks so much for offering to be David's mentor. He is having a hard time letting go of cannabis... tried to convince me to try (spent 3 hours) and flew into a rage. Currently, he is off antipsychotics which were prescribed for his schizophrenia. Any advice you have we will gratefully accept.

Thank you,

Olivia"

Supporting David

David is a bright young man who has an addiction to cannabis, which led to him being admitted under my care as a psychiatrist during his undergraduate studies. He is pleasant, friendly, and gifted.

I replied:

Hello Olivia,

Thank you for reaching out and sharing David's situation. It sounds like a challenging time for both him and your family. Here's a general approach that might help, considering the complexities of his condition:

Understanding the Situation

1. **Schizophrenia Management**: As a psychiatrist, it is crucial to communicate with him to reassess the need for antipsychotics. Schizophrenia can have serious consequences if not managed properly.

2. **Cannabis and Schizophrenia**: Cannabis use can exacerbate schizophrenia symptoms. Reducing or eliminating cannabis use is a priority.

3. **Communication**: Maintain open lines of communication with David. Express empathy and understanding, rather than judgment, to foster trust.

Building Support Networks

1. **Family Support**: I encourage family members to educate themselves about schizophrenia and addiction to support him better.

2. **Peer Support Groups**: I urge you to consider support groups for both psychosis and cannabis addiction. These can provide David with a sense of community and shared experience.

3. **Therapeutic Support**: Explore therapy options. Cognitive Behavioural Therapy (CBT) can be effective for both managing addiction and schizophrenia.

Creating a Management Plan

1. **Professional Guidance**: Regular consultation with mental health professionals, including psychiatrists, addiction specialists, and therapists, is crucial.

2. **Structured Routine**: Encourage a structured daily routine to provide stability and predictability.

3. **Identify Triggers**: Work with David to identify and understand triggers that lead to cannabis use, and develop coping strategies.

Positive Reinforcement

1. **Highlight Strengths**: Focus on his positive attributes and achievements to build self-esteem and motivation.

2. **Goal Setting**: Help David set realistic and achievable short-term and long-term goals.

Holistic Approach

1. **Physical Health**: Encourage a healthy lifestyle, including exercise, nutrition, and sleep hygiene.

2. **Mindfulness and Relaxation**: Techniques such as meditation or yoga can reduce stress and improve mental clarity.

Patience and Persistence

Recovery and management of schizophrenia and addiction are long-term processes that require patience and persistence from both David and his support network.

Professional Assistance

As his mentor and psychiatrist, I can provide tailored strategies and interventions, aligning them with David's specific needs and circumstances.

I should stress that progress may be gradual, and setbacks are part of the journey. Celebrate small victories along the way.

Feel free to ask more specific questions or reach out if you need anything else. I am here to support you and David through this process.

Warm regards,

Francis

Is There a Cannabis Antagonist Drug?

As of now, there is no approved cannabis antagonist specifically developed to counteract the effects of cannabis. However, research in this area is ongoing. Cannabis antagonists are compounds designed to block the effects of cannabinoids, primarily THC (the psychoactive component of cannabis), at cannabinoid receptors in the brain.

One of the most well-known compounds studied as a potential cannabis antagonist is **Rimonabant**. It was designed to block CB1 receptors, which mediate many of the psychoactive effects of THC. However, it was withdrawn from the market due to psychiatric side effects, such as depression and anxiety.

Researchers continue to explore other potential cannabinoids and compounds that could act as antagonists with fewer side effects, but as of now, these are still in the experimental and research stages. If you are interested in treatment for cannabis use disorder, focusing on behavioural therapies and seeking professional guidance would be the most recommended approach currently.

Into the Future: What Are the Current Research Studies on Cannabis Antagonists?

Current research on cannabis antagonists primarily focuses on developing compounds that can effectively block the psychoactive effects of THC while minimising side effects. Here are some key areas of research:

1. **Selective CB1 Antagonists**: Scientists are working on creating selective compounds that target the CB1 receptor, aiming to reduce THC's psychoactive effects without causing adverse psychiatric effects. These could potentially help treat cannabis use disorder.

2. **Inverse Agonists**: Research is exploring inverse agonists that block and induce an opposite response at the receptor site. These could help counteract the effects of THC more effectively.

3. **Allosteric Modulators**: These compounds bind to a different part of the CB1 receptor, potentially providing a way to modulate its activity rather than completely blocking it. This might offer a more controlled approach to managing THC's effects.

4. **Biphasic Regulation**: Studies are examining how cannabinoids exhibit biphasic effects—having different effects at varying doses—and how antagonists can be used to manage these.

5. **Clinical Trials**: Clinical trials are ongoing to test the efficacy and safety of potential cannabis antagonists in real-world settings, often focusing on treating cannabis use disorder or reducing withdrawal symptoms.

Researchers are also investigating the role of cannabis antagonists in treating various conditions, such as obesity, given the known effects of cannabinoids on appetite regulation.

While promising, these studies are still in early stages, and further research is necessary to develop safe and effective treatments.

ICD-10 Codes for Cannabis Use Disorder (CUD):

- **F12.10**: Cannabis abuse, uncomplicated
- **F12.20**: Cannabis dependence, uncomplicated
- **F12.90**: Cannabis use, unspecified, uncomplicated
- **F12.93**: Cannabis use, unspecified with withdrawal
- **F12.29**: Cannabis dependence with other cannabis-induced disorders

LET'S TALK ABOUT CANNABIS: APPRAISAL OF CANNABIS CLINICS

Cannabis clinics are specialised medical facilities that often focus on prescribing and guiding the use of medical cannabis for patients with specific health conditions.

The appraisal of these clinics involves looking at various aspects:

1. **Professionalism and Expertise**:
    - Staffed by trained healthcare professionals, usually with experience in pain management, oncology, neurology, or psychiatry.

- They often provide personalised treatment plans, adjusting cannabis dosage and strain according to individual needs.

2. **Accessibility and Cost**:
    - Location and availability can vary widely; access might be limited in certain regions.
    - Costs can potentially be high, especially if not covered by insurance, although some clinics operate on sliding scales.

3. **Quality of Care**:
    - Clinics may offer comprehensive consultations, ongoing monitoring, and follow-up care to adjust treatments.
    - They often prioritise patient education about cannabis use, benefits, and potential risks.

4. **Legal and Ethical Considerations**:
    - Operate under strict legal frameworks, ensuring compliance with state and federal laws.
    - Ethical practices involve safeguarding patient privacy and ensuring informed consent.

5. **Patient Outcomes**:
    - Many patients report positive outcomes in pain management, anxiety reduction, and improved quality of life.
    - Evidence supporting efficacy varies, and results can be subjective, varying from person to person.

6. **Variety of Services**:
    - Often provide a range of cannabis products (oils, edibles, capsules) to suit patient preferences and needs.
    - Additional services may include nutritional advice and complementary therapies.

Cannabis Clinics

Cannabis clinics serve an important role in healthcare for patients seeking alternative treatments. Their appraisal varies based on the individual clinic's reputation, the expertise of their staff, and the success of their patient outcomes.

While they provide an essential service, potential patients should research and consult with healthcare providers to ensure they select a reputable clinic that meets their needs.

1. **Maudsley Cannabis Clinic**: Focuses on young adults with psychosis linked to high-potency cannabis use. It combines addiction treatments with psychosis care, showing success in reducing cannabis use and improving mental health outcomes.

2. **Private Rehab Centres** (e.g., Primrose Lodge, UKAT): Offer detox, therapy (CBT, group therapy), and personalised recovery plans in supportive environments. These centres emphasise long-term recovery, addressing underlying causes of addiction.

Visiting a cannabis clinic for the first time can be an informative and structured experience. Here's what you can typically expect:

1. **Initial Registration**:
   - You might need to fill out forms with personal information, medical history, and details about your current medications and conditions.

2. **Consultation with a Healthcare Professional**:
   - You'll meet with a doctor or healthcare expert who will review your medical history and discuss your specific health problems and goals.
   - The professional will assess whether cannabis is a suitable treatment option for you, considering your symptoms, prior treatments, and potential benefits.

3. **Discussion of Cannabis Knowledge**:
   - The healthcare provider may educate you about how medical cannabis works, its effects, and any risks involved.
   - You'll learn about different strains, CBD-to-THC ratios, and methods of consumption (oils, edibles, vaping, etc.).

4. **Developing a Treatment Plan**:
   - You will create a personalised treatment plan with the healthcare professional, including recommended products, dosages, and consumption methods.
   - They will probably emphasise starting with a low dose and gradually increasing it to monitor its effects.

5. **Addressing Questions and Concerns**:
   o You'll have the opportunity to ask questions or express any concerns you might have about using cannabis for your condition.
   o This might include discussions about potential side effects, drug interactions, or lifestyle considerations.

6. **Follow-up Arrangements**:
   o A follow-up appointment might be scheduled to assess how the treatment is working for you and make any needed adjustments.
   o The clinic may also offer resources or support services to aid in your treatment process.

7. **Compliance and Legal Guidance**:
   o You'll be informed about the legal aspects of using medical cannabis, including possession limits and any relevant state laws.
   o The clinic will likely guide you on obtaining a medical cannabis card if required in your region.

8. **Visit to Dispensary (if applicable)**:
   o In some clinics, you might then visit an on-site dispensary or receive guidance on where to legally purchase your recommended cannabis products.

Preparation and understanding are key to maximising the benefits of your visit, and feeling free to communicate openly with the healthcare professionals will help tailor the experience to your needs.

Are Such Clinics Helpful in Cannabis Use Disorder (CUD)?

Therapy Options for Cannabis Use Disorder

There are several therapy options that have proven effective for treating cannabis use disorder (CUD). Here are some of the most common approaches:

1. **Cognitive-Behavioural Therapy (CBT):**
    - CBT focuses on identifying and changing negative thought patterns and behaviours. It helps individuals develop coping skills and strategies to manage cravings and avoid triggers.

2. **Motivational Enhancement Therapy (MET):**
    - MET is designed to enhance an individual's motivation to change their cannabis use by evoking personal reasons and emphasising the benefits of quitting. It typically involves a limited number of sessions.

3. **Contingency Management (CM):**
    - CM uses a reward-based system to reinforce positive behaviours, such as abstinence from cannabis. Rewards might include vouchers or other incentives for meeting treatment goals.

4. **Behavioural Couples Therapy (BCT):**
    - For individuals in relationships, BCT involves both partners and focuses on improving communication and support for overcoming substance use.

5. **Mindfulness-Based Interventions**:
   - Mindfulness practices, such as meditation and yoga, can help increase awareness of thoughts and behaviours, reducing the likelihood of relapse by promoting relaxation and stress reduction.

6. **12-Step Programs**:
   - Although these programs are typically associated with other substances, some people find support and structure through groups like Marijuana Anonymous, which follows a similar 12-step framework.

7. **Support Groups**:
   - Peer support groups provide a community of individuals with similar experiences, facilitating shared knowledge and encouragement throughout recovery.

Each therapy option can be tailored to meet individual needs and can often be combined for more comprehensive treatment.

Working with a healthcare professional or therapist is important to determine the most suitable approach for your situation.

Treatment of Cannabis Use Disorder

Cannabis use disorder (CUD) is a condition characterised by the problematic use of cannabis, leading to significant impairment or distress. Treatment for CUD typically involves a combination of behavioural therapies, medication, and support groups.

Here's a brief overview:

1. **Behavioural Therapies:**

    o **Cognitive-Behavioural Therapy (CBT):** Helps individuals identify and change negative thought patterns and behaviours associated with cannabis use.

    o **Motivational Enhancement Therapy (MET):** Focuses on building motivation to quit by exploring the pros and cons of cannabis use and setting personal goals.

    o **Contingency Management:** Provides tangible rewards for staying abstinent and attending treatment sessions, encouraging continued sobriety.

2. **Medications:**

    o Currently, there are no FDA-approved medications specifically for cannabis use disorder. However, some medications used off-label may help manage withdrawal symptoms or reduce cravings, including antidepressants or anti-anxiety medications.

3. **Support Groups:**

    o Participating in groups like Marijuana Anonymous can offer community support and shared experiences, aiding in recovery.

    o Online forums and virtual meetings can also provide accessible support.

4. **Lifestyle Changes and Self-Care:**

    o Encouraging a healthy lifestyle, such as regular exercise, good nutrition, and sufficient sleep, can help improve overall well-being and reduce the urge to use cannabis.

- o Developing coping strategies for stress, such as mindfulness and meditation, can be beneficial.

5. **Family and Social Support**:
    - o Involving family members or close friends in the treatment process can provide additional support. Family therapy may help repair relationships affected by cannabis use.

6. **Professional Support**:
    - o Working with a mental health professional or addiction specialist can provide personalised guidance and treatment plans.

Recovery from cannabis use disorder is possible with the right support and treatment. Each individual's path to recovery is unique, and treatment plans should be tailored to meet personal needs and circumstances.

From a Man with Schizophrenia:

"One more thing. Last year the Lord told me not to get involved with mental health when I decided to obey what the angel came into my hospital room at the hospital and told me to go back to my church."

Reflection:

The man is expressing a personal and spiritual experience. What you may not know is that for someone with schizophrenia, experiences that involve visions or messages can be particularly vivid and meaningful. It's important to approach such discussions with sensitivity and understanding.

We must find a way to ensure that they have access to professional mental health services, which would be beneficial, as well as encouraging them to talk openly with mental health professionals about their experiences. This can help in managing their condition effectively. Maintaining a supportive and non-judgmental relationship with them is also key.

The intersection of faith and mental health can be deeply personal and complex, especially for individuals with schizophrenia. In this case, the patient appears to draw on their faith as a source of guidance and comfort. Their experiences with visions or messages might be interpreted through their religious beliefs, which can significantly influence how they perceive their mental health and treatment.

Here are a few considerations when supporting someone in this situation:

1. **Respect Spiritual Beliefs**: Recognising and respecting the patient's spiritual experiences and beliefs can build trust and rapport.

2. **Holistic Approach**: Balancing mental health treatment with respect for spiritual beliefs can be beneficial. Encouraging the patient to discuss both aspects with their healthcare providers can help integrate their care.

3. **Open Communication**: Encouraging open, judgment-free conversations about mental health and spiritual experiences can foster understanding and clarify how these experiences affect their well-being.

4. **Support Systems**: Understanding that religious communities can be a source of support, the patient might benefit from involvement with supportive peers within these communities while continuing to receive appropriate medical care.

5. **Professional Guidance**: Consult with mental health professionals who can navigate these overlapping areas with sensitivity and expertise, possibly integrating spiritual care jointly with religious leaders if the patient wishes.

Balancing faith and treatment in the care for those with schizophrenia should be done with careful consideration and respect for the individual's values and beliefs.

THE SPIRITUAL CHALLENGES YOU WILL FACE IN BRINGING FAITH INTO YOUR MENTAL RECOVERY

Bringing faith into your mental recovery can present several spiritual challenges, including:

1. **Crisis of Faith**: Undergoing mental health struggles might lead to questioning or doubting your spiritual beliefs. It's natural to wonder why you're facing difficulties, and figuring out where faith fits in can be challenging.

2. **Finding Meaning**: Searching for spirituality's role or meaning in your mental health journey may be difficult. Balancing your faith with the reality of your struggles is a deeply personal process.

3. **Conflicting Emotions**: You might experience emotions like anger or guilt if you feel that your faith isn't providing the comfort or answers you seek. Navigating these emotions while staying true to your beliefs requires resilience.

4. **Balancing Practices**: Determining how to balance spiritual practices and rituals with therapeutic treatments can

challenge maintaining an integrated and holistic recovery approach.

5. **Isolation**: Feeling isolated from your faith community, especially if they don't fully understand mental health challenges, can hinder your recovery. Building a bridge between your needs and your community's understanding is crucial.

6. **Spiritual Discipline**: Maintaining discipline in spiritual practices may require extra effort when mental health issues are present. Ensuring regularity might involve adapting these practices to suit your mental and emotional state.

7. **Integration with Therapy**: Successfully integrating faith with psychological therapy can pose a challenge, especially if your therapist isn't familiar with faith's role in mental health.

8. **Expectation vs. Reality**: Having high expectations for spiritual healing could lead to disappointment if recovery takes time or doesn't progress as hoped. Managing these expectations is essential.

9. **Inner Conflict**: Internal conflicts about faith and mental health can arise, especially if your beliefs suggest solutions that conflict with medical advice. Finding harmony between the two can be complex.

10. **Acceptance of Vulnerability**: Accepting that having faith does not render you invulnerable to mental health challenges is key, embracing vulnerability as a part of the human experience.

Facing these spiritual challenges involves patience, self-reflection, and open-mindedness. Seeking guidance from faith leaders who understand mental health, engaging with supportive communities, and nurturing your spiritual and psychological well-being can provide healing. Remember, blending faith with mental recovery is a journey, and it's okay to seek help and adapt your approach along the way.

Mental health legislation in the next decade and beyond

In the UK, the future of mental health legislation over the next decade and beyond will likely focus on enhancing accessibility, integration, and protection of mental health services. Here are some key trends and focus areas that might shape future legislation:

1. Increased Funding and Resources: The UK government might continue to allocate more resources to mental health services, aiming to reduce waiting times, improve treatment facilities, and ensure equitable access to care across the country.

2. Integration with Physical Health: Legislation is likely to support the integration of mental health services with physical health care, promoting collaboration between healthcare providers to treat patients holistically.

3. Workplace Mental Health Support: New laws may require businesses to implement mental health policies, provide training for staff, and ensure employees have access to mental health resources and support.

4. Digital and Telehealth Services: With the expansion of digital health services, legislation will likely address the regulation of telehealth platforms, ensuring they are secure, accessible, and offer parity with in-person services.

5. Youth and School-Based Mental Health: There may be increased focus on the mental health of children and adolescents, with potential legislation mandating mental health education and support services in schools.

6. Research and Innovation: Supporting research into new treatments and mental health technologies will continue to be a legislative priority, encouraging innovation and evidence-based practices.

7. Crisis Intervention and Support: Developing robust crisis intervention services and legislation to improve emergency mental health responses, possibly shifting towards more non-police involvement and community-centred support.

8. Data Privacy and Security: Ensuring the protection of personal mental health data will be a critical area of focus as digital services expand, with legislation potentially enforcing stringent privacy regulations.

9. Anti-Stigma and Anti-Discrimination: Strengthening laws to combat stigma and discrimination faced by individuals with mental health conditions in employment, healthcare, and society.

10. Community-Based Support Systems: Emphasis on community-based care models may lead to legislative support for local mental health initiatives, encouraging grassroots participation and resource sharing.

11. Global Trends and Cooperation: The UK may work towards aligning its mental health policies with global standards, sharing best practices, and addressing mental health at an international level.

12. Rights and Protections: Expanding and reinforcing patient rights in mental health care settings, ensuring individuals are treated with dignity and respect, and can voice their care preferences.

These future legislative trends reflect a comprehensive approach to mental health in the UK, aiming to create a society where mental health is a priority and resources are accessible and equitable for all individuals.

Recent changes in UK mental health legislation have focused on modernising policies to provide better patient-centred care, safeguarding rights, and improving access to services. Here are some key developments:

1. Mental Health Act Reform: The UK government has been working on reforming the Mental Health Act, emphasising patient autonomy and enhancing safeguards. Proposed changes aim to give individuals more control over their treatment and reduce the use of compulsory detention.

2. Improved Community Support: There's a push towards enhancing community-based mental health services to provide better support and reduce hospital admissions. This includes increasing funding and developing mental health hubs.

3. Workforce Expansion: Efforts have been made to expand the mental health workforce, ensuring more professionals are available to meet the growing demand for mental health services.

4. Access to Services: There have been initiatives to improve access to mental health services, particularly for young people and marginalised groups, through digital platforms and targeted programs.

5. Crisis Services Enhancement: Developing and expanding mental health crisis services, including 24/7 helplines, to support people experiencing acute mental health crises.

These changes aim to create a more equitable, accessible, and effective mental health care system in the UK.

The reform of the Mental Health Act in the UK is centred around improving patient rights and ensuring that mental health care is more personalised and responsive to individual needs.

Here are some of the key aspects of the proposed reform:

1. Patient Autonomy: One of the main goals is to give patients greater autonomy over their treatment choices. This means enhancing patients' rights to make decisions about their care, including when and how they receive treatment.

2. Criteria for Detention: The reform aims to tighten the criteria for detaining individuals under the Mental Health Act, ensuring that detention is used as a last resort and only when absolutely necessary. This involves reassessing the conditions under which individuals can be sectioned.

3. Community Treatment Orders: There's a proposal to make changes to Community Treatment Orders (CTOs) to ensure they are used appropriately and that their duration and conditions are justified and reviewed regularly.

4. Role of Families and Caregivers: The reform seeks to strengthen the role of families and caregivers in decision-making processes, ensuring that they are more involved and informed about the treatments and care of their loved ones.

5. Reducing Disparities: Addressing the disparities in the way the Act is applied to different demographic groups, particularly focusing on reducing the disproportionate detention of individuals from Black and minority ethnic communities.

6. Improved Access to Advocacy: Ensuring that patients have better access to independent advocates who can represent their interests and help them understand their rights and options.

7. Advance Choice Documents: Encouraging the use of Advance Choice Documents, which allow patients to outline their treatment preferences in advance, should they become unable to make decisions in the future.

8. Review Processes: Establishing more robust review processes to regularly assess the necessity and appropriateness of continued detention or treatment under the Act.

Overall, the aim of the reform is to create a more compassionate, fair, and effective mental health care system in the UK, focusing on the dignity and rights of individuals receiving care.

4

STRESS AND BURNOUT

With academic pressures, career uncertainties, and social expectations, stress and burnout are highly relatable issues. Techniques for managing stress are widely sought after.

MENTAL HEALTH CHALLENGES OF YOUNG PEOPLE

Anxiety and depression

Let's talk about something real: depression. It's like having a cloud follow you around even on the sunniest days.

1. **What is Depression?**
   It's not just feeling blue. It's like your brain is stuck on a playlist of sad songs, and you can't hit skip.

2. **Signs We Might Miss:**
   Being extra tired, losing interest in things you love—like your favourite show suddenly being "meh." It's like your inner Wi-Fi is down.

3. **Why Do We Feel This Way?**
   Sometimes it's life stuff, like stress or heartbreak. Other

times, it's just how our brain's wired. Think of it like a phone glitch that needs fixing.

4. **Let's Get Moving:**
Physical activity is like magic for your mood. Even a quick walk can be like restarting your computer when it's lagging.

5. **Art of Expression:**
Dive into something creative. Draw, write, or play music. It's like letting those bottled-up feelings out in a cool blackout poem or a new track.

6. **Reach Out:**
Chat with someone you trust—a friend, family, or a counsellor. It's like unloading a heavy backpack you didn't realise you were carrying.

7. **Our Digital World:**
Social media's great for connection, but it can also be overwhelming. Notice how it makes you feel, and take breaks when needed. Consider it a mini digital detox.

8. **Mood Foods:**
Believe it or not, what you eat affects how you feel. Loading up on fruits, vegetables, and water is like giving your brain a refreshing splash.

9. **Sleep's Superpower:**
Quality sleep is your secret weapon. It's like plugging in and recharging your whole system. Try a chill bedtime routine to help.

10. **You're Not Alone:**
So many people are in this with you. Reaching out for help is like calling tech support for your mind. You deserve to feel better.

Remember, you're awesome just as you are. If you want to talk more about it or anything else, I'm all ears!

Faith as a Tool for Anxiety and Depression:

Young people today face a variety of mental health challenges, some of which include:

1. **Anxiety:** Many young people experience anxiety related to school pressure, social interactions, and the future. Social media can exacerbate these feelings by creating pressure to maintain a certain image.

2. **Depression:** Feelings of sadness, hopelessness, and a lack of interest in activities they once enjoyed are common. These can be fuelled by academic stress, social stressors, or family issues.

3. **Stress:** The demands of school, extracurricular activities, and sometimes part-time work can lead to high levels of stress.

4. **Body Image Issues:** Influenced by social media and societal standards, young people may struggle with body image, which can lead to eating disorders or low self-esteem.

5. **Social Anxiety:** This involves intense fear or anxiety of being judged or negatively evaluated in social situations.

Social Anxiety: Breaking Down Walls, One Step at a Time

Imagine walking into a room full of people, and it feels like the walls are closing in. Your heart races, your palms sweat, and you wonder – is anyone else feeling this too?

You're Not Alone!

Social anxiety is more common than you think. It's like that uninvited guest who pops up just when you want to be chill. But here's the good news – it's something you can manage and overcome!

Let's Dive In:

1. **What's Really Happening?**
    - Understand that social anxiety is your brain's way of protecting you from potential embarrassment.
    - It's more about how we perceive situations rather than their actual difficulty.

2. **Small Steps, Big Wins!**
    - Start with baby steps. Try smiling at a stranger or asking a simple question.
    - Celebrate these small victories – they're big deals!

3. **Mindfulness Magic!**
    - Practice mindfulness exercises to keep your anxious thoughts in check.
    - Apps and videos can guide you in focusing on the present moment.

4. **Breathe, Believe, Achieve!**
    - Deep breathing can help calm those jitters.
    - Believe in yourself and the power of progress!

5. **Find Your Tribe**
    - Surround yourself with supportive people who understand and respect your journey.
    - Join groups or forums where people share similar experiences.

6. **Get Creative!**
    - Express yourself through art, writing, or any hobby that allows you to channel energy positively.
    - These outlets can be therapeutic and confidence-boosting.

7. **Professional Help is Cool!**
    - Sometimes talking to a counsellor or therapist can make a world of difference.
    - They bring insights and tools tailored to help you succeed.

Remember This:

Social anxiety doesn't define you. You have the power to write your own story and conquer the awkwardness, one step at a time. Here are some challenges below:

1. **Identity and Sexual Orientation:** Figuring out one's identity and sexual orientation can be challenging, and may lead to confusion, stress, or fear of acceptance.

2. **Substance Abuse:** Some turn to substances as a way to cope with their mental health issues, leading to further complications.

3. **Bullying and Cyberbullying:** Both in-person and online bullying can have severe effects on mental health, leading to increased anxiety, depression, and even suicidal thoughts.

4. **Academic Pressure:** The pressure to perform well in school and gain admission to top universities can lead to chronic stress and burnout.

5. **Loneliness and Isolation:** Despite being constantly connected through technology, many young people feel isolated and struggle to form meaningful connections.

6. **Family Issues:** Divorce, financial troubles, or conflict within the family can heavily impact a young person's mental well-being.

These challenges can vary in intensity and impact, depending on the individual's environment, history, and available support systems. Access to mental health resources, supportive family, and an understanding community play vital roles in helping young people navigate these challenges.

Stress Management

High levels of stress from school, work, and relationships are a major concern, leading to interest in stress-relief techniques. Stress-related paranoia or severe dissociative symptoms may occur.

Let's talk about stress management – something that's super important but often overlooked, especially by young people. Life can get pretty hectic with school, social life, side hustles, and everything in between, right? Here are some cool tips to help you tackle stress like a pro:

1. **Mindfulness and Meditation:**
   Ever tried meditation? It's like a mini-vacation for your brain! Apps like Headspace and Calm can make meditation easy and fun with guided sessions. Just ten minutes a day can help you chill out.

2. **Get Moving:**
   Exercise isn't just for your body, it's awesome for your mind too. Whether it's dancing, playing a sport, or just a walk around the block, keeping active can bust stress big time.

3. **Creative Outlets:**
   Do you like to draw, write, or play music? Creative activities are great for reducing stress. They let you express yourself and can be a perfect escape from daily pressures.

4. **Connect with Friends:**
   Spending time with friends can boost your mood and reduce stress. Plan a fun outing or even just a virtual hangout to unwind and share your feelings.

5. **Sleep Well:**
   Never underestimate the power of good sleep. Aim for 7-9 hours each night, and try sticking to a sleep schedule. It helps your body recover and keeps stress at bay.

6. **Stay Organised:**
   Sometimes stress comes from feeling overwhelmed. Use a planner or a digital app to keep track of tasks and deadlines. Breaking things into smaller, manageable chunks can make a huge difference.

7. **Tech Breaks:**
   Constant notifications can be stressful. Set boundaries on screen time or take regular tech breaks to stay grounded and present. Protect your mind!

8. **Practice Gratitude:**
   Start or end your day by jotting down three things you're

grateful for. Focusing on the positives can shift your mindset and reduce stress.

9. **Talk It Out:**
   Don't bottle things up. If you're feeling stressed, talk to someone you trust—friends, family, or a counsellor. Sometimes, just sharing how you feel can lighten the load.

10. **Laugh:**
    Laughter is an awesome stress-buster. Watch a funny movie, listen to a comedy podcast, or hang out with someone who makes you smile.

Remember, it's okay to feel stressed sometimes, but you have the power to handle it. You've got this!

Body Image and Eating Disorders: These issues are prevalent, with many young people looking for healthier ways to perceive their bodies and manage eating habits.

What are some tips for dealing with negative body image thoughts?

Dealing with negative body image thoughts can be tough, but there are some strategies that might help flip those thoughts into positive ones. Here are some tips:

1. **Challenge the Critic:** Question its validity when a negative thought pops up. Ask yourself, "Is this thought based on fact or just a perception?"

2. **Positive Affirmations:** Start your day with positive affirmations. Repeat phrases like "I am strong," "I am capable," or "I love my body for all it does."

3. **Limit Social Media:** If scrolling through social media makes you feel bad, take a break. Follow accounts that promote body positivity and diverse bodies.

4. **Practice Gratitude:** Focus on what your body can do, rather than how it looks. Be grateful for health, strength, and abilities.

5. **Surround Yourself with Positivity:** Spend time with people who uplift you and make you feel good about yourself.

6. **Wear What Makes You Comfortable:** Choose clothes that make you feel confident and reflect your personal style.

7. **Seek Support:** If negative thoughts are overwhelming, talking to a friend, family member, or therapist can help.

8. **Mindfulness and Meditation:** Practice mindfulness and meditation to stay present and reduce anxiety over appearance.

9. **Creative Expression:** Engage in creative activities that make you feel good and distract from negative self-talk.

10. **Celebrate Small Wins:** Recognise and celebrate your achievements, no matter how small.

Remember, it's a journey, and being kind to yourself is key. You're not alone, and taking steps to improve your self-image is a big move towards a happier, healthier you!

Let's dive into a chat about something super important yet often overlooked – body image. Ever find yourself standing in front of a mirror, questioning how you look or comparing yourself to others on social media? You're not alone, my friend! In today's world, where filters and edits are just a swipe away, embracing and accepting your true self can be challenging.

But here's the scoop: everybody is unique, and that's what makes us all so amazing! Let's talk about the ups and downs of navigating body image, share tips on self-love and body positivity, and explore how to feel more confident in your own skin.

Jump in whenever you're ready to chat, ask questions, or share your thoughts. Remember, it's all about embracing yourself, flaws and all!

Eating Disorders

Key Statistics on Eating Disorders

- **Prevalence:** 9% of the U.S. population (28.8 million) will experience an eating disorder in their lifetime. In the UK, 1.25–3.4 million people are affected.

- **Mortality:** Eating disorders cause 10,200 deaths annually in the U.S., with anorexia having the highest mortality rate among psychiatric disorders.

- **Demographics:** Females are 2–3 times more likely to have eating disorders than males. Adolescents and young adults are most affected.

- **Co-morbidities:** PTSD and anxiety are common among sufferers.

- **Treatment Gaps:** Less than 27% of sufferers receive treatment.

The most common eating disorders among adolescents are:

- **Binge Eating Disorder (BED):** The most prevalent, affecting up to 1.6% of teens, characterised by episodes of overeating without compensatory behaviours.

- **Bulimia Nervosa:** Affects about 0.9% of teens, involving cycles of bingeing and purging through vomiting, laxatives, or excessive exercise.

- **Anorexia Nervosa:** Affects 0.3–0.6% of adolescents, marked by extreme food restriction, fear of weight gain, and distorted body image.
- **Subthreshold Eating Disorders:** These are also common.

Faith can play a significant role in eating disorder recovery by providing emotional and spiritual support. Positive religious beliefs, such as seeing the body as sacred, are linked to lower rates of disordered eating and improved body satisfaction. Faith can foster a sense of purpose, community, and hope, which aids recovery through prayer, trust in a higher power, and reframing self-worth. However, struggles with faith, such as guilt or viewing the body as needing control, can complicate recovery. Tailored treatment integrating faith and therapy can help balance religious practices with recovery needs.

Eating Disorders in Young People

Eating disorders in young people are serious mental health conditions that can affect anyone, regardless of age, gender, or background. Families need to understand the complexity of these disorders. Here's a brief overview:

Signs and Symptoms

- **Physical Changes:** Noticeable weight fluctuations, fatigue, dizziness, or digestive issues.
- **Emotional Symptoms:** Anxiety around food, low self-esteem, or perfectionism.
- **Behavioural Signs:** Skipping meals, eating in secret, or becoming overly focused on dieting.

Common Types

- **Anorexia Nervosa:** Characterised by restricted eating, extreme thinness, and an intense fear of gaining weight.
- **Bulimia Nervosa:** Involves cycles of binge eating followed by purging through vomiting or excessive exercise.
- **Binge Eating Disorder:** Consuming large quantities of food without purging, leading to feelings of guilt.

Underlying Causes

- **Biological Factors:** Genetics and hormone imbalances may play a role.
- **Psychological Factors:** Stress, trauma, or a history of dieting can contribute.
- **Social Influences:** Pressure from peers or societal expectations around body image.

Impact on Life

Eating disorders can affect every aspect of a young person's life, from their health and academic performance to relationships and self-image. They can lead to serious medical complications if not addressed.

How Families Can Help

- **Listen Without Judgment:** Create an open and supportive environment where your loved one feels safe to share their feelings.
- **Educate Yourselves:** Understanding the nature of eating disorders can help you recognise the signs and provide appropriate support.

- **Encourage Professional Help:** Seek guidance from healthcare providers who specialise in treating eating disorders.

Promoting Recovery

- **Build Trust:** Establish a non-judgemental and empathetic communication channel.
- **Focus on Positives:** Encourage talents and strengths beyond appearance.
- **Be Patient:** Recovery is a long process that requires support, understanding, and patience.

Important Notes

- **Avoid Blame:** Eating disorders are complex and not a result of poor parenting.
- **Celebrate Small Victories:** Every positive step is a move towards recovery.

Talking about eating disorders can be challenging, but understanding these key points can help families support their loved ones more effectively.

Faith and Eating Disorders

Discussion of ethical issues, such as respecting diverse beliefs in a mental health care setting.

Faith and belief can be particularly important for individuals or families dealing with eating disorders, offering unique forms of support and healing. Here's how:

Emotional and Spiritual Support

- **Hope and Healing:** Faith can instil hope and reinforce the belief in recovery, providing a sense of spiritual healing.
- **Inner Strength:** Belief can help individuals tap into a deeper reservoir of strength to combat the challenges of an eating disorder.

Community and Connection

- **Support Networks:** Faith communities can offer a supportive network, providing understanding, encouragement, and accountability.
- **Shared Struggles:** Connecting with others who share similar beliefs can reduce feelings of isolation and promote a sense of belonging.

Coping Mechanisms

- **Mindfulness and Meditation:** Prayer or meditation can serve as a grounding technique, reducing anxiety and promoting self-awareness.
- **Rituals and Routine:** Faith-based practices can offer structure and routine, which can be comforting and stabilising.

Moral and Ethical Guidance

- **Self-Worth and Acceptance:** Spiritual teachings often emphasise the inherent worth of each individual, encouraging self-love and acceptance.
- **Empathy and Compassion:** Faith can foster compassion towards oneself, countering the self-critical thoughts that often accompany eating disorders.

Contribution to Personal Growth

- **Reflective Practices:** Faith encourages introspection, helping individuals confront fears and develop healthier relationships with food and body image.

- **Purpose and Identity:** Belief systems can provide a sense of purpose and identity beyond physical appearance, focusing on inner qualities and strengths.

Family Dynamics

- **Unity and Support:** Shared beliefs can strengthen family bonds, creating a unified approach to coping with the disorder.

- **Communication and Understanding:** Faith-based frameworks can facilitate open, honest discussions about feelings, struggles, and recovery goals.

Access to Resources

- **Faith-Based Counseling:** Many faith communities offer counselling services that align with spiritual beliefs, integrating them into the healing process.

- **Inspirational Narratives:** Stories of recovery and redemption within religious texts or teachings can inspire and motivate individuals on their journey to wellness.

While faith and belief are personal, embracing them can provide significant emotional and psychological benefits during the recovery process from an eating disorder. They can complement medical and therapeutic interventions, offering a holistic approach to healing and growth.

Specific Examples of Faith Practices That Can Help with Eating Disorders

Christian Practices

- **Prayer:** Engaging in regular prayer can provide solace, clarity, and a deeper connection to one's spiritual beliefs, offering strength and comfort during recovery.
- **Bible Study:** Reflecting on scripture can inspire hope and encouragement, highlighting themes of self-worth and God's love for all individuals.
- **Communion:** Participating in communion can reinforce community ties and spiritual reflection, focusing on nourishment in a sacred context.

Jewish Practices

- **Shabbat:** Observing the Sabbath can promote rest and mindfulness, encouraging individuals to focus on spiritual nourishment rather than physical consumption.
- **Meditation on Torah:** Studying the Torah can provide wisdom and guidance, offering perspectives on self-care and inner value.
- **Community Support:** Engaging in synagogue events can foster community support, cultivating a network of understanding and care.

Islamic Practices

- **Salah (Prayer):** Daily prayers can offer routine and spiritual grounding, enhancing mindfulness and reflection.

- **Fasting:** During Ramadan, fasting is paired with reflection and charity, teaching discipline and the importance of spiritual over physical needs.
- **Quranic Recitation:** Reciting the Quran can bring peace and focus, emphasising compassion and self-respect.

Buddhist Practices

- **Mindfulness Meditation:** Practising meditation enhances self-awareness and promotes a balanced mind-body connection, reducing anxiety around eating.
- **Loving-kindness (Metta) Meditation:** This practice fosters self-compassion and empathy, encouraging positive body image and self-acceptance.
- **Noble Eightfold Path:** Following the path helps develop ethical living and mental discipline, aiding individuals in finding balance and inner peace.

Hindu Practices

- **Yoga:** Incorporating yoga can improve physical and mental well-being, fostering mindfulness and a healthy body image.
- **Bhajan/Kirtan:** Devotional singing or chanting can provide a sense of community and emotional release, enhancing feelings of joy and spiritual connection.
- **Scriptural Reflection:** Studying texts like the Bhagavad Gita can offer insights into living a balanced and harmonious life.

Indigenous Spiritual Practices

- **Ceremonial Rituals:** Engaging in traditional ceremonies can reinforce cultural identity and community support, promoting holistic healing.

- **Nature Walks:** Connecting with nature can restore balance and inner peace, emphasising the importance of harmony with the earth.

- **Storytelling:** Sharing ancestral stories can strengthen identity and impart wisdom about resilience and self-respect.

These faith practices, integrated with professional treatment and support, can promote resilience, enhance self-understanding, and reinforce a holistic approach to healing and recovery.

Community Resources for Support in Eating Disorders

1. **Beat:** The UK's leading eating disorder charity offers helplines, online support, and local support groups. They provide resources for both individuals and families.

2. **NHS Services:** The NHS provides support through General Practitioners (GPs), who can refer individuals to specialists, and local mental health services. They also offer eating disorder-specific treatment in many areas.

3. **Mind:** This mental health charity offers information and support, including local Mind branches that may have resources for eating disorders.

4. **Seed:** Provides support and information to individuals and families affected by eating disorders. They offer a support group and have downloadable resources.

5. **SHINE (Self-Help, Independence, Nutrition, and Exercise):** A programme designed for young people dealing with eating disorders, providing group support and activities.

6. **Local University and College Support Services:** Many academic institutions in the UK offer counselling and support for students experiencing eating disorders.

7. **Online Support Forums and Communities:** Forums such as those found on websites and social media for people in recovery can be helpful for finding peer support.

8. **Support Networks and Community Groups:** Local groups dedicated to mental health and well-being might have programmes or meetings specific to eating disorders.

9. **Counselling and Therapy Services:** Private therapists and counsellors who specialise in eating disorders can provide support.

10. **Mindfulness and Health Clubs:** Organisations focusing on wellness, like yoga studios or meditation groups, may offer additional support for mental health.

These resources can provide valuable support and information. Always ensure that any group or service is reputable and follows health and safety guidelines.

How Faith Can Be Integrated into Eating Disorder Treatment
Faith can be integrated into eating disorder treatment through the following approaches:

Faith-Based Programs:
Facilities like The Renfrew Center offer faith-based options, integrating Christian or Jewish practices into evidence-based treatments. These include rituals, prayers, and discussions on faith-related topics like body image and identity.

Spiritual Identity:
Programs encourage reclaiming identity through faith, such as trusting in God's design of the body and rejecting harmful societal messages. This fosters self-worth and healing.

Cultural Sensitivity:
Treatment plans can incorporate religious dietary laws (e.g., kosher or halal) while balancing recovery needs, ensuring cultural and spiritual alignment.

5

ANXIETY AND DEPRESSION

These are common mental health conditions among young people. Open discussions about symptoms, treatments, and personal experiences can draw significant attention.

Anxiety and Depression in Young People

Depression is another prevalent issue. Young people seek information on how to recognise depression, cope with it, and support peers who might be struggling.

Anxiety

In the context of the Christian faith, the mental health of young people can be influenced in several ways:

1. **Identity and Belonging:** Christianity offers a clear sense of identity as children of God. This understanding can foster a sense of belonging and acceptance, which is important for mental health.

2. **Moral and Ethical Framework:** The teachings of Christianity, such as love, forgiveness, and compassion, provide young people with guidance and a framework for making ethical decisions, reducing moral dilemmas and stress.

3. **Hope and Purpose:** Christian beliefs in redemption, eternal life, and divine purpose can instil hope and a sense of purpose, helping young people find meaning even in difficult circumstances.

4. **Community Support:** Church communities can offer fellowship, support networks, and mentorship opportunities, which are vital for providing emotional and social support to young people.

5. **Prayer and Meditation:** Practices like prayer and meditation are essential aspects of Christian spirituality that can help young people manage anxiety, stress, and depression by fostering a sense of peace and connection to God.

6. **Forgiveness and Healing:** The concept of forgiveness in Christianity can be powerful for mental health, enabling young people to handle guilt, resentment, and past traumas constructively.

7. **Challenges and Pressures:** It's also important to acknowledge that some young people might feel pressured by religious expectations or norms, which can affect their mental well-being. Open discussions and supportive environments are necessary for addressing these issues.

8. **Spiritual Counselling:** Churches often provide pastoral counselling, which can be a resource for young people to discuss their mental health concerns in a faith-based context.

Integrating Christian faith with mental health approaches can be beneficial, but it requires sensitivity to individual experiences and needs. Supporting young people in their spiritual and mental health journey involves listening, understanding, and providing access to both spiritual and mental health resources.

Youth Groups and Mental Health Awareness

Youth groups can play a significant role in supporting mental health awareness through various initiatives and activities. Here are some ways they can contribute:

1. **Creating a Safe Space:** Establish an open and non-judgemental environment where young people feel comfortable sharing their thoughts and experiences related to mental health.

2. **Education and Workshops:** Organise sessions that educate youth about mental health issues, symptoms, and coping strategies. Bringing in mental health professionals for talks can provide valuable insights and resources.

3. **Peer Support Programs:** Encourage peer mentoring and support systems where young people can support each other, share experiences, and provide empathy and understanding.

4. **Awareness Campaigns:** Initiate campaigns that normalise conversations about mental health, breaking down stigma and encouraging more openness in discussing these issues.

5. **Mental Health Days/Events:** Plan special events focused on mental well-being. These could involve activities like yoga, meditation, art therapy, or any activity that promotes mental relaxation and stress relief.

6. **Integration of Faith and Mental Health:** For faith-based youth groups, integrate spiritual practices with mental health discussions, highlighting how aspects of faith can promote mental well-being.

7. **Collaboration with Mental Health Organisations:** Partner with professional mental health organisations to provide resources, helplines, and opportunities for direct intervention or counselling if needed.

8. **Resource Sharing:** Provide access to mental health resources, such as books, articles, or online courses, that can help young people learn more about mental health care.

9. **Leadership Training:** Offer training for youth leaders to recognise signs of mental distress among group members and effectively guide them to appropriate resources or support.

10. **Encourage Expression:** Facilitate clubs or activities like writing, art, or drama that allow young people to express emotions creatively and therapeutically.

By actively engaging in these activities, youth groups can create a culture of awareness and support where mental health is openly discussed and prioritised, empowering young individuals to seek help and support each other.

Why is Everyone Talking About Mindfulness and Self-Care?

Let's dive into the world of mindfulness together. You might be wondering, "Why is everyone talking about mindfulness?" It's all about being present and enjoying the moment without distractions. It's like hitting pause on the hustle and bustle of life to focus on what truly matters.

Think of mindfulness as a superpower for your mind. Whether you're studying, playing games, or just chilling with friends, it helps you stay in the moment and fully enjoy it. Plus, it's super helpful in dealing with stress and anxiety. Who doesn't want a bit of peace in their life, right?

Imagine you're listening to your favourite song. Being mindful means hearing each beat, every lyric, and feeling the music rather than letting it pass you by. If you're into tech, there are tons of cool apps that can guide you through meditation or breathing exercises—Headspace and Calm are popular favourites. Or if you're a creative soul, mindfulness can be about drawing, painting, or writing, allowing you to express yourself and feel centred.

Mindfulness is super flexible. You don't have to sit still, although you can if that's your thing. You can practice it while jogging, cooking, or even gaming. It's all about paying attention to how you feel and what you're doing.

Want to try a simple mindfulness exercise? Here we go:

1. **Find a comfy spot:** Sit or lie down somewhere you feel relaxed.
2. **Breathe:** Take a slow, deep breath in through your nose and out through your mouth. Feel your chest rise and fall.
3. **Focus:** Notice how your body feels. Is there tension anywhere? What can you hear around you?
4. **Let go:** If thoughts pop up, just notice them and then gently bring your mind back to your breath.
5. **Repeat:** Do this for a couple of minutes, or however long you're comfortable.

In just a few minutes a day, you can feel more relaxed, focused, and happy!

Let's dive into the fascinating world of the brain!

First up, did you know that your brain is a constant buzz of activity, even when you're just relaxing? It's like a never-ending conversation happening at lightning speed among neurons (the tiny cells that make up your brain). They send messages back and forth, faster than you can imagine.

Now, let's talk about the parts of this super-powered organ. The brain is like a video game controller, with different sections for different actions. The **frontal lobe** is like the main player—helping you make decisions and understand consequences. Then there's the **hippocampus**, your memory bank, keeping track of everything, from your first ice cream cone to last night's dream.

Imagine you're playing a sport, and suddenly you dodge a ball without thinking— that's your **cerebellum** making sure you stay balanced and coordinated like a pro.

Then there's the brain's special effects team: the **limbic system**, which controls your emotions. Have you ever felt nervous about something, or excited about an adventure? That's your limbic system at work.

Ever wonder why you feel hungry or tired? That's your **hypothalamus**, like your personal life coach, telling your body when to eat, sleep, or even when it's time for fight or flight.

What's even cooler is the brain's ability to change and adapt – this is known as **brain plasticity**. When you learn something new, like a language or an instrument, it actually rewires and strengthens connections in your brain. Imagine upgrading your game console while you're playing!

The brain uses about 20% of your body's total energy, which is why after a long day of studying or thinking hard, you might feel like you've run a marathon.

Finally, here's something interesting—dreams! Scientists still don't fully understand why we dream, but it's believed to help us process emotions and problem-solve. Your brain is still working while you sleep!

So, how about that? The more you understand about how your brain works, the more you can harness its power to learn, create, and live your best life. Want to explore more brainy topics? Let's talk!

1. Stress Management and Relaxation Techniques:

- Teach practical stress-relief exercises such as deep breathing, progressive muscle relaxation, or meditation.

2. Mindfulness Practices:

- Educate on mindfulness practices and how regular meditation can improve focus and reduce anxiety.

3. Understanding Anxiety and Depression:

- Provide insights into recognising signs of anxiety and depression, along with coping strategies and resources for help.

4. Building Resilience and Emotional Strength:

- Explore techniques for developing resilience, handling setbacks, and maintaining a positive outlook.

5. Healthy Communication and Relationships:

- Focus on building healthy communication skills, understanding emotional boundaries, and fostering supportive relationships.

6. Self-Esteem and Confidence Building:

- Engage in activities that boost self-confidence and help youth recognise their strengths and achievements.

7. Digital Well-being and Online Safety:

- Discuss the impact of social media on mental health and strategies for maintaining a healthy digital life.

8. Coping with Peer Pressure and Bullying:

- Provide guidance on handling peer pressure and dealing with bullying effectively and safely.

9. Creative Expression through Art and Writing:

- Offer workshops that use art and writing to express emotions and process feelings.

10. Goal Setting and Motivation:

- Teach techniques for setting realistic goals and staying motivated amidst challenges and pressures.

11. Mental Health First Aid:

- Train participants to support peers in crisis by recognising warning signs and understanding how to respond appropriately.

12. Nutrition and Mental Health:

- Explore the connection between diet and mental well-being, emphasising nutrition's role in maintaining a healthy mind.

These workshops can be tailored to suit the needs and interests of the group, ensuring they resonate with participants and provide beneficial tools for mental well-being.

Let's talk about mindfulness workshops for young people.

Running a mindfulness workshop for young people can be a rewarding and enriching experience. Here's a step-by-step guide to help you organise and conduct such a workshop:

Planning Phase:

1. **Define Objectives:**
   - Decide on the core objectives. For example, introducing mindfulness, teaching practical exercises, and highlighting its benefits.
2. **Select a Venue:**
   - Choose a quiet and comfortable space conducive to relaxation and focus.
3. **Prepare Materials:**
   - Gather materials such as yoga mats, cushions, notebooks, pens, and any audio equipment for guided meditations.
4. **Create a Schedule:**
   - Plan a structured timeline for the workshop, including introduction, practice sessions, discussions, and breaks.

Workshop Components:

1. **Introduction (10-15 minutes):**
   - Explain mindfulness and its benefits, focusing on how it can help reduce stress and improve focus.

2. **Warm-Up Activity (5 minutes):**
   - Begin with a simple icebreaker to make participants comfortable. This could be a short breathing exercise or a focus game.

3. **Guided Meditation Session (10-15 minutes):**
   - Lead a guided meditation practice. You can use scripts or recordings, covering basic techniques like focusing on the breath or body scan.

4. **Mindfulness Activities (20-30 minutes):**
   - Conduct activities such as mindful walking, mindful eating exercises, or creative activities like drawing with focus on the present moment.

5. **Discussion and Sharing (15 minutes):**
   - Allow participants to share their experiences. Encourage discussions around how they felt during exercises and any challenges they faced.

6. **Techniques for Daily Practice (10 minutes):**
   - Teach simple techniques for integrating mindfulness into daily life, like taking mindful pauses or using mindfulness apps.

7. **Q&A Session (10 minutes):**
   - Open the floor for questions to address any doubts or provide further clarification on practising mindfulness.

8. **Closing Reflection (5 minutes):**
   - Conclude with a brief reflection or gratitude exercise, encouraging participants to note one takeaway they will apply.

Post-Workshop:

1. **Feedback Collection:**
   - Distribute feedback forms to understand participant experiences and gather suggestions for improvement.

2. **Resources:**
   - Provide participants with handouts, app recommendations, or online resources to continue practising mindfulness.

3. **Follow-Up:**
   - Consider organising regular follow-up sessions to support continued practice and reinforce the skills learned.

Facilitators of mindfulness workshops should be trained or experienced in mindfulness techniques and maintain a calm, respectful atmosphere throughout the session.

Let's explore mindfulness activities that are perfect for young people.

1. **Deep Breathing:** Encourage slow, deep breaths in through the nose and out through the mouth. This calms the nervous system and helps focus the mind.

2. **Mindful Walking:** Take a walk and focus on the sensation of each step, the surroundings, and the sounds. It's a great way to connect with nature.

3. **Body Scan:** Guide them to close their eyes and visualise scanning their body from head to toe, noticing any tension or relaxation along the way.

4. **Gratitude Journaling:** Spend a few minutes each day writing down three things they are grateful for. This builds a positive mindset.

5. **Mindful Eating:** Focus on the taste, texture, and smell of each bite, eating slowly and without distractions to fully enjoy the meal.

6. **Guided Imagery:** Use a peaceful image or scene in the mind to promote serenity. Many apps and videos offer guided imagery exercises.

7. **Mindful Listening:** Sit quietly and focus on the sounds around without labelling or judging them. This enhances listening skills and patience.

8. **Simple Yoga or Stretching:** Engage in a series of slow, mindful stretches or yoga poses focusing on the breath and body sensations.

9. **Creative Expression:** Drawing, painting, or crafting while fully immersing in the process can be a calming and centring activity.

10. **Mindfulness in Daily Activities:** Encourage them to do everyday activities like brushing teeth or washing hands mindfully, paying full attention to the action.

11. **Progressive Muscle Relaxation:** Tense and then relax different muscle groups, noticing the sensation of release and relaxation.

These activities can help young people develop a sense of calm, increase their concentration, and foster emotional well-being.

Mindful Walking

Mindful walking is a simple yet profound practice that can help young people connect more deeply with the present moment. Here's a detailed guide on how to get started:

1. **Choose a Location:** It can be a park, a quiet street, or even your backyard. The key is to be in a place where you feel comfortable and safe.

2. **Set an Intention:** Before starting, set a simple intention for your walk. It could be gratitude, peace, or simply being present.

3. **Start Slowly:** Begin walking at a slow and deliberate pace. Allow yourself to feel the connection between your feet and the ground.

4. **Focus on Sensations:** Pay attention to the sensations in your feet and legs as you walk. Notice how the ground feels beneath you with each step.

5. **Breathe Deeply:** As you walk, take deep breaths in through your nose and out through your mouth. You can synchronise your breath with your steps, perhaps inhaling for two steps and exhaling for two steps.

6. **Engage Your Senses:** Notice the sounds around you, like the rustling of leaves or the chirping of birds. Observe the colours and textures of your surroundings. Smell the air and notice any scents.

7. **Stay Present:** If your mind starts to wander, gently bring your attention back to your breath or the sensations of walking. It's normal for thoughts to drift; just notice them and return to the present.

8. **Gratitude Practice:** As you walk, think of something you're grateful for with each step. It can be as simple as the ability to walk or the beauty around you.

9. **Observe Your Thoughts:** Notice any feelings or thoughts as they arise without judgment. Acknowledge them and let them pass like clouds in the sky.

10. **End with Reflection:** After your walk, take a moment to sit quietly and reflect on how you feel. Notice any changes in your mood or perspective.

Mindful walking is about experiencing the simple act of walking with full awareness and appreciation. It's a fantastic way to reduce stress, improve concentration, and enhance overall well-being.

Let's talk about mindful walking for beginners.

If you're new to mindful walking, here are some tips to get started:

1. **Start Small:** Begin with just a few minutes of mindful walking, gradually increasing the duration as you become more comfortable with the practice.

2. **Choose a Quiet Spot:** It can be helpful to start in a quieter area where there are fewer distractions, especially when you're just beginning.

3. **Focus on Your Body:** Pay attention to how each part of your body feels as you walk. Notice the movement of your feet, legs, and arms.

4. **Walk Slowly:** Slow down your pace more than usual. Mindful walking is not about covering distance but experiencing the act of walking itself.

5. **Use a Mantra:** Sometimes, repeating a calming word or phrase, such as "peace" or "relax," can help maintain focus and concentration.

6. **Incorporate Breathing:** Focus on your breathing. Count your steps as you inhale and exhale to keep your mind engaged with the process.

7. **Bring Curiosity:** Approach the walk with a sense of curiosity. Notice things you've never seen before and appreciate the small details.

8. **Stay Comfortable:** Wear comfortable clothing and shoes suitable for walking to avoid any discomfort or distractions.

9. **Accept Imperfections:** Your mind will wander, and that's okay. Gently bring your attention back to the walking experience without judgment.

10. **Join a Group:** If you're having trouble staying motivated, consider joining a mindfulness or walking group for support and community.

11. **Set a Regular Schedule:** Practice mindful walking at the same time each day to help make it a habit.

12. **Be Patient:** Like any new practice, it takes time to become comfortable and proficient. Be patient with yourself and enjoy the process.

These tips can help you ease into mindful walking and start enjoying its many benefits. Happy walking!

Mindfulness and Self-Care

Practices that promote self-awareness and relaxation are especially appealing as young people look for ways to improve their mental health.

Suggested Coping Strategies for Anxiety

Here are some effective coping strategies for managing anxiety:

1. **Deep Breathing:** Practice breathing exercises to calm your nervous system. Inhale deeply through your nose, hold for a few seconds, and exhale slowly through your mouth.

2. **Mindfulness and Meditation:** Engage in mindfulness or meditation practices to focus on the present moment, which can help reduce anxious thoughts.

3. **Exercise:** Physical activity releases endorphins that improve mood. Regular exercise can help reduce anxiety levels over time.

4. **Healthy Lifestyle:** Maintain a balanced diet, get enough sleep, and limit caffeine and alcohol, as these can exacerbate anxiety.

5. **Journaling:** Write down your thoughts and feelings. This can help you identify triggers and better understand your anxiety.

6. **Time Management:** Plan and prioritise tasks to reduce feeling overwhelmed. Break tasks into smaller, manageable steps.

7. **Social Support:** Connect with friends or family members who understand and support you. Talking to someone can provide relief and perspective.

8. **Therapy:** Consider speaking with a therapist or counsellor who can provide professional guidance and support.

9. **Limit Screen Time:** Take breaks from screens, especially if social media contributes to your anxiety. Engage in offline activities.

10. **Relaxation Techniques:** Try yoga, tai chi, or progressive muscle relaxation to ease tension in the body.

11. **Set Realistic Goals:** Avoid setting overly ambitious goals. Break them down into smaller, achievable steps.

12. **Positive Affirmations:** Use affirmations to challenge negative thoughts and reinforce a positive mindset.

13. **Learn Coping Skills:** Familiarise yourself with coping skills that work for you, like creative outlets, hobbies, or relaxing activities.
14. **Limit Worry Time:** Set aside a specific "worry time" each day to devote to your anxious thoughts, and try to avoid worrying outside of that allotted time.

It's important to remember that what works varies from person to person. Experiment with different strategies to see which suits you best, and consult a mental health professional if needed.

Positive Affirmations Based on Faith

Here are some faith-based positive affirmations that can help reinforce self-worth and positivity:

1. "I am created in God's image, and I am beautiful and unique."
2. "God has a plan and purpose for my life, and I am worthy of love and respect."
3. "I am a beloved child of God, and my value is limitless."
4. "God's love strengthens me and gives me confidence in who I am."
5. "My worth is defined by God's love, not by appearance."
6. "I am fearfully and wonderfully made, deserving of love and acceptance."
7. "God's grace surrounds me, and I am enough just as I am."
8. "I trust in God's plan for my life and embrace my unique journey."
9. "With God's help, I am growing more kind, loving, and accepting of myself every day."

10. "God's peace fills my heart, and I radiate His love to the world."

These affirmations can be integrated into daily prayer, meditation, or reflection to help reinforce a positive self-image grounded in faith.

Deep Breathing Exercises Explained

Deep breathing exercises are a simple yet effective way to manage anxiety and stress. The goal is to focus on slow, deliberate breaths to calm your mind and body. Here's a step-by-step guide to practising deep breathing:

1. **Find a Comfortable Position:** Sit or lie down in a comfortable position. Make sure your posture allows your chest and abdomen to expand freely.

2. **Close Your Eyes:** This can help minimise distractions and help you focus inward.

3. **Inhale Deeply:** Breathe in slowly through your nose. Aim to fill your lungs, feeling your abdomen rise as you take in air. Count to four or five as you inhale.

4. **Hold the Breath:** Gently hold your breath for a brief pause, about two to three seconds. This helps in maximising the oxygen intake.

5. **Exhale Slowly:** Exhale slowly through your mouth, releasing the air gently. Try to make the exhalation longer than the inhalation, counting to six or seven if possible. You can purse your lips slightly to control the flow of air.

6. **Repeat the Process:** Continue this cycle for about five to ten minutes. Focus on the rhythm of your breath and the sensation of air entering and leaving your body.

7. **Return to Normal Breathing:** Once you feel more relaxed, gradually return to your normal breathing pattern.

Tips:

- **Visualise Calmness:** While doing deep breathing, you can imagine a peaceful scene or repeat a calming word or phrase in your mind.

- **Practice Regularly:** Regular practice can make it more effective, so try to incorporate it into your daily routine.

- **Adapt as Needed:** Modify your breathing speed and depth if you feel dizzy or uncomfortable.

Deep breathing can be done anywhere—whether you're at home, work, or on the go—and can serve as a powerful tool to help navigate anxiety and stress when they arise.

DEPRESSION

"It is during our darkest moments that we must focus to see the light." — Aristotle

How to Know You Might Be Depressed

Recognising depression in young people can be challenging, but being aware of certain signs can help you identify if someone might be struggling. Here are some key indicators to watch for:

1. **Changes in Mood:** You might notice consistent feelings of sadness, hopelessness, or irritability. Instead of just occasional bad days, these moods linger and disrupt daily life.

2. **Loss of Interest:** Activities and hobbies that used to bring joy now seem uninteresting or burdensome. You might witness someone withdrawing from social interactions or losing enthusiasm for things they once loved.

3. **Changes in Sleep Patterns:** Pay attention if someone is sleeping too much or too little. Insomnia or frequent oversleeping can both be signs of depression.

4. **Appetite and Weight Changes:** Noticeable changes in eating habits, whether it's a loss of appetite or overeating, can lead to significant weight changes.

5. **Decreased Energy and Fatigue:** You may see someone experiencing constant fatigue or low energy, even performing simple tasks can seem exhausting.

6. **Difficulty Concentrating:** If someone struggles with focus, memory, or decision-making, it might affect their performance in school or other areas of life.

7. **Feelings of Worthlessness or Guilt:** They might express a relentless sense of worthlessness or excessive guilt over situations out of proportion to the event itself.

8. **Physical Symptoms:** Watch for unexplained aches and pains, headaches, or stomach aches that don't seem to have a clear physical cause.

9. **Thoughts of Death or Suicide:** Any mention of self-harm, death, or suicide, even in a seemingly casual or joking manner, should be taken seriously and addressed immediately.

If you recognise these signs in someone, it's important to approach the situation with care and empathy. Encourage them to talk about what they're feeling and seek professional help if necessary. Your support can make a significant difference in their journey to healing.

How to Help Someone Heal from Depression

Supporting a friend who might be experiencing depression can be challenging, but your care and attention can be incredibly valuable. Here are some practical steps you can take:

1. **Be There:** Reach out and make it clear that you're available to listen. Sometimes just knowing someone cares can make a big difference.

2. **Listen Actively:** When they're ready to talk, listen without interrupting or offering immediate advice. Your goal is to understand their feelings and provide a safe space for expression.

3. **Express Concern:** Gently express your concern without sounding judgmental. Use "I" statements like, "I've noticed you seem down lately, and I'm worried about you."

4. **Encourage Professional Help:** Suggest speaking to a mental health professional. Offer to help them find resources or accompany them to their first appointment if they're comfortable with that.

5. **Stay Connected:** Regularly check in to show that your support is ongoing, whether through a text, call, or invitation to hang out. Your consistent presence can be reassuring.

6. **Offer Practical Help:** Assist with tasks that seem overwhelming. Offering to help with errands, homework, or simply spending time together can provide relief.

7. **Encourage Healthy Habits:** Gently encourage them to engage in activities that promote well-being, like getting enough sleep, eating well, and exercising. Join them in physical activities if possible, like going for a walk.

8. **Educate Yourself:** Learn about depression to better understand what your friend is going through. This knowledge can help you provide more informed support.

9. **Avoid Dismissing Feelings:** Don't minimise their feelings with statements like "it's not that bad" or "you'll get over it." Validate their emotions to show that you understand the seriousness of their situation.

10. **Be Patient:** Recovering from depression can take time, and progress may be slow. Be patient and maintain your support as they work through their struggles.

11. **Know Emergency Protocols:** Learn how to recognise crisis situations, such as suicidal thoughts or behaviours. In an emergency, don't hesitate to contact mental health professionals or emergency services.

Remember, taking care of your own mental health is also important. Supporting a friend can be emotionally taxing, so ensure you're also getting the support you need through your social network or a mental health professional. Your efforts in being there for your friend can make a meaningful difference in their life.

What to Avoid Saying to Someone with Depression

When speaking to someone with depression, it's important to be supportive and sensitive. Here are some things you should avoid saying:

1. "Just snap out of it": Depression is a complex mental health condition and not something someone can simply overcome through willpower.

2. "Everyone feels this way sometimes": This can trivialise their experience and make them feel misunderstood.

3. "It's all in your head": This suggests that their feelings are not real or valid.

4. "Think about all the good things in your life": While well-intentioned, this can make them feel guilty for not being happy despite the positives in their life.

5. "Other people have it worse": Comparisons can invalidate their feelings and add to their burden.

6. "Stop being so negative": This can make them feel worse for having a hard time seeing things positively.

7. "You're just lazy": Depression can cause fatigue and a lack of motivation; labelling them as lazy is harmful and inaccurate.

8. "You should get out more": While social activities can help, it might oversimplify their condition and ignore their personal struggles.

Instead, try offering support and understanding. You can say:

- "I'm here for you."
- "How can I help?"
- "I care about you and want to understand."
- "It's okay to feel how you're feeling."

Remember that empathy, patience, and active listening can go a long way in providing support.

High Functioning Depression – When All Is Not as It Seems

High functioning depression is a term often used to describe individuals who, despite experiencing symptoms of depression, continue to meet the demands of daily life. These individuals appear to be functioning normally in their professional, social, and personal lives. However, internally they may be facing feelings of emptiness, sadness, or fatigue.

Here are some key aspects of high functioning depression:

1. **Hidden Symptoms:** On the surface, the individual might seem fine, but they could be dealing with persistent low mood, lack of interest in activities they once enjoyed, and a general feeling of being overwhelmed.

2. **Performance Pressure:** Often, individuals push themselves to maintain appearances. This pressure can exacerbate feelings of worthlessness or inadequacy.

3. **Isolation:** They might withdraw from friends or social activities, not because they don't care, but because social interaction demands energy they do not have.

4. **Perfectionism:** There's often an underlying desire to be perfect, which can contribute to their depressive symptoms if things don't go as planned.

5. **Coping Mechanisms:** They might rely on unhealthy coping mechanisms, like overworking, to distract themselves from their internal struggles.

6. **Seeking Help:** Since they appear functional, they might not seek help or support from professionals, friends, or family. Acknowledging the problem is often the first step toward recovery, and reaching out for support is essential.

7. **Treatment Options:** Therapy, medication, lifestyle changes such as exercise or a healthy diet, and mindfulness practices can be effective in managing symptoms.

If you or someone you know might be experiencing high functioning depression, it's important to talk to a professional. While they might seem fine on the outside, internally they could be struggling significantly, and professional intervention can provide much-needed support.

Signs That Someone Might Be Experiencing High-Functioning Depression

High functioning depression can be difficult to recognise because individuals often appear to be managing life well. However, there are certain signs that might indicate someone is experiencing this condition:

1. **Persistent Low Mood:** Despite outward appearances, the individual may consistently feel sad, empty, or hopeless.

2. **Fatigue and Low Energy:** They may feel constantly drained and physically exhausted even with adequate rest.

3. **Irritability or Frustration:** They might be more irritable or easily frustrated, even with minor issues.

4. **Loss of Interest:** Activities they once enjoyed no longer bring pleasure or satisfaction.

5. **Changes in Sleep Patterns:** They might experience insomnia or sleep more than usual.

6. **Changes in Appetite:** Noticeable changes in appetite or weight, whether increase or decrease, can occur.

7. **Difficulty Concentrating:** Even simple tasks might demand more focus, and decision-making could feel overwhelming.

8. **Perfectionism:** To outsiders they may seem driven and hardworking, but internally they may struggle with a need to perform perfectly and fear failure.

9. **Isolation:** They may pull back from social interactions or engagements, preferring solitude over company.

10. **Negative Self-Talk:** Internally, they might engage in harsh self-criticism or feel a sense of unworthiness.

11. **Overcompensating:** They might overextend themselves at work or in social situations to maintain appearances.
12. **Physical Aches:** Headaches, stomach issues, or unexplained aches and pains can accompany their emotional symptoms.

Talking Therapies

Each of these therapies has a unique approach and can be suited for different types of emotional and mental health challenges. They all aim to help individuals gain better control over their emotions, thoughts, and interactions with others.

DBT (Dialectical Behaviour Therapy)

1. **What it is:** DBT is a type of talk therapy designed to help people manage intense emotions and improve relationships.
2. **Main Focus:** It teaches skills in four main areas:
    - **Mindfulness:** Being present and fully engaged in the moment.
    - **Distress Tolerance:** Handling difficult situations without making them worse.
    - **Emotion Regulation:** Understanding and managing intense feelings.
    - **Interpersonal Effectiveness:** Communicating and interacting in a healthy way.

CBT (Cognitive Behavioural Therapy)

1. **What it is:** CBT is a common type of therapy that focuses on changing negative thought patterns and behaviours.

2. **Main Focus:** It helps you recognise unhelpful thoughts and replace them with more positive, realistic ones.

3. **How it works:**
    - Identify negative thoughts.
    - Challenge and change these thoughts.
    - Develop better habits and coping strategies.

MBT (Mentalisation-Based Therapy)

1. **What it is:** MBT is a therapeutic approach that helps people better understand their own thoughts and feelings and those of others.

2. **Main Focus:** It enhances your ability to mentalise, or see yourself from the outside and others from the inside.

3. **How it works:**
    - Focus on understanding mental states and intentions.
    - Improve empathy and emotional awareness.
    - Enhance interpersonal relationships by understanding different perspectives.

PEOPLE IN THE BIBLE WHO STRUGGLED WITH MENTAL ILLNESS

- **King David** experienced prolonged bouts of depression.

- **Elijah the prophet** fell into despair and asked God to take his life.

- **Job's** life is a profound meditation on human suffering.

- **Hannah's** life is marked by the anguish of unfulfilled longing.

Who Was Bipolar in the Bible?

This may indicate that Saul's condition was more serious than depression. If the above two brief excerpts are accepted as signifying manic episodes, then perhaps Saul qualifies for a DSM–IV diagnosis of bipolar affective disorder.

One notable response to this effect came from pastor Jarrid Wilson. He died by suicide a year and a half later after tweeting the following:

Jarrid Wilson (September 19, 1988 – September 9, 2019) was an American pastor, author, and mental health advocate. He served as an associate pastor at Harvest Christian Fellowship in California and previously pastored at churches in Tennessee. Wilson co-founded Anthem of Hope, a program supporting those struggling with depression and suicidal thoughts. Known for his openness about his own mental health challenges, Wilson frequently spoke on faith and mental health. Tragically, he died by suicide at age 30. He is survived by his wife, Juli, and their two sons, Denham and Finch.

Jarrid Wilson significantly contributed to mental health advocacy, particularly within faith communities. He co-founded Anthem of Hope, a nonprofit aimed at supporting individuals facing depression and suicidal thoughts. Wilson was open about his own struggles with mental health, which encouraged discussions around these issues in churches, challenging the stigma associated with mental illness. His advocacy highlighted the need for compassion and understanding in religious contexts, prompting many church leaders to confront mental health issues more openly following his tragic death.

According to some research, in the US, more individuals with mental health concerns seek out help from religious leaders and clergy than from psychologists and psychiatrists combined.

Christian Saints Who Suffered with Mental Health Challenges

- **Saint Dymphna:**
  Saint Dymphna is a Christian saint honoured in the Roman Catholic and Eastern Orthodox traditions. She is traditionally depicted as a maiden with a book and a sword, symbolising her holiness and martyrdom. Saint Dymphna is the patron saint of mental illness and nervous disorders because of her own struggles and eventual martyrdom. Her story is one of faith, courage, and the search for refuge.

- **Saint Thérèse of Lisieux** faced several specific mental challenges, including:

  - **Anxiety and Sensitivity:** Thérèse was known for her sensitive nature, which led her to experience intense emotional reactions to situations. This sensitivity sometimes resulted in anxiety and emotional turmoil.

  - **Scrupulosity:** She struggled with scrupulosity, an obsessive concern with her own sins and a fear of being unable to achieve spiritual perfection. This made her feel an intense need to confess even minor faults, leading to inner conflict and distress.

- - **Doubts and Spiritual Darkness:** Thérèse sometimes experienced periods of doubt and spiritual dryness, feeling distant from God. This spiritual darkness challenged her faith, yet she continued to trust in God through these trials.

- **Saint Benedict Joseph Labre** faced significant mental health challenges, including depression and anxiety. Despite his desire for religious community life, his mental state often led him to isolation and wandering.

  - **Pilgrimage and Homelessness:** After being rejected by religious communities, Labre adopted a life of pilgrimage. He travelled to various shrines across Europe, living as a homeless beggar and relying entirely on the charity of others. His choice to embrace poverty and wandering was a radical expression of his faith.

  - **Spiritual Depth:** Labre exhibited profound spiritual insight and humility despite his mental struggles. His surrender to God's will, acceptance of suffering, and devotion to prayer earned him a reputation for holiness among those he encountered.

  - **Legacy:** Saint Benedict Joseph Labre was canonised in 1881. He is often invoked as a patron saint by those suffering from mental illness, homelessness, and wanderers. His life serves as a testament to the idea that holiness can be found in unexpected places and that God's grace can work through our struggles.

- **Saint John of God:**

  - **Early Life and Turmoil:** John experienced a tumultuous early life, marked by abandonment and wandering. He served as a soldier, and these experiences left him with significant emotional scars and mental struggles.

- **Crisis and Conversion:** At the age of 40, John underwent a profound religious conversion that dramatically changed his life. This turning point was marked by a deep crisis where he exhibited erratic behaviour and intense emotional turmoil.

- **Saint Christina the Astonishing:**
Saint Christina the Astonishing's life was marked by actions and behaviours that might be considered symptoms of mental struggles in today's context. However, mental health and spirituality perceptions differed during the 12th century. Here's how her mental struggles were expressed and perceived:

    - **Experiences of Detachment:** After her resurrection, Christina often seemed detached from reality. Her behaviours, such as climbing trees or perching on rooftops, were perceived as startling and unusual, possibly indicating a different mental state or altered perception of reality.

    - **Severe Penances:** Christina subjected herself to extreme forms of asceticism, which included physical deprivation and entering dangerous situations. These actions, possibly expressions of deep spiritual conviction or a sign of psychological distress, highlighted her complex relationship with the physical world.

    - **Visions and Mystical Experiences:** Christina claimed to have vivid spiritual experiences, including travelling to heaven and visiting purgatory and hell. These visions were central to her mission, though they might be examined today through different psychological lenses.

- **Reclusion and Isolation:** Her tendency to live in isolation, avoiding human interaction, and living in seclusion could indicate social withdrawal. However, this behaviour was also common in monastic life, emphasising her commitment to prayer and contemplation.

- **Public Perception:** People in her time were both fascinated and bewildered by her actions. Some saw her as divinely inspired, while others might have viewed her conduct as unexplainable or misunderstood.

- **Posthumous Reflection:** Modern reflection allows us to consider Christina's life choices as an intersection of mysticism and mental health. Her experiences bridge the gap between spiritual ecstasy and what could be seen as psychological challenges. Her narrative offers an opportunity for contemporary audiences to explore the connections and distinctions between faith, mysticism, and mental health.

Neuroscience and Psychology:

Younger audiences are increasingly interested in understanding the scientific aspects of how the brain works in relation to mental health.

Having a Faith Commitment as a Christian Does Not Prevent a Person from Having Serious Mental Disorders

This idea suggests that being a 'good Christian' might provide some form of protection against serious mental disorders due to their faith, community support, and their belief systems. Here are some thoughts on this viewpoint:

Faith as Support

1. **Spiritual Beliefs:** Faith can offer a sense of purpose and hope, which might contribute to emotional resilience. Many believers find comfort and strength in their relationship with God, which can be a stabilising factor.

2. **Community Support:** The community aspect of religion can provide social support and a sense of belonging, which are known to be protective factors for mental health. Valued relationships and shared values can help people cope with life's challenges.

Coping Mechanisms

1. **Rituals and Prayer:** Regular religious practices like prayer and rituals can offer emotional release and a mechanism to express one's feelings. They might also provide routine and structure, which can be beneficial for mental well-being.

2. **Moral Framework:** Adhering to a set moral framework can guide individuals in making decisions and managing stress, potentially reducing feelings of guilt or confusion.

Limitations and Considerations

1. **No Immunity to Disorder:** It's essential to note that religion is not a guaranteed protection against mental health disorders. Factors such as genetics, environment, and life experiences play significant roles in mental health.

2. **Impact of Disconnect:** If someone feels they are not living up to their religious principles or if they experience doubt, this could potentially increase stress and emotional turmoil, rather than decrease it.

3. **Variation in Experience:** People's experiences with religion and its impact on their mental health can vary

widely. Cultural, personal belief strength, and individual resilience are all variables.

Ethical Implications

1. **Seeking Help:** It is crucial for individuals experiencing mental health issues to seek professional help, regardless of their faith background. Relying solely on spiritual intervention may not address all aspects of a mental health condition.

2. **Stigma:** In some religious communities, there might be stigma attached to mental illness, which could discourage individuals from seeking the help they need.

Conclusion

While religion can offer various protective and coping mechanisms, it is not a panacea for mental health disorders. The complex interplay of different factors affecting mental health underscores the importance of a holistic approach that includes faith, community, and professional mental health support. Recognising the value and limitations of spiritual guidance can help form balanced perspectives on mental well-being.

6

THE INTRICATE RELATIONSHIP BETWEEN FAITH AND MENTAL HEALTH

Faith and public mental health are intricately connected. Many individuals find that their faith provides them with a framework for understanding and coping with life's challenges, contributing positively to their mental well-being.

1. **Community Support:** Places of worship often serve as supportive communities, offering social connections that can alleviate feelings of isolation.

2. **Meaning and Purpose:** Faith can provide a sense of purpose, helping individuals navigate difficult times by giving meaning to their experiences.

3. **Rituals and Traditions:** These can offer stability through routine, which is particularly beneficial for mental health. Rituals provide comfort and a sense of belonging.

4. **Spiritual Practices:** Activities like prayer and meditation can reduce stress and anxiety levels, promoting a more peaceful state of mind.

5. **Hope and Resilience:** Faith often instils hope, encouraging resilience. This hope can be pivotal in overcoming mental health struggles.

However, it's important to balance faith and public mental health. While faith can be a strong support, mental health professionals are essential in providing evidence-based treatments for mental illnesses. Integrating faith with traditional mental health care can lead to comprehensive and effective support for individuals, respecting both scientific and personal beliefs. It is essential to be sensitive to the diversity of religions and faiths.

Some patients value their faith, and incorporating faith into mental health treatment can benefit them. Let's explore some ways mental health professionals can integrate faith into treatment:

1. **Cultural Competence:** Understand the patient's faith background and how it influences their worldview. This demonstrates respect and helps build trust.

2. **Open Dialogue:** Encourage patients to discuss their faith openly. Create a safe space where they can share how their beliefs affect their mental health.

3. **Collaborative Approach:** Work alongside faith leaders and communities. This can ensure that spiritual needs are met in conjunction with mental health support.

4. **Incorporate Spiritual Practices:** If suitable, encourage practices like prayer, meditation, or mindfulness that align with the patient's beliefs.

5. **Tailored Treatment Plans:** Integrate faith-based considerations into treatment plans, ensuring they align with the patient's values and promote healing.

6. **Respect Belief Systems:** Be sensitive to and respectful of the patient's beliefs, even if they differ from your own. Avoid imposing personal beliefs.

7. **Faith-Based Resources:** Recommend books, groups, or activities that align with the patient's faith and can provide additional support.

8. **Education and Training:** Mental health professionals should seek education in spiritual care and cultural competency to provide informed and respectful treatment.

By thoughtfully integrating faith into treatment, mental health professionals can offer more holistic and personalised care that honours the patient's identity and promotes well-being.

Faith and Mental Health: Intersecting and Complementary

Faith and mental health do indeed intersect, overlap, and complement each other in various ways, each relationship shaped by individual beliefs and cultural contexts. Here are a few key aspects of their relationship:

1. **Support System:** Faith often provides a strong support network through community activities like religious gatherings. These interactions can offer emotional support, reducing feelings of isolation and loneliness. This communal aspect can be vital in maintaining mental well-being.

2. **Coping Mechanism:** Many people turn to their faith during challenging times. Religious practices, such as prayer or meditation, can serve as coping mechanisms, promoting calmness and helping individuals manage stress and anxiety.

3. **Meaning and Purpose:** Faith can offer a sense of meaning and purpose, which is crucial for mental health. Believing in something greater than oneself can provide direction and a framework for understanding life's challenges, which can be both grounding and uplifting.

4. **Moral and Ethical Guidance:** For some, faith provides moral and ethical guidelines that can assist in making life choices, thereby reducing anxiety about decision-making and encouraging positive behaviour.

5. **Psychosocial Benefits:** Religious doctrine often encourages forgiveness and gratitude, which are linked to better mental health outcomes. Forgiveness can help release negative emotions, while gratitude can foster a positive outlook.

6. **Potential Challenges:** While faith can positively impact mental health, there can also be potential challenges. Unrealistic expectations set by religious beliefs or guilt associated with perceived religious shortcomings might contribute to mental distress for some individuals.

7. **Holistic Healing:** Some mental health treatments incorporate spiritual components, recognising the holistic nature of healing. Integrating spirituality with conventional treatments may enhance the effectiveness of interventions for some patients.

8. **Diverse Perspectives:** The impact of faith varies greatly among individuals. While some find comfort and strength in faith, others might not resonate with spiritual approaches, pointing to the importance of personalised mental health care.

9. **Research Insights:** Studies suggest that people with strong spiritual beliefs may experience lower rates of depression and anxiety and higher levels of satisfaction and well-

being. However, these benefits are not universal, highlighting the need for further research into the nuanced influences of faith on mental health.

In summary, faith can complement mental health by offering support, meaning, and coping strategies, though it may also pose challenges for some. The relationship between the two is complex, and while many find them harmonious, individual experiences can vary widely. Respectful integration and consideration of a person's faith and spiritual beliefs can enhance mental health practices, emphasising the value of holistic and individualised approaches.

SLEEP, MENTAL HEALTH, AND THE BIBLE

Sleep plays a critical role in mental health by regulating mood, emotions, and cognitive functions. Poor sleep is linked to conditions like depression, anxiety, and stress, while improving sleep quality can enhance mental well-being.

Spiritually, the Bible emphasises sleep as a gift from God that brings peace and renewal (Psalm 4:8). Trusting in God's sovereignty and meditating on scripture can alleviate anxiety and promote restful sleep.

Integrating faith-based practices with healthy sleep habits fosters both emotional and spiritual resilience. When Elijah was running for his life (complaining and wanting to die), the first thing Elijah needed was sleep (1 Kings 19:5).

Elijah Flees to Horeb

19:4-5: "4 While he himself went a day's journey into the wilderness. He came to a broom bush, sat down under it and prayed that he might die. 'I have had enough, Lord,' he said. 'Take my life; I am no better than my ancestors.' 5 Then he lay down under the bush and fell asleep.

All at once an angel touched him and said, 'Get up and eat.' 6 He looked around, and there by his head was some bread baked over hot coals, and a jar of water. He ate and drank and then lay down again.
7 The angel of the Lord came back a second time, touched him, and said, 'Get up and eat, for the journey is too much for you.' 8 So he got up and ate and drank. Strengthened by that food, he travelled forty days and forty nights until he reached Horeb, the mountain of God. 9 There he went into a cave and spent the night."

Throughout the Old and New Testaments, sleep was also a time where God interacted through dreams, which was an ancient standard (Job 33:14-15).

Job 33:14-15 (NIV)

"14 For God does speak—now one way, now another—though no one perceives it.
15 In a dream, in a vision of the night, when deep sleep falls on people as they slumber in their beds..."

How Does the Bible Address the Relationship Between Sleep and Mental Well-being?

The Bible addresses the relationship between sleep and mental well-being in several ways, emphasising its importance for overall health and spiritual vitality:

- **Sleep as a Divine Gift:** Scripture portrays sleep as a blessing from God. Psalm 127:2 states, "He gives to his beloved sleep," indicating that rest is a gift from God rather than solely a result of human effort.

- **Rest for Emotional Restoration:** The Bible recognises sleep's role in emotional healing. When the prophet Elijah experienced depression, God's initial remedy was sleep and nourishment before addressing his spiritual needs (1 Kings 19:4-6).

- **Sleep and Spiritual Health:** Good sleep habits are linked to spiritual well-being. Proverbs suggests that wisdom leads to good rest (Proverbs 3:24), implying a connection between spiritual maturity and quality sleep.

- **Physical and Mental Rejuvenation:** Scripture acknowledges sleep's restorative properties. It's seen as essential for physical, mental, and spiritual health, contributing to our ability to serve God and others effectively.

Building Self-Worth and Overcoming Self-Doubt

Self-esteem and mental health are vital aspects of overall well-being, with many individuals seeking ways to boost their confidence and overcome self-doubt.

Self-Esteem and Mental Health and What the Bible Says – The Mind Garden

Your mind is like a garden.

Imagine a serene and lush garden, filled with vibrant flowers and tall, sturdy trees. This garden symbolises your mind. Just like the garden, it requires nurturing and care. Every flower represents a positive thought, and every tree is a strong pillar of self-belief. This is your inner sanctuary, where self-esteem is built.

The Holy Bible speaks to your value and worth. Psalm 139:14 says, "I praise you because I am fearfully and wonderfully made." This reminds you that you are cherished and uniquely crafted, a tapestry woven with purpose and love.

Picture a gentle stream flowing through this garden, representing peace and clarity. Philippians 4:6-7 encourages you, "Do not be anxious about anything, but in every situation, by prayer and petition, with thanksgiving, present your requests to God." This stream symbolises the peace that transcends understanding, guarding your heart and mind.

In the corner of the garden is a comfortable bench, symbolising rest and reflection. Here, you can sit and reflect on Jeremiah 29:11, where God says, "For I know the plans I have for you, plans to prosper you and not to harm you, plans to give you hope and a future." This assures you that a loving plan guides your journey.

As you walk through this garden, remember that maintaining mental health and self-esteem is a journey. Like any garden, it may have weeds of doubt and storms of anxiety, but through patience and faith, it flourishes.

Additional Faith-Based Mental Health Resources

Here are some additional faith-based mental health resources that you might find helpful:

1. **Faith-Based Counselling Centres:** Many churches and religious communities offer counselling services or can recommend faith-integrated therapists who emphasise spiritual growth alongside mental health support.

2. **Books:**
    - *The Anxiety Cure* by Dr. Archibald Hart: A Christian perspective on dealing with anxiety.

- *Unglued: Making Wise Choices in the Midst of Raw Emotions* by Lysa TerKeurst: This book blends faith with practical strategies for managing emotions.

3. **Online Courses and Workshops:**

    - Consider faith-based mental health workshops offered by organisations like Focus on the Family and the American Association of Christian Counsellors (AACC).

4. **Podcasts:**

    - *The Next Right Thing* by Emily P. Freeman: A podcast offering guidance and encouragement through a Christian lens.

    - *God-Centred Mom* hosted by Heather MacFadyen: Addresses mental health topics, parenting, and spiritual growth.

5. **Support Groups:**

    - Some churches and religious organisations host support groups where participants can share struggles and find encouragement through faith-focused discussions.

6. **Christian Mental Health Organisations:**

    - **Grace Alliance:** Provides groups, resources, and training for integrating faith and mental health recovery.

- **Mental Health Grace Alliance:** Offers a range of resources addressing mental health challenges from a Christian perspective.

By exploring these resources, you can find guidance and community support that aligns with your faith and mental wellness journey.

Bipolar Disorder and Energy Drinks

When dealing with bipolar disorder, it is important to be cautious with the consumption of energy drinks. Here's why:

1. **Caffeine and Stimulants:** Energy drinks typically contain high levels of caffeine and other stimulants, which can potentially trigger manic or hypomanic episodes in some individuals with bipolar disorder.

2. **Sleep Disruption:** The stimulating effects can interfere with sleep patterns, which are critical for managing mood stability in bipolar disorder. Lack of sleep can exacerbate mood swings.

3. **Anxiety and Jitters:** The ingredients in energy drinks can increase anxiety and cause jitteriness, which may worsen symptoms or trigger a mood episode.

4. **Interaction with Medication:** Energy drinks can interact with medications used to treat bipolar disorder, potentially affecting their efficacy or causing side effects.

5. **Mood Swings:** The initial energy boost can lead to a subsequent crash, contributing to mood swings and emotional instability.

6. **Dehydration and Heart Concerns:** Ingredients in some energy drinks can lead to dehydration and strain on the

cardiovascular system, which can be concerning for overall health.

Key Mental Health Challenges Facing the Black Community

In the UK, mental health issues in the Black community present unique challenges and disparities. Here are some key statistics:

1. **Prevalence of Mental Health Issues:** Black individuals in the UK are more likely to be diagnosed with mental health disorders compared to their white counterparts. A study found that Black people are more than four times more likely to be detained under the Mental Health Act.

2. **Higher Rates of Psychosis:** Black Caribbean people are estimated to be nearly three times more likely to experience psychosis compared to the white British population.

3. **Access to Services:** Black individuals often face barriers to accessing mental health services due to stigma, discrimination, and lack of cultural competence within the healthcare system.

4. **Involuntary Hospitalisation:** Black people are significantly more likely to be sectioned under the Mental Health Act, indicating systemic biases in treatment approaches.

5. **Discrimination and Racism:** Racial discrimination and socioeconomic disadvantage contribute to higher stress levels, impacting mental well-being in the Black community.

6. **Suicide Rates:** While specific statistics on suicide rates among the Black community in the UK might not be as comprehensive, underlying factors like discrimination and

lack of adequate care contribute significantly to mental health crises.

These statistics highlight critical areas where improvements in mental health services are needed, emphasising culturally aware practices and better access to mental health care for the Black community in the UK.

Mental Health Challenges in the Black Community: Key Issues

The mental health challenges in the Black community are complex and multifaceted, influenced by historical, cultural, and socioeconomic factors. Here are some key challenges:

1. **Stigma and Mistrust:** Mental health issues often carry a stigma in the Black community, discouraging individuals from seeking help. Historical events, such as unethical experimentation on Black patients, have also led to mistrust in the healthcare system.

2. **Access to Care:** There is often a lack of access to culturally competent mental health care providers. This can result from living in areas with limited healthcare resources or a lack of providers who understand or respect cultural differences.

3. **Socioeconomic Factors:** Poverty, unemployment, and low educational attainment are prevalent in many Black communities, contributing to stress and mental health issues. Economic disadvantages can hinder access to appropriate care and support.

4. **Racial Trauma and Discrimination:** Experiences of racism and discrimination can lead to racial trauma, adversely impacting mental health. These experiences can

be ongoing and cumulative, affecting psychological well-being, self-esteem, and stress levels.

5. **Cultural Differences in Perception:** Mental health might be perceived differently across cultures. In some Black communities, emotional distress may be expressed through physical symptoms or viewed through a spiritual lens, affecting diagnosis and treatment.

6. **Inadequate Representation in Research:** There is often inadequate representation of Black individuals in mental health research, leading to a lack of understanding of how mental health conditions may manifest differently in this community.

7. **Youth-Specific Challenges:** Young Black individuals might face unique challenges, such as identity struggles or peer pressure, exacerbated by societal and cultural expectations.

Addressing these challenges requires a multifaceted approach that includes increasing access to culturally competent care, improving mental health education and awareness within the community, advocating for policy changes, and supporting community-led mental health initiatives.

Common Mental Health Disorders Affecting Black Individuals in the UK

Black individuals in the UK, like other communities, face a range of mental health disorders. Some of the most common ones include:

1. **Depression:** A prevalent mental health condition that affects mood, leading to persistent feelings of sadness and loss of interest. Social and economic factors can exacerbate its impact among Black individuals.

2. **Anxiety Disorders:** Characterised by excessive worry or fear, anxiety disorders such as generalised anxiety disorder or panic disorder can be aggravated by racial discrimination and social stressors.

3. **Psychosis and Schizophrenia:** These are particularly significant, with Black individuals being disproportionately diagnosed. Psychosis involves a disconnection from reality, which can manifest as hallucinations or delusions.

4. **Post-Traumatic Stress Disorder (PTSD):** Often resulting from exposure to trauma, PTSD symptoms may include flashbacks, severe anxiety, and uncontrollable thoughts. Experiences of racism and discrimination can contribute to PTSD.

5. **Bipolar Disorder:** Featuring mood swings between depressive lows and manic highs, bipolar disorder can be misdiagnosed or misunderstood due to cultural differences in expressing emotions.

6. **Substance Use Disorders:** Stress and discrimination can increase the vulnerability to substance misuse, leading to related mental health issues.

The Relationship Between Faith and Mental Health: Survey Insights

A survey of more than 2,000 American adults, conducted by Morning Consult on behalf of the APA, assessed the relationship between faith and mental health. Among those belonging to a religious community, nearly three in five (57%) said they would be likely to reach out to a faith leader if they were struggling with their mental health. An even larger share (68%) said they would be likely to seek mental health care if a leader in their religious community recommended it. Of the surveyed adults, 67% indicated that religion or spirituality was important to them, whereas 28% identified religion as "not too important" or "not important at all."

"Many of us rely on our faith communities for support in times of mental and emotional difficulty, whether we are struggling ourselves or we are supporting a loved one with a mental health condition," said Marketa M. Wills, M.D., M.B.A., CEO and Medical Director of the APA. "When a faith leader supports and encourages conversations around mental health, it makes a difference to that community, and as psychiatrists, we welcome that approach."

The APA Foundation has convened experts on the role of faith and mental health through its **Mental Health & Faith Community Partnership** for nearly a decade. This partnership brings psychiatrists and other mental health professionals together with faith leaders to create dialogue, which informs the development of educational resources and training for both disciplines.

In conjunction with the poll, the APA Foundation is releasing the second edition of its resource guide, *Mental Health: A Guide for Faith Leaders*. The resource guide provides faith leaders with insights and tools to understand mental health concerns and support congregants with mental health challenges. The updated edition of the guide adapts the APA Foundation's existing **Notice. Talk. Act.®** framework for a faith community setting and offers advice to faith leaders on caring for themselves to avoid compassion fatigue, as well as some noteworthy post-pandemic tools and resources. The guide is available on the Foundation website.

Additionally, in conjunction with the Partnership, the APA is developing a continuing medical education (CME) module for psychiatrists to learn more about the connection between faith and mental health, and how to provide meaningful care within faith communities.

"The results from this APA poll underscore the trust congregants place in faith leaders to give advice and counsel, and to know when additional mental health support is necessary," said Rawle Andrews Jr., Esq., the executive director of the APA Foundation. "By giving faith leaders the resources they need to make these connections to care, and in turn giving psychiatrists the CME training they need to provide culturally competent care, we are creating more equitable mental health outcomes for patients and their families."

To learn more about the APA Foundation's Mental Health & Faith Community Partnership, visit www.apaf.org/faith. The poll was conducted from August 16-17, 2024, among a sample of 2,201 adults.

American Psychiatric Association

The American Psychiatric Association, founded in 1844, is the oldest medical association in the country. The APA is also the largest psychiatric association in the world with more than 38,900 physician members specialising in the diagnosis, treatment, prevention, and research of mental illnesses. APA's vision is to ensure access to quality psychiatric diagnosis and treatment. For more information, please visit www.psychiatry.org.

The American Psychiatric Association Foundation is the philanthropic and educational arm of the APA. The APA Foundation promotes awareness of mental illnesses and the effectiveness of treatment, the importance of early intervention, access to care, and the need for high-quality services and treatment through a combination of public and professional education, research training, grants, and awards.

7

Cultural and Spiritual Sensitivity

Considering how different cultural backgrounds influence faith and mental health perceptions and the importance of culturally sensitive care

The intersection of cultural, social, and economic factors means that diagnosis and treatment in the Black community require cultural competence and sensitivity to address these disorders effectively.

Cultural Factors That Significantly Influence Mental Health Treatment

Cultural factors can significantly influence mental health treatment in various ways:

1. **Perception of Mental Health**: Cultural beliefs and values shape individuals' understanding and perception of mental health issues. In some cultures, mental illness may be stigmatised or not recognised as a medical condition, leading to reluctance in seeking help.

2. **Communication Styles**: Different cultures have unique ways of expressing emotions and discussing personal matters. Misunderstandings can arise if mental health

practitioners are not culturally aware, potentially affecting diagnosis and treatment.

3. **Trust and Authority**: Cultural attitudes towards authority figures, including healthcare providers, can influence a patient's willingness to engage in treatment. A lack of representation or understanding in the mental health field may lead to distrust among minority groups.

4. **Coping Strategies**: Cultural backgrounds can influence preferred coping mechanisms and support systems, such as relying on family or community networks rather than professional help.

5. **Stigma**: The stigma surrounding mental health can vary widely between cultures, affecting how individuals seek and adhere to treatment. In some cultures, mental health issues are seen as a personal or family failure, leading to increased isolation and reduced treatment-seeking behaviour.

6. **Cultural Competence of Providers**: Providers with cultural competence are better able to tailor treatments to fit cultural contexts, improving effectiveness. Cultural competence includes understanding cultural beliefs, behaviours, and values, and applying this understanding in clinical practice.

7. **Language Barriers**: Language differences can hinder communication for effective diagnosis and treatment. Misinterpretation of symptoms due to language differences can lead to misdiagnosis or inappropriate treatment plans.

8. **Access to Services**: Socioeconomic disparities correlated with cultural backgrounds can affect access to quality mental health services. Financial constraints, lack of insurance, or geographical barriers might prevent individuals from accessing the care they need.

Integrating cultural awareness into mental health care improves diagnostic accuracy, enhances treatment adherence, and fosters a more inclusive, supportive healthcare environment. Cultural beliefs and values shape how individuals understand and perceive mental health issues. In some cultures, mental illness may be stigmatised or not recognised as a medical condition, leading to reluctance to seek help.

Examples of Cultural Beliefs Affecting Mental Health

Here are some examples of cultural beliefs that can affect mental health:

1. **Shame and Honour Cultures**: In many cultures, mental illness is seen as a family disgrace. This belief can prevent individuals from seeking help due to fear of bringing shame upon their family.

2. **Spiritual or Religious Beliefs**: Some cultures may view mental health issues as spiritual problems or a form of religious punishment. As a result, individuals might prioritise religious or spiritual healing practices over psychological treatment.

3. **Mind-Body Connection**: In certain Asian cultures, mental health is viewed as interconnected with physical health. This belief might lead individuals to seek medical treatment for physical symptoms rather than addressing underlying psychological issues.

4. **Collectivism vs. Individualism**: In collectivist cultures, emphasising group harmony and family obligations might result in individuals neglecting their mental health to fulfil perceived social responsibilities. In contrast, individualistic cultures may promote personal fulfilment and autonomy, potentially reducing stigma.

5. **Acceptance of Expression**: In some cultures, open expression of emotions is discouraged, leading individuals to suppress feelings. This suppression can exacerbate mental health issues like depression and anxiety.

6. **Concept of Personal Control**: Cultures that value personal control might interpret mental health challenges as a lack of willpower, resulting in less empathy and support for those experiencing such challenges.

7. **Views on Fate and Destiny**: In cultures where life events are seen as predestined, individuals may feel powerless to change their mental health situation, potentially reducing motivation to seek help.

8. **Nature and Nurture Beliefs**: Some cultures emphasise genetic or biological explanations for mental illness, while others focus on environmental or sociocultural factors. These beliefs can influence the types of treatments individuals consider acceptable.

These cultural beliefs highlight the importance of culturally sensitive mental health care that respects and integrates diverse perspectives into treatment and support systems.

Schizophrenia

Schizophrenia is a complex mental health disorder that affects how a person thinks, feels, and behaves. It can lead to a loss of touch with reality, causing individuals to experience hallucinations or delusions.

1. **What is Schizophrenia?** Schizophrenia is characterised by symptoms that distort the way an individual perceives reality. This may include hearing voices, seeing things, or having false beliefs about oneself or the world.

2. **Who Can Have It?**: Schizophrenia can develop in anyone, but it typically appears in late adolescence or early adulthood. Approximately 1 in 100 people will experience schizophrenia at some point in their lives.

3. **Living with Schizophrenia**: While schizophrenia can be challenging, many individuals with the condition lead fulfilling lives with the right support. Treatment options include therapies, medications, and community support systems.

4. **Myths and Facts**: There are many misconceptions about schizophrenia. For instance, schizophrenia is not the same as multiple personality disorder, and individuals with schizophrenia are not more violent than others.

5. **Famous People with Schizophrenia**: Many renowned individuals, including artists, writers, and scientists, have lived with schizophrenia and contributed significantly to their respective fields.

It is important to engage with empathy and understanding when supporting individuals with schizophrenia. By becoming better informed, we can offer better support and contribute to a more compassionate society.

Schizophrenia Is Over diagnosed in Black Communities In The UK

Research suggests that schizophrenia and other psychotic disorders may be over diagnosed in Black communities in the UK. Several studies have highlighted that Black individuals are more likely to be diagnosed with schizophrenia compared to their White counterparts. This discrepancy is often attributed to a variety of factors, including:

1. **Cultural Bias**: Mental health professionals may have cultural biases that affect their diagnostic practices, leading to misinterpretation of cultural behaviours or expressions.

2. **Socioeconomic Factors**: Social determinants of health, such as economic disadvantage and systemic racism, may contribute to higher diagnosis rates.

3. **Access to Services**: Differences in access to mental health services and support can impact diagnosis, with Black individuals more likely to encounter crisis services rather than preventative care.

4. **Presentation**: Symptoms may be expressed differently across cultures, and clinicians may not always accurately interpret these expressions in Black patients.

Efforts are being made to address these disparities through cultural competency training and more inclusive mental health practices. However, it is an ongoing issue that requires continued attention and research.

Dawn Edge: New Hope to End Black Schizophrenia Care Crisis

A groundbreaking talking treatment has been developed and successfully trialled with a group of Black and minority ethnic (BME) schizophrenia service users, carers, community members, and health professionals. Dr Dawn Edge from The University of Manchester led a team that developed the model in a study funded by the National Institute for Health Research (NIHR), which she says could be a breakthrough for BME patients whose mental healthcare is both sub-optimal and costly for the NHS.

The new therapy, called Culturally-Adapted Family Intervention, or 'CaFI' for short, emerges in the context of decades of poor engagement between Black communities and mental health services. People of African-Caribbean origin, including those of 'Mixed' heritage, are nine times more likely to be diagnosed with schizophrenia than White British people. Black Africans' risk of diagnosis is six times greater.

https://doi.org/10.3310/hsdr06320

Signs of Schizophrenia: Churchgoer with Schizophrenia

Dear Doctor Francis, thank you for your kind reply. However, I am not sure what you mean by the phrase "Where is your faith?" I am unsure if it is the Lord speaking to rebuke me, or your observation based on your own mature experience of spiritual matters.

I gave my life to Jesus Christ at the age of ten. Then Satan attacked. First, he tried to draw me into the homosexual lifestyle by sexually abusing me within a paedophile group in my mother's church. It was no ordinary abuse. It was a ritual in order to draw me into the Satanic cult that is so hidden in Europe. I was chosen by Satan to be his cult leader. He killed eight members of my family, amputated the legs of my niece, and left her brain damaged for life.

At the time of the abuse, evil spirits were transferred to my soul, which is the root of my mental illness and the addiction to pornography that the Lord is healing me from.

When I came back to London in 1991 after a prolonged battle in America with supernatural forces such as giant spiders, giant insects, Medusa, and many more devices that he used to try to force me to give up my faith in Christ, I joined Morris Cerullo Victorious Army. I have been partnering with MCWE for the last 34 years.

Instead of going to California in January 1995, I was sectioned under the Mental Health Act. It was my first section of many. After I was released from Lambeth Hospital, I walked on Clapham Common to a tent meeting by Pastor Chambers. I looked up into the sky and I saw it change. A loud voice told me I would become a mighty warrior. I should know that no power or man will be able to stand against me because the Lord is with me.

I thought this voice was the principality my family had been fighting for three generations. This is the dream that I received about what Morris Cerullo prophesied over my life in 1994.

I talked to my aunt and told her that I had to go back to England. I told her about Trevor and David. But I called Trevor a different name. I told her that David had blotches on his skin. She said that he was emaciated and thin. She said that Trevor had children. Then she changed to a white man wearing beige/brown trousers and a tie. He also wore a white shirt. He began to talk about Job—how in thirty days he went away to reflect on his suffering. It happened in daylight, and the window was opened.

Date Given: 4th March 2020

I thought that it was from the devil. Many years later, the Lord forced me to use it, and I have been very cautious about using this anointing in my street pastoral ministry with those who have the faith to receive it.

Examples: Cassie was healed from a slipped disc. Grace received £5,000. Tintin was able to sleep at night after many years of not being able to sleep and walking the streets of Clapham at night for many years, and there are many more.

My fear is that it may not be from God, even though it was given by true men of God and is being rejected.

In my professional experience, not every word a person says is delusional. Almost always, there are shades of reality.

Another Example: A very pleasant Christian woman from Gen Z with bipolar disorder who wrote a piece to me:

"This is my story, this is my soul. I hope for agape = joyful. I like Benjamin Zephaniah. Alpha courses will help."

In Christianity, "agape" refers to a specific type of love, often considered the highest form, characterised by selflessness, sacrifice, and unconditional love for others. It's seen as the love God has for humanity and the love that Christians are called to have for one another. Agape is distinct from other Greek words for love like "eros" (romantic love) and "philia" (brotherly love).

Here's a more detailed explanation:

- **Unconditional and Unwavering**: Agape love is not based on feelings or reciprocity, but on a commitment to the well-being of others, even when they are not deserving of love.
- **Selfless and Sacrificial**: Agape love is characterised by a willingness to give, serve, and sacrifice for the benefit of others, putting their needs before one's own.
- **Love of God and Neighbour**: Agape is seen as the love God has for all humans and the love that Christians are called to show to their neighbours and to God in return.
- **Contrast with Other Forms of Love**: Agape is distinct from romantic love (eros) and brotherly/sisterly love (philia) because it is not conditional, emotional, or based on personal preferences.

In the midst of mental illness, a young woman with bipolar expressed her faith. You can see a struggle for faith despite mental distortions of thinking.

BIPOLAR AFFECTIVE DISORDER

Bipolar disorder is a mental health condition that causes unusual shifts in mood, energy, activity levels, and the ability to carry out daily tasks. It isn't just about the regular mood swings that everyone experiences but involves intense emotional states known as mood episodes.

Mood Episodes: Understanding the Highs and Lows

1. **Manic Episodes**: These episodes can make an individual feel overly energetic, euphoric, or irritable. During these periods, individuals may take on numerous projects or feel like they are unstoppable.

2. **Depressive Episodes**: On the other hand, depressive episodes can cause feelings of sadness and low energy. Activities that were once enjoyable may seem dull, and simple tasks may become overwhelming.

3. **Hypomanic Episodes**: These episodes are milder than manic episodes but can still have an impact on daily functioning.

Who Can Experience This?

Bipolar disorder affects people of all ages, races, and backgrounds. While it commonly begins in late adolescence or early adulthood, it can occur at any stage of life.

Why Should We Talk About It?

Discussing bipolar disorder reduces stigma and promotes understanding, enabling individuals to support those experiencing the condition. Additionally, awareness helps individuals manage their own mental health and recognise when something may be amiss.

The Science Behind It

Bipolar disorder is not a result of personal fault. It is typically caused by a combination of genetic, environmental, and brain structural factors. Research continues to improve our understanding of the condition, and there is hope as treatment options continue to evolve.

Treatment and Management

Bipolar disorder can be managed effectively. Treatment often includes a combination of medication, therapy, lifestyle changes, and support networks. It is important to identify the treatment plan that works best for each individual.

Reach Out

If you suspect that you or someone you know is experiencing symptoms of bipolar disorder, seeking professional help is the first important step. There are numerous resources, support groups, and hotlines available to provide guidance and assistance. It is important to remember that support is always available.

Get Involved

Empower yourself and others by learning about the condition, sharing experiences, and being part of a community that views mental health as a vital component of overall health.

Remember

Bipolar disorder does not define a person. While it is a part of the individual's experience, there is much more to their story. It is important to embrace one's uniqueness and continue progressing forward.

Imagine a person named Alex who has bipolar disorder.

At times, Alex experiences periods of extreme energy and elation, commonly referred to as manic episodes. During these episodes, they may engage in rapid speech, feel an influx of new ideas, and remain awake through the night without feeling tired. These periods often lead to impulsive behaviour such as taking on large projects or spending money unwisely.

At other times, Alex experiences depressive episodes, where they feel low and lack the motivation to get out of bed. Activities they usually find enjoyable may seem unappealing, and they may struggle with feelings of hopelessness or worthlessness.

While Alex may experience stable periods between these extremes, the dramatic mood shifts can be challenging. To manage these fluctuations, Alex works closely with healthcare professionals, often using a combination of medication, therapy, and lifestyle changes to maintain balance and well-being.

Supporting someone with bipolar disorder requires understanding their unique needs and challenges. Here are some ways to offer support:

1. **Educate Yourself**: Learning about bipolar disorder, its symptoms, and treatments can enhance understanding and improve your ability to offer support.

2. **Encourage Treatment and Therapy**: Support individuals in adhering to their treatment plan, which may include medication, therapy, and counselling. Offering assistance with appointments or medication management can also be helpful.

3. **Show Empathy and Understanding**: It is important to be patient and understanding of the mood fluctuations. These mood shifts are part of the disorder and should not be seen as a reflection of the individual's true character.

4. **Maintain Open Communication**: Actively listen without judgement. Encourage the individual to share their thoughts and feelings, and ensure they know you are there for them.

5. **Help with Daily Structure**: Encouraging a structured routine can assist in managing the symptoms of bipolar disorder. This includes promoting regular sleep patterns, healthy eating, and consistency in daily activities.

6. **Encourage a Healthy Lifestyle**: Promote healthy habits such as regular physical activity and stress-reducing techniques, both of which can positively impact mood stability.

7. **Be Prepared for Emergencies**: Recognise the signs of a manic or depressive episode and be prepared to take necessary steps in an emergency, including seeking professional help if needed.

8. **Encourage Social Interaction**: Encourage participation in social activities or support groups to combat isolation and promote healthy interpersonal relationships.

9. **Take Care of Your Own Well-being**: Supporting someone with bipolar disorder can be demanding. It is important to prioritise self-care and seek support when needed.

Providing support with empathy and understanding can significantly improve the individual's ability to manage bipolar disorder and lead a fulfilling life.

Specific Lifestyle Changes That Can Help Manage Bipolar Disorder

Several lifestyle changes can support the management of bipolar disorder. These include:

1. **Consistent Routine**: Establishing and maintaining a regular daily routine for sleep, meals, and activities helps stabilise mood swings.

2. **Sleep Hygiene**: Prioritising quality sleep is essential. Consistently going to bed and waking up at the same time each day can help manage mood fluctuations.

3. **Healthy Diet**: Eating a balanced diet, rich in fruits, vegetables, whole grains, and lean proteins, supports both overall health and brain function.

4. **Regular Exercise**: Engaging in physical activity, such as walking, jogging, or yoga, can improve mood and reduce stress levels.

5. **Stress Management**: Practising techniques such as mindfulness, meditation, or deep-breathing exercises can help manage emotional stress.

6. **Avoiding Alcohol and Drugs**: Avoiding substances such as alcohol and recreational drugs is crucial, as they can exacerbate mood swings and interfere with medications.

7. **Monitoring Moods**: Tracking mood changes and identifying potential triggers can help predict and manage mood shifts more effectively.

8. **Social Support**: Cultivating a strong support network of family, friends, or support groups provides emotional support and helps reduce feelings of isolation.

9. **Therapy and Education**: Participating in therapy, such as cognitive behavioural therapy (CBT), and learning about bipolar disorder empowers individuals to manage their symptoms more effectively.

10. **Medication Adherence**: Following prescribed medication regimens and maintaining regular communication with healthcare providers is crucial for managing bipolar disorder.

Each individual's experience with bipolar disorder is unique, and it is important to work with healthcare professionals to develop a personalised lifestyle plan that complements other treatments.

Faith-Based Mindfulness for Borderline Personality Disorder (BPD)

Faith-based mindfulness can be a valuable tool for individuals with Borderline Personality Disorder (BPD). This approach combines spiritual practices and beliefs with mindfulness techniques, providing a holistic way to manage emotions and behaviours. Here's how it can help:

1. **Integration of Belief and Mindfulness**: This approach merges religious or spiritual faith with mindfulness practices. It encourages individuals to focus on the present moment while drawing strength and comfort from their faith.

2. **Grounding Practices**: Mindfulness helps individuals stay grounded in the present moment, reduce anxiety, and think more clearly. Faith can offer a sense of purpose and hope, which can be especially uplifting for someone experiencing intense emotions.

3. **Compassion and Acceptance**: Many faiths emphasise compassion and acceptance towards oneself and others. This can reduce self-criticism and help in developing healthier relationships.

How It Helps in BPD

1. **Emotional Regulation**: BPD is characterised by emotional instability. Mindfulness helps individuals observe their emotions without judgment, making it easier to manage and regulate intense feelings.

2. **Reduction of Impulsive Behaviour**: Mindfulness can help reduce impulsive behaviours, a common challenge in BPD, by fostering a thoughtful response rather than a reactive approach.

3. **Enhancement of Interpersonal Relationships**: Faith often emphasises empathy and understanding, which can improve communication and relationship skills.

4. **Promoting Acceptance and Letting Go**: Faith-based mindfulness encourages acceptance of suffering and letting go of things beyond one's control, easing the emotional turbulence often experienced in BPD.

By combining the centering and calming techniques of mindfulness with the emotional and spiritual support of faith, individuals with BPD can find a more balanced way to navigate their emotions. This holistic approach encourages a sense of peace, purpose, and connection, which is essential for well-being and recovery. It's important to work with a mental health professional who understands BPD to integrate faith-based mindfulness appropriately into treatment plans.

What Are Some Successful Case Studies of Faith-Based Mental Health Interventions?

Case studies of faith-based mental health interventions that have shown positive outcomes:

1. **The Sanctuary Model**: Originating in the United States, the Sanctuary Model integrates trauma-informed care with spiritual support. It's been used in various settings, including hospitals and schools, and emphasises creating safe, supportive communities for healing, often involving faith leaders in the process.

2. **The Holy Cross Health System in Uganda**: This initiative collaborates with local churches to provide mental health services. Churches serve as the first point of contact, offering counselling, support groups, and referrals to professional services, significantly increasing access to mental health care in remote areas.

3. **Islamic Counselling Centres**: Islamic counselling centres integrate traditional religious teachings with modern psychological practices in some parts of the Middle East and Southeast Asia. These centres have successfully helped individuals by aligning therapeutic practices with their faith, reducing stigma and encouraging treatment.

4. **The Mental Health Chaplaincy Program**: In Seattle, Washington, this program combines chaplaincy and mental health services to assist people experiencing homelessness. By offering spiritual guidance alongside mental health support, the program has effectively engaged individuals who might otherwise resist conventional mental health treatments.

5. **Faith-Based CBT Programs**: Cognitive Behavioural Therapy (CBT) programs that incorporate Christian principles have been successfully implemented in several U.S. communities. These programs align therapeutic concepts with spiritual teachings, increasing receptiveness among participants who hold their faith as central to their lives.

6. **Interfaith Network on Mental Illness (INMI)**

   This U.S.-based initiative brings together diverse faith communities to address mental health issues. By fostering interfaith dialogue and collaboration, they have created workshops and support networks that respect varying spiritual beliefs while providing mental health education and resources.

7. **Hindus for Human Rights: Support Networks**

   This organisation in the U.S. offers support groups that integrate Hindu principles and practices to address mental health and stress. By aligning with religious values and offering culturally sensitive resources, they've improved community engagement and support for those struggling with mental health issues.

These case studies demonstrate how integrating faith-based approaches with mental health interventions can enhance accessibility, reduce stigma, and offer culturally and spiritually informed support, leading to improved outcomes for individuals from diverse backgrounds.

Feeling Unheard or Not Being Truly Listened To

Feeling unheard or not being truly listened to by mental health professionals can be incredibly frustrating and disheartening. It often leads to a sense of isolation, as if your experiences and feelings are being invalidated. Here are some common emotions and thoughts that might arise in such situations:

1. **Frustration**: You might feel that your attempts to communicate are falling on deaf ears. This can be especially challenging when you're trying to articulate complex emotions or experiences.

2. **Isolation**: Feeling unheard can lead to a sense of loneliness, as though no one truly understands or is willing to understand what you're going through.

3. **Invalidation**: You might feel as though your experiences, emotions, or even your understanding of your own situation are being dismissed or not taken seriously.

4. **Helplessness**: When you're not listened to, it can sometimes feel like you're stuck in your current situation with no way out, as though the support meant to help feels inaccessible.

5. **Distrust**: Continuous experiences of not being listened to may lead to a lack of trust in the professional or mental health system.

6. **Anger or Resentment**: You may feel anger towards the professional for not fulfilling their role to provide support and understanding. This can also develop into resentment over time.

7. **Reduced Self-Esteem**: Feeling ignored can lead you to question the worth of your own experiences and whether you're worthy of help or support.

Mental health professionals must set a foundation of trust, empathy, and understanding. If you find yourself in this position, it might be beneficial to:

- Express your feelings directly, letting the professional know that you don't feel heard.

- Seek a second opinion or another professional who might better suit your needs.

- Reach out to support groups or communities where you may feel more understood.

Your experiences and feelings are valid, and it's important to find the support that acknowledges and respects them.

Feeling Misunderstood by a Mental Health Professional

Feeling misunderstood by a mental health professional can be challenging, but there are steps you can take to address the situation:

1. **Communicate Clearly**: Express your feelings openly to your therapist or counsellor. Let them know you feel misunderstood and provide specific examples of where this occurred. Clear communication can sometimes resolve misunderstandings quickly.

2. **Ask for Clarification**: If something the professional says doesn't feel right to you, ask them to elaborate.

Understanding their perspective fully might help bridge the gap between your views.

3. **Reflect on Your Own Needs**: Consider what you want to achieve from your sessions and whether your current professional is equipped to help with those needs. Reflecting on this can provide clarity on whether it's a communication issue or a mismatch in therapeutic approaches.

4. **Provide Feedback**: Share what methods or communication styles have worked for you in the past. Professionals often appreciate feedback as it allows them to adjust their approach and better support you.

5. **Take Notes**: Jot down what you want to discuss before sessions and note any points where you felt misunderstood. This can help guide conversations and ensure important topics aren't overlooked.

6. **Seek a Second Opinion**: If resolution seems elusive, consider consulting another mental health professional. Different professionals may offer different perspectives, and it might help you find someone whose style aligns better with your needs.

7. **Use Support Networks**: Talk to friends, family, or support groups about your experiences. Sometimes an outside perspective can provide valuable insights or suggestions.

8. **Explore Different Therapies**: Consider whether another form of therapy or a different specialist might be more suited to your situation. Sometimes exploring options like cognitive-behavioural therapy (CBT), dialectical behaviour therapy (DBT), or other therapeutic modalities can lead to better understanding.

9. **Trust Your Instincts**: If after trying several strategies, things don't improve, trust your intuition. Your mental

health is crucial; finding the right professional is key to your growth and healing.

Remember, feeling heard, understood, and supported in your therapeutic journey is important. Finding the right fit can make a significant difference in your mental health journey.

Strategic and Pivotal Role of Faith Communities, Including Churches

Faith communities play a significant role in public mental health by offering social support, reducing stigma, and connecting individuals to care. Faith leaders often act as "first responders" for mental health crises, particularly in underserved areas, helping to dispel misconceptions and facilitate treatment access. Initiatives like FaithAction's "Friendly Places" encourage faith groups to create welcoming environments for mental health support. Additionally, religiosity is associated with improved well-being, lower depression rates, and recovery from mental illness, highlighting the potential for collaboration between faith leaders and mental health professionals.

How Can Faith Leaders Effectively Reduce Stigma Around Mental Health?

Faith leaders can effectively reduce stigma around mental health by:

- **Modelling Openness**: Sharing personal experiences with mental health challenges to normalise seeking help and reduce shame.
- **Dispelling Myths and Misconceptions**: Educating congregations through workshops, sermons, or discussions to dispel myths about mental illness and promote awareness.

- **Collaborating with Professionals**: Partnering with mental health experts to deliver culturally sensitive interventions and provide accurate information.

- **Creating Safe Spaces**: Establishing welcoming environments for open conversations and peer-led support groups within faith communities.

How New Testament Stories Relate to Modern Life

Several New Testament stories relate to modern life in various ways, as they address themes and challenges that remain relevant today:

1. **The Temptation of Jesus**: This story is relevant in the context of self-control and resilience against temptation. In modern life, individuals often face temptations, whether it be unhealthy food, shortcuts in ethical practices, or addictive substances. This story encourages prioritising long-term well-being and spiritual integrity over immediate gratification.

2. **The Rich Young Ruler**: This encounter speaks to the modern craving for wealth and material possessions. In a consumer-driven society, people often equate success and happiness with material accumulation. This story challenges individuals to consider what they truly value and encourages finding fulfilment beyond material wealth.

3. **The Prodigal Son**: The tale is timeless in its portrayal of failure, repentance, and forgiveness. Modern life is filled with opportunities for mistakes, especially during youth. The story reassures that no matter how far one strays, there's always a path back, emphasising forgiveness, reconciliation, and the enduring bonds of family.

4. **The Teaching on Worry**: This teaching addresses common anxieties about basic needs and future security. In

contemporary life, people are often stressed about finances, career, and daily living. Jesus' advice to prioritise spiritual and meaningful pursuits over constant worry offers a perspective that encourages trust and balance.

Overall, these stories and teachings from the New Testament offer insights into human nature and provide moral and ethical guidance that many find relevant in navigating the complexities of modern life. They encourage reflection on priorities, self-control, resilience, and compassion, which are timeless values applicable in any era.

FAITH SUPPORT WORKER

A **faith support worker** is a professional who integrates spiritual and religious beliefs with mental health care to provide emotional, psychological, and spiritual support to individuals. They assist clients by offering guidance through faith-based practices, such as prayer, scripture, or other religious teachings, while also addressing emotional well-being and mental health concerns. Faith support workers are often trained in both mental health principles and spiritual care, and they help individuals navigate life's challenges by aligning their faith with therapeutic practices. Their role involves offering comfort, promoting resilience, and supporting personal growth, while respecting the client's beliefs and values.

Core Competencies of a Faith Support Worker

A faith support worker should possess a combination of formal education, spiritual understanding, and interpersonal skills. Here are some qualifications that can help ensure they are effective in their role:

1. **Educational Background**: A degree in psychology, counselling, or social work provides a foundation in mental health principles and therapeutic techniques. Additional

education in theology or religious studies is needed to understand faith-based perspectives deeply.

2. **Faith-Based Training**: Training or certification in spiritual caregiving, pastoral counselling, or a related field, ensuring competence in integrating faith with mental health practices. Understanding and respect across various religious traditions if working in interfaith settings.

3. **Clinical Experience**: Practical experience through internships or supervised practice in environments that require the integration of faith and mental health support. Experience in conducting individual and group therapy sessions.

4. **Licensing and Certification**: Licensure as a therapist, counsellor, or social worker, depending on regional requirements, ensuring adherence to professional standards in mental health care. Certification from relevant religious or spiritual organisations affirming their capability and integrity in spiritual guidance.

5. **Ethical Competence**: A strong ethical foundation to navigate complex situations where religious beliefs intersect with mental health needs, ensuring client welfare is always prioritised. Commitment to maintaining client confidentiality and professional boundaries.

6. **Interpersonal Skills**: Strong communication and listening skills to understand clients effectively and provide empathetic support. Ability to build trust and rapport with clients, creating a safe and welcoming environment for discussion.

7. **Cultural Sensitivity**: Awareness and respect for diverse cultural backgrounds and beliefs, ensuring inclusive and respectful treatment of all clients.

8. **Continuous Learning**: Commitment to ongoing education in both mental health advancements and evolving spiritual insights, ensuring current knowledge and practice standards.

By combining these qualifications, a faith support worker can provide effective and compassionate support, helping individuals navigate life's challenges through the interconnected lenses of faith and mental health.

A Christian Faith-Based Support Worker

A Christian faith-based support worker integrates Christian beliefs and principles with traditional psychological techniques to offer holistic mental health support. This approach considers individuals' spiritual, emotional, and psychological aspects, often incorporating prayer, scripture, and Christian teachings into therapy. Practitioners are typically licensed professionals who respect diverse beliefs while offering a faith-aligned therapeutic experience. Organisations like the Association of Christians in Counselling and Linked Professions (ACC) support these practitioners by promoting ethical practices and providing resources. This integration aims to provide comfort, hope, and a sense of purpose rooted in Christian faith.

Core Competencies of a Faith Mental Support Worker

The core competencies of a faith mental support worker include:

1. **Relational Skills**: Ability to engage empathetically, actively listen, and communicate effectively with clients, fostering mutual trust and respect.

2. **Knowledge and Understanding**: Awareness of mental health issues, trauma-informed care, and the integration of faith-based perspectives in supporting mental health.

3. **Supportive Techniques**: Skills in facilitating personal recovery, promoting client autonomy, and helping clients develop coping strategies.

4. **Ethical Practice**: Understanding of confidentiality, consent, and safeguarding procedures, while maintaining professional boundaries.

5. **Self-Care**: Ability to practice self-care and utilise supervision to prevent burnout and ensure effective support delivery.

How Faith Mental Support Workers Can Support Clients in Developing Coping Skills

Faith mental support workers can support clients in developing coping skills through several strategies:

1. **Faith Integrated Techniques**: Encourage the use of prayer, meditation on scripture, and reliance on spiritual beliefs to manage stress and build resilience.

2. **Goal Setting and Action Planning**: Help clients set goals aligned with their faith, breaking them into actionable steps incorporating spiritual practices.

3. **Self-Reflection and Awareness**: Facilitate self-reflection activities that enhance spiritual awareness and understanding of one's identity within their faith.

4. **Education and Skill Development**: Teach coping skills like emotional regulation and decision-making, integrating biblical principles to support holistic well-being.

5. **Community and Connection**: Promote a sense of belonging and support through community involvement and faith-based activities, which can enhance resilience and provide a network of support.

What Role Goal Setting Plays in the Work of Faith Mental Support Workers?

Goal setting plays a crucial role in the work of faith mental support workers by providing structure and direction for clients' personal growth and recovery. It helps clients align their therapeutic goals with their spiritual beliefs, enhancing motivation and engagement in the therapeutic process. By setting meaningful and achievable goals, clients can experience a sense of purpose and progress, which is vital for behaviour change and emotional well-being. Additionally, goal setting fosters a collaborative relationship between the support worker and client, promoting open communication and trust. This approach not only supports mental health but also integrates spiritual growth.

Benefits of Involving a Faith Leader (Minister, Pastor, Vicar) in the Goal-Setting Process for Clients

Involving a faith leader in the goal-setting process for clients offers several benefits:

1. **Clarification of Worldview**: Faith leaders help clients articulate and integrate their spiritual beliefs into their goals, providing a clearer sense of purpose and direction.

2. **Holistic Support**: By addressing spiritual, existential, and emotional needs, faith leaders ensure that goals are comprehensive and aligned with clients' values and beliefs, enhancing overall well-being.

3. **Ethical Guidance**: Faith leaders provide ethical and moral support, helping clients navigate complex decisions and align their goals with personal and organisational values.

4. **Meaningful Goal Setting**: Faith leaders assist in setting meaningful and personalised goals, ensuring they resonate deeply with clients' fundamental beliefs and aspirations.

Faith and Digital Mental Health

Faith and digital mental health are interesting subjects that intersect in various ways. Here's how these areas connect:

1. **Supportive Communities**: Many religious groups have online communities and forums where members can share experiences, seek support, and connect with others who share their beliefs. These digital platforms can provide a sense of belonging and community, which is beneficial for mental health.

2. **Mental Health Resources**: Some faith-based organisations offer digital resources like apps or websites that focus on mental wellness from a religious perspective. These resources might include prayer guides, meditation techniques, or religious teachings that promote peace and mental clarity.

3. **Online Counselling**: Digital mental health services incorporate faith-based counselling. These services blend professional mental health support with spiritual guidance, addressing the client's psychological and spiritual needs.

4. **Mindfulness and Meditation**: Many religions emphasise practices like mindfulness and meditation, which have been shown to positively impact mental health. Digital platforms often provide guided meditations and mindfulness exercises rooted in religious traditions.

5. **Inclusivity and Accessibility**: Digital platforms make faith-based resources accessible to a broader audience, including those who can't physically attend religious gatherings. This

accessibility ensures that more people can benefit from religious communities' mental health support.

6. **Balanced Approach**: Faith-based approaches can offer support, but balancing them with professional mental health services when necessary is essential. Digital platforms can provide information on when to seek professional help and how to combine it with spiritual practices.

It's fascinating to see how faith and technology are merging to create supportive environments that enhance mental wellness.

Online Faith-Based Recovery Programs

1. **Celebrate Recovery Online**: This Christian-based recovery program often offers online meetings, where participants can connect over video calls to work through the principles of recovery in a supportive, faith-centred environment.

2. **Alcoholics Anonymous (AA) Online Intergroup**: Although AA is not strictly faith-based, its spiritual principles appeal to many religious individuals. There are numerous online AA meetings, some of which might focus on incorporating faith traditions more prominently.

3. **Narcotics Anonymous (NA) Online Meetings**: Similar to AA, NA provides online meetings accessible to those seeking a spiritually influenced path to recovery from drug-related issues.

4. **Recovery Dharma Online**: While not strictly aligned with a single faith, Recovery Dharma incorporates Buddhist practices and principles, offering meditation and mindfulness as tools for recovery. Online meetings are available.

5. **Christian 12-Step Programs Online**: Various Christian organisations offer online versions of 12-step recovery

programs. These meetings often integrate Bible study and prayer alongside the 12-step process.

6. **Faith Partners Online Support Groups**: Some interfaith organisations provide online support that caters to various faith traditions, offering a diverse spiritual perspective in recovery.

7. **JACS Virtual Meetings**: Jewish Alcoholics, Chemically Dependent Persons, and Significant Others offer virtual support meetings, focusing on Jewish spiritual traditions.

8. **Buddhist Recovery Network Online**: This network provides online resources and meetings for individuals interested in applying Buddhist principles to recovery.

These online options allow individuals to access support from the comfort of their homes, providing flexibility and privacy while maintaining a strong spiritual foundation. It's recommended that the availability and schedule of these online meetings be verified, as they can vary.

Some Faith-Based Mental Health Apps

Here are a few faith-based mental health apps that combine spiritual guidance with mental wellness support:

1. **Abide**: A Christian meditation app that provides guided prayers and meditation based on Bible scriptures. It helps users find peace and encouragement through faith-driven content.

2. **Soultime**: This app offers Christian meditation sessions, journaling features, and mood tracking to help users address their emotional well-being through a biblical lens.

3. **Glorify**: Designed for Christians, Glorify provides daily devotionals, Bible readings, and meditation practices to support spiritual and mental wellness.

4. **Serene**: A faith-based mindfulness app that includes exercises and reflections to promote mental health, rooted in Christian teachings.

5. **CalmCatholic**: An app that blends Catholic teachings with mental wellness advice, including scriptures, prayers, and meditations designed to alleviate stress and enhance spiritual growth.

Remember to explore each app to see which one aligns best with your beliefs and mental wellness needs.

Free Christian Faith-Based Mental Health Apps

There are free faith-based mental health apps, although some may offer premium features or subscriptions. Here are a few you can try out:

1. **Pray.com**: While rooted in community prayer, this app offers a range of free audio prayers and meditative stories to enhance both faith and mental well-being.

2. **YouVersion Bible App**: While primarily a Bible app, it includes daily devotionals and plans that emphasise mental health and emotional support through scripture.

Many young people don't understand mental health and tend to shy away from talking about any issues they may have.

"My grace is sufficient... my power is made perfect in weakness" (2 Cor. 12:9).

Exploring Young People's Perspectives on Mental Health Support: A Qualitative Study Across Three Geographical Areas in England, UK - PMC

The mentioned study seems to explore the perspectives of young people regarding mental health support in three different geographical areas of England. While I don't have direct access to external studies or databases like PMC (PubMed Central), I can suggest a general idea of what such a study might entail:

1. **Objective**:
   - To understand how young people perceive mental health support.
   - To identify barriers and facilitators to accessing mental health services.

2. **Methodology**:
   - Conducting qualitative research through interviews or focus groups.
   - Participants comprise young individuals from diverse backgrounds in three different geographical areas.

3. **Key Areas of Focus**:
   - Accessibility of mental health services.
   - Quality and effectiveness of the support provided.
   - Stigma surrounding mental health issues and its impact on seeking help.
   - Preferences for types of support (in-person, online, group therapy, etc.).

4. **Potential Findings**:
    - Variations in experiences and opinions related to geographical or socio-economic differences.
    - Common themes around the need for more approachable and youth-friendly services.
    - Insights into how mental health education and awareness can be improved among young people.
5. **Implications**:
    - Recommendations for policymakers to enhance mental health support for young people.
    - Providing evidence to inform the development of targeted interventions.

I would recommend reading the full study on PMC or similar academic platforms to get more detailed insights. Feel free to ask if you have specific questions or need help with a summary or analysis!

What Are the Common Barriers Young People Face in Accessing Mental Health Support?

Young people often encounter various barriers when trying to access mental health support. Some of the common challenges include:

1. **Stigma and Shame**:
    - Fear of judgment or being labelled can deter individuals from seeking help.
2. **Lack of Awareness**:
    - Young people may not recognise the signs of mental health issues or know where to find help.

3. **Accessibility**:
    - Limited availability of nearby services or long waiting times can be discouraging.

4. **Financial Constraints**:
    - Cost of services can be a barrier, especially if they are not covered by insurance.

5. **Confidentiality Concerns**:
    - Worries about privacy and parental notification may prevent seeking support.

6. **Cultural and Social Factors**:
    - Cultural beliefs and societal norms can influence attitudes towards mental health.

7. **Peer Influence**:
    - Pressure from friends or a lack of understanding in social circles can inhibit reaching out.

8. **Lack of Trust**:
    - Mistrust in mental health professionals or the system may discourage engagement.

9. **Insufficient Youth-Specific Services**:
    - A lack of tailored services for young people can lead to inadequate support.

10. **School and Time Constraints**:
    - Busy schedules and academic pressures may make it difficult to prioritise mental health care.

Addressing these barriers involves increasing awareness, enhancing accessibility and affordability, fostering supportive environments, and developing youth-focused mental health initiatives.

What Are Some Effective Ways to Raise Awareness About Mental Health Issues Among Youth?

Raising awareness about mental health issues among youth requires a multi-faceted approach that's engaging, educational, and relatable. Here are some effective strategies:

1. **Social Media Campaigns**:
    - Using platforms like Instagram, TikTok, and Facebook to share information, personal stories, and resources can quickly reach a wide audience.
2. **School Programs**:
    - Implementing mental health education in schools through workshops, classes, and seminars can provide valuable knowledge and destigmatise mental health issues.
3. **Peer Support Groups**:
    - Encouraging the formation of peer-led support groups where young people can share experiences and support one another.
4. **Collaborate with Influencers**:
    - Partnering with popular influencers and celebrities who can speak openly about mental health and reach their followers in a meaningful way.

5. **Interactive Workshops**:
   - Hosting workshops that involve role-play, discussions, and activities to engage youth and increase understanding.

6. **Art and Expression**:
   - Using art, music, and theatre as mediums to creatively express and explore mental health topics.

7. **Parents and Guardians Involvement**:
   - Educating parents and guardians to recognise signs and provide support, creating a more understanding environment at home.

8. **Create Safe Spaces**:
   - Establishing safe environments where young people feel comfortable discussing their mental health without fear of judgment.

9. **Online Resources and Apps**:
   - Developing and promoting digital resources, apps, and websites that offer information, support, and self-assessment tools.

10. **Community Events**:
    - Organising events such as mental health fairs, awareness runs, or youth conventions to engage the community and spark conversation.

11. **Storytelling and Personal Narratives**:
    - Sharing personal stories and narratives can help normalise mental health discussions and make them more relatable.

By implementing these strategies, we can foster a supportive community that encourages open conversation and reduces the stigma surrounding mental health among youth.

What Activities Can We Organise for a Mental Health Awareness Event?

Organising activities for a mental health awareness event can make it engaging, informative, and impactful. Here are some activities you can include:

1. **Workshops and Seminars**:
    - Host sessions on stress management, mindfulness, and coping strategies led by mental health professionals.
2. **Panel Discussions**:
    - Invite experts, mental health advocates, and individuals with lived experiences to share their insights and answer questions.
3. **Art Therapy Sessions**:
    - Provide art supplies for participants to express their emotions creatively, facilitated by an art therapist.
4. **Yoga and Meditation Classes**:
    - Offer sessions that focus on relaxation and mental well-being through guided practices.
5. **Storytelling and Open Mic**:
    - Create a platform for participants to share personal stories, poetry, or spoken word on mental health topics.

6. **Interactive Exhibit:**
   o Set up an exhibit with interactive displays, information booths, and resource materials on mental health issues.

7. **Stress Relief Stations:**
   o Include activities like colouring, journaling, or crafting where attendees can unwind and relax.

8. **Mindfulness Walk:**
   o Organise a guided mindfulness walk where participants practice being present and aware of their surroundings.

9. **Q&A with Professionals:**
   o Allow attendees to ask anonymous questions to mental health professionals and receive expert advice.

10. **Role-Playing Scenarios:**
    o Conduct role-playing exercises to practise effective communication and empathy in mental health conversations.

11. **Resource Fair:**
    o Feature booths from local mental health organisations offering resources, support, and volunteer opportunities.

12. **Fitness Activities:**
    o Host group fitness classes like Zumba or dance as physical activity is beneficial for mental health.

13. **DIY Self-Care Stations**:
    - Provide materials for participants to create self-care kits, including stress balls or lavender sachets.

14. **Nutrition and Mental Health Talk**:
    - Feature a session on the connection between diet and mental well-being, including tips for healthy eating.

By incorporating these activities, you can create a dynamic and engaging mental health awareness event that educates and supports attendees while fostering a sense of community and empathy.

How to Know When Your Teen Needs Help with Mental Health

Recognising when your teenager might need help with their mental health can be challenging, but there are some signs to watch for:

1. **Mood Changes**: Look for shifts in mood, such as persistent sadness, irritability, or mood swings that are more severe than typical teenage moodiness.

2. **Withdrawal**: Notice if your teen is withdrawing from friends, family, or activities they used to enjoy.

3. **Drop in Performance**: Keep an eye on their performance at school or in sports, looking for drops in grades or missed activities.

4. **Changes in Sleep Patterns**: Be aware of changes in their sleep habits, such as insomnia or sleeping too much.

5. **Appetite Changes**: Take note if they have an increase or decrease in appetite, which can affect weight.

6. **Extreme Risk-Taking Behaviours**: Watch for behaviours that could be harmful, such as drug or alcohol use or extreme risk-taking.

7. **Difficulty Concentrating**: Observe if they have trouble focusing on tasks, seem forgetful, or can't concentrate.

8. **Physical Symptoms**: Look for unexplained physical complaints, like headaches or stomach aches, which might be stress-related.

9. **Expressions of Hopelessness**: Listen for statements about feeling hopeless, worthless, or excessively guilty.

10. **Self-harm or Talk of Suicide**: Be vigilant about any signs of self-harm or discussions about death or suicide.

11. **Avoidance**: Notice if they are avoiding certain places, people, or situations due to anxiety or fear.

12. **Changes in Appearance**: Pay attention to any dramatic changes in the way they dress or care for their personal hygiene.

If you notice any of these signs, having an open and supportive conversation with your teenager is important. Let them know you're there for them and willing to listen without judgment. Seeking help from a mental health professional can also be beneficial. Often, early intervention can lead to better outcomes.

What Should I Say to My Teen if I'm Worried?

When talking to your teen about your concerns regarding their mental health, it's important to approach the conversation with care, empathy, and openness. Here's a guide on what you might say:

1. **Express Concern Calmly**:
    - "I've noticed some changes in your mood/behaviour lately, and I'm concerned. How have you been feeling?"

2. **Be Supportive and Open**:
    - "I'm here for you, and you can talk to me about anything. I'm willing to listen without judgment."
3. **Ask Open-ended Questions**:
    - "Is there something that's been bothering you that you'd like to talk about?"
4. **Validate Their Feelings**:
    - "It's okay to feel upset or stressed. Everyone feels that way sometimes."
5. **Offer Help and Resources**:
    - "If you ever want to talk to someone other than me, I can help you find someone, like a counsellor or therapist."
6. **Reassure Them**:
    - "You're not alone in this, and it's brave to talk about what's going on. We'll figure this out together."
7. **Avoid Pressuring Them**:
    - "Whenever you feel ready to talk, I'll be here, and we can take each step as it comes."
8. **Be Patient**:
    - "I understand if you don't want to talk about it right now. Just know I'm always here for you."
9. **Acknowledge Their Autonomy**:
    - "I trust you to know what you need, and I want to support you in the way that feels right for you."

Keeping the conversation supportive and non-judgemental creates a safe space for your teen to open up. Remember, the goal is to let them know you care and that they have options and support.

Research Priorities and Findings from NIHR on Public Mental Health and Faith or Churches

The NIHR's Public Mental Health programme addresses mental health inequalities and improves well-being across diverse populations. While faith or churches are not explicitly mentioned in the search results, the programme emphasises community-based interventions and leveraging local assets to support mental health. Key priorities include:

- **Community Engagement**: Utilising local resources, such as community groups, to promote mental health and reduce disparities.

- **Inequality Reduction**: Targeting at-risk populations through tailored interventions, often involving collaborative efforts with local organisations.

- **Evidence Generation**: Evaluating effective approaches for improving mental health in various settings, including schools and communities.

Faith communities are increasingly involved in public mental health research and interventions, as evidenced by several initiatives:

- **Faith-Based Partnerships**: Research highlights the potential of partnerships between mental health professionals and faith communities to reduce stigma, enhance mental health literacy, and provide culturally sensitive care. Faith leaders play a key role in prevention, education, and referrals.

- **PRiSM Project**: This project explored the role of Black Majority Churches in Southeast London, emphasising the importance of culturally appropriate policies and collaboration between faith communities and mental health services.

- **NIHR-Funded Programmes**: The NIHR supports faith-based interventions, such as a project targeting young Muslim women, integrating spiritual practices to address mental health challenges.

Several successful examples demonstrate faith communities partnering with mental health services to support well-being and reduce stigma:

1. **Bridges to Care and Recovery (St. Louis, USA)**: African American churches were mobilised to reduce mental health stigma through education, outreach, and training "Wellness Champions" to provide support, referrals, and crisis intervention.

2. **North London Mental Health Partnership (UK)**: Collaborated with local faith groups to establish walk-in clinics and open dialogues for children and youth, improving access to mental health services while reducing stigma.

3. **Santa Clara County Faith-Based Training (USA)**: Tailored training programmes for diverse faith leaders improved their ability to refer individuals and integrate spirituality into recovery processes.

8

FUTURE DIRECTIONS

SPECULATE ON THE FUTURE OF FAITH AND MENTAL HEALTH COLLABORATION AND THE POTENTIAL FOR NEW RESEARCH AND UNDERSTANDING

Let's dive into a fascinating conversation about the future of faith and mental health collaboration. This is a journey into the unknown but with great promise.

1. **A New Horizon in Healing:** Imagine a future where mental health support is not just about therapy and medication. Picture faith leaders and mental health professionals working together to enhance well-being. The blend of spiritual and psychological support could offer a more holistic healing process.

2. **Innovative Research Opportunities:** The intersection of faith and mental health opens the door to groundbreaking research. New studies could explore how spiritual practices such as meditation, prayer, or community gatherings impact mental wellness. Could these practices become a standard part of mental health treatment? The possibilities are considerable.

3. **Breaking Stigmas, Building Bridges:** Collaboration between these fields could help dismantle the stigmas surrounding mental health issues within faith communities.

Faith leaders advocating for mental wellness could influence perceptions and encourage more people to seek help.

4. **Tech Meets Tradition:** As technology advances, we may see digital platforms that merge religious teachings with mental health insights, offering support that is accessible anytime, anywhere. Virtual reality, apps, and AI could become tools to bridge the gap between faith and mental health.

5. **Global Movement:** Around the world, different cultures approach healing in diverse ways. As collaborations grow, there is potential for a global movement – a blend of diverse spiritual and mental wellness practices benefiting everyone.

Into The Future

FAITH AND MENTAL HEALTH IN THE NEXT DECADE

There are growing calls for greater religious sensitivity among mental health clinicians, to help unlock the potentially healing aspects of religiosity. Until recently, most literature from English-speaking countries has focused on Christianity and mental health, with little attention paid to Muslim mental health. Islam is the fastest-growing religion in English-speaking countries, yet the mental health of Muslims in these regions remains under-researched, poorly understood, and under-resourced.

Negative aspects of religiosity

While there are many positive aspects of religiosity, research also indicates potential harmful effects. For example, religiosity can sometimes lead to excessive feelings of guilt, fear, shame, and death anxiety. In my own practice, I have encountered patients who feel they do not deserve God's mercy. At the other extreme, high levels of religiosity may lead some individuals to consult religious leaders instead of seeking professional help during mental distress. This is where faith leaders and mental health professionals need to work together holistically.

In conclusion, there is growing evidence that the influence of religion on mental health is largely positive. This challenges outdated notions, such as those expressed by Sigmund Freud, about the negative effects of religion on mental health. Freud's view of religion was sceptical and at times hostile, despite his grounding in Jewish religious thought and life-long fascination with the religious impulse. This growing evidence strengthens the case for new models of cooperation between religious leaders and mental health professionals.

In an ideal world, this would involve cooperation and education. Faith ministers could receive basic mental health training to improve understanding and increase referrals to mental health professionals. Educational and public outreach campaigns could also target religious and minority communities, with participation from those communities themselves. Similarly, mental health professionals need better training in religious matters, including taking a spiritual history as part of mental state assessment and working with culture brokers and community religious leaders. Such training could be co-delivered by clinical experts and religious leaders as a form of co-production.

New Mental Health Bill

As of the latest updates, the new Mental Health Bill progressing through Parliament aims to significantly overhaul the existing framework for mental health care and treatment. Here's an overview of its key aspects:

Or: The UK Mental Health Bill, currently under consideration in the House of Lords, aims to modernise the Mental Health Act to enhance patient rights and care quality. Key reforms include granting patients more autonomy over their treatment, introducing statutory care and treatment plans, and ending inappropriate detentions, especially for autistic individuals and those with learning disabilities. The Bill also seeks to eliminate the use of police and prison cells for mental health crises and improve racial disparities in detention rates. These changes align with recommendations from an independent review conducted in 2018.

1. **Patient-Centred Approach:** The Bill focuses on enhancing patient rights and ensuring individuals undergoing mental health treatment have greater agency in their care decisions. It emphasises patient consent and involvement in treatment planning.

2. **Reduction of Involuntary Admissions:** A major shift is the reduction of involuntary admissions and treatments. The Bill seeks to implement stricter criteria for compulsory sections, aiming to make such treatment a last resort. This respects patient autonomy and stresses the importance of voluntary engagement.

3. **Elimination of Discrimination:** The Bill acknowledges disparities in treatment based on race, gender, and ethnicity. It proposes measures to address and rectify these inequalities, ensuring fair and impartial care.

4. **Strengthening Community-Based Services:** There is a strong push to enhance community-based mental health services. This includes better support for local mental health teams and community centres to provide effective alternatives to hospital admissions.

5. **Increased Funding and Resources:** The Bill includes proposals for increased funding and resources, covering financial support for mental health facilities, practitioner training, and infrastructure to support the community care model.

6. **Integration of Health Services:** It encourages integration of mental health services with general healthcare, promoting a holistic approach to health.

7. **Safeguarding Children's Mental Health:** Special attention is given to children and adolescents, including early intervention programmes and school-based mental health services.

8. **Advancements in Technology and Innovation:** The Bill emphasises technology for mental health care, including telehealth, digital mental health tools, and data-driven approaches to personalised treatment plans.

9. **Focus on Prevention and Early Detection:** It advocates for preventive measures and early detection initiatives, with public health campaigns to raise awareness and reduce stigma.

10. **Ongoing Review and Evaluation:** The Bill mandates regular assessments of mental health policies to ensure they remain effective, adapting to new research and patient feedback.

If passed, this Bill could mark a transformative step in mental health care, aligning legal frameworks with modern, compassionate approaches to treatment.

Faith and the Proposed New Mental Health Bill

The connection between faith and mental health legislation, such as a proposed new mental health bill, can be multifaceted. Here are some potential intersections:

1. **Support Systems:** Faith communities often provide strong support networks, which can be vital for individuals dealing with mental health issues. These communities can also advocate for improved mental health services and support legislative change.

2. **Stigma Reduction:** Faith leaders can play a key role in reducing the stigma surrounding mental health by discussing it openly within their communities. This aligns with the goals of mental health legislation that seeks to normalise seeking support.

3. **Access to Services:** A new mental health bill may aim to improve access to services, including those that are culturally and spiritually sensitive, recognising the role of faith in many people's lives.

4. **Holistic Approaches:** Legislation may encourage or fund holistic approaches that integrate spiritual practices with traditional mental healthcare, acknowledging the positive impact faith can have on mental wellness for some individuals.

5. **Advocacy and Awareness:** Faith-based organisations often engage in outreach and advocacy, helping to raise awareness and encourage communities to support policy change.

6. **Training for Leaders:** The bill might include provisions for training faith leaders to recognise and address mental health issues, enabling them to offer initial support and referrals to professionals.

The relationship between faith and mental health legislation is about finding a balance that respects individual beliefs while ensuring access to effective care. This synergy can enhance community well-being and ensure that mental health policies are inclusive and supportive of all.

Criticisms of the New Mental Health Bill

Critics of the proposed bill raise concerns in several areas:

1. **Lack of Funding:** The bill may not allocate enough funding to implement changes effectively or support already underfunded services.

2. **Insufficient Access:** It may fail to address significant access issues, particularly in rural or underserved areas where services are scarce.

3. **Privacy Concerns:** Some provisions may raise concerns about data sharing between agencies without adequate safeguards for patient confidentiality.

4. **Focus on Institutionalisation:** Critics note a perceived overemphasis on hospital or institutional care rather than more effective community-based services.

5. **Stigma Reinforcement:** Certain language or provisions could inadvertently reinforce stigma rather than promote understanding and acceptance.

6. **Inadequate Workforce Provisions:** There may be insufficient measures to tackle the shortage of mental health professionals, particularly in high-demand areas.

7. **Complex Bureaucracy:** Additional layers of bureaucracy could make it harder for patients to navigate the system or for practitioners to deliver care efficiently.

8. **Neglect of Preventive Measures:** The bill could do more to include robust preventive strategies aimed at reducing the incidence of mental health issues before they require intensive treatment.

These criticisms vary depending on specific provisions and the context of the bill's debate or implementation.

Proposed Community-Based Solutions in the Bill and the Opportunity for Faith Communities

Community-based solutions in mental health bills often focus on improving accessibility, integration, and local support. Common proposals include:

1. **Expansion of Local Services:** Increasing funding and resources for community mental health centres to provide therapy, counselling, and crisis intervention.

2. **Integration with Primary Care:** Encouraging integration of mental health services into primary care settings so patients can receive comprehensive care in one location.

3. **Support for Community Programmes:** Funding local initiatives focused on education, awareness, and stigma reduction to foster more supportive environments.

4. **Peer Support Networks:** Expanding peer support services where individuals with lived experience offer guidance and assistance.

9

MENTAL HEALTH STIGMA

Breaking down stigma around mental health and encouraging help-seeking are essential.

Overcoming Stigma in Faith Communities

Within some faith communities, stigma around mental illness persists. Addressing it requires proactive, inclusive strategies.

How to Destigmatise Mental Illness?

Destigmatising and rebranding mental illness involves reshaping public perceptions to foster understanding, acceptance, and compassion:

1. **Language Change:** Use respectful, non-judgemental terms such as "mental health conditions" or "challenges" to replace negative language.

2. **Awareness Campaigns:** Public campaigns can normalise mental health issues by highlighting their prevalence and equating them with physical health conditions.

3. **Storytelling and Media Representation:** Share personal experiences and ensure fair representation in films, television, and literature.

4. **Education and Training:** Introduce mental health education in schools and training programmes in workplaces and communities.

5. **Promote Open Conversations:** Create spaces for open discussion to reduce fear of judgement.

6. **Role of Influencers and Celebrities:** Public figures speaking about their own mental health can reduce stigma and widen engagement.

7. **Integrate Mental Health into Healthcare:** Give mental health parity with physical health, including routine check-ups.

8. **Positive Messaging:** Focus on resilience, recovery, and empowerment, not just challenges.

9. **Cultural Sensitivity:** Adapt approaches to reflect cultural differences in understanding mental health.

10. **Peer Support Systems:** Establish or strengthen peer support programmes to lower barriers to help-seeking.

11. **Policy and Advocacy:** Push for policies protecting rights, increasing funding, and providing resources for mental health services.

By taking these steps, society can reframe mental illness in ways that encourage understanding, acceptance, and empathy, creating a more inclusive environment.

There are growing calls for greater religious sensitivity among mental health clinicians, to help unlock the potentially healing aspects of religiosity. Until recently, most literature from English-speaking countries has focused on Christianity and mental health, with little attention paid to Muslim mental health. Islam is the fastest-growing religion in these countries, yet the mental health of

Muslims remains under-researched, poorly understood, and under-resourced.

Negative aspects of religiosity
While there are many positive aspects, some research points to potential harmful effects. Religiosity can sometimes lead to excessive feelings of guilt, fear, shame, and death anxiety. In my own practice, I have encountered patients who feel they do not deserve God's mercy. At the other extreme, high levels of religiosity may lead some individuals to consult religious leaders instead of seeking professional help in times of mental distress. This is where faith leaders and mental health professionals must work together holistically.

In conclusion, there is growing evidence that the influence of religion on mental health is largely positive. This challenges outdated notions, such as those of Sigmund Freud, who was sceptical and at times hostile towards religion, despite having a grounding in Jewish religious thought and a lifelong fascination with the religious impulse. This evidence supports the development of new models of cooperation between religious leaders and mental health professionals.

In an ideal world, this would involve cooperation and education. Faith ministers could receive basic mental health training to improve understanding and increase referrals to mental health professionals. Educational and outreach campaigns could target religious and minority communities, with their cooperation and participation. Mental health professionals would also benefit from better education in religious matters, including taking a spiritual history during mental state assessments and working with culture brokers and community religious leaders. Such training could be co-delivered by clinical experts and religious leaders in a co-production model.

Destigmatising Mental Illness

What role do social media platforms play in destigmatising mental illness?

Social media can play a significant role in destigmatising mental illness in several ways:

1. **Awareness and Education:** Platforms such as Instagram, Facebook, and Twitter allow organisations and advocates to share information and resources widely, helping to dispel myths and misconceptions.

2. **Community and Support:** Online spaces allow people with similar experiences to connect, providing belonging and reducing feelings of isolation.

3. **Storytelling and Personal Narratives:** Personal stories humanise mental illness, foster empathy, and encourage others to seek help.

4. **Challenging Stigmas:** Campaigns like *MentalHealthAwareness* or *EndTheStigma* use social media to normalise discussion and promote acceptance.

5. **Access to Resources:** Platforms can share therapy apps, helplines, and other support tools.

6. **Influencer Impact:** Celebrities and influencers who speak openly about their struggles can help shift public attitudes.

7. **Advocacy and Mobilisation:** Social media can mobilise people to support mental health causes and influence policy.

However, it is a double-edged sword. Misinformation, cyberbullying, and harassment can harm mental health, making moderation, education, and responsible use essential.

How to start a conversation about mental health on social media

1. **Be Genuine:** Share your thoughts or experiences if comfortable.
2. **Choose the Right Platform:** Select the platform best suited to your audience.
3. **Use Hashtags:** Include relevant hashtags to join wider conversations.
4. **Share Educational Content:** Post articles, infographics, or statistics.
5. **Ask Open-Ended Questions:** Invite others to share experiences.
6. **Highlight Resources:** Share helplines, websites, and apps.
7. **Share Inspiring Stories:** Offer hope through resilience and recovery examples.
8. **Engage Responsibly:** Respond with empathy and signpost to professional help where appropriate.
9. **Collaborate:** Partner with advocates or organisations to amplify your message.
10. **Create a Safe Space:** Encourage respect and kindness in discussions.

Open-ended questions to initiate conversations about mental health

1. How do you prioritise your mental well-being in your daily routine?
2. What strategies have you found helpful in managing stress or anxiety?
3. How do you feel social media impacts your mental health?

4. Can you share a moment when someone's support made a difference to your mental health journey?

5. What misconceptions about mental health do you think need more attention?

6. How do you practise self-care, and which activities work best for you?

7. In what ways could our community better support individuals struggling with mental health issues?

8. How do you approach conversations about mental health with friends or family?

9. What advice would you give to someone hesitant to speak about their mental health challenges?

10. How has mental health awareness changed in recent years, and what more could be done?

Suggested activities for a church to engage the community in mental health discussions

Here are a few activities a church could organise to engage the community in mental health discussions:

1. **Workshops and Seminars:** Invite mental health professionals to lead workshops on topics such as stress management, coping strategies, and understanding mental health conditions.

2. **Support Groups:** Establish regular support group meetings for different demographics, such as young people, parents, or older adults. This provides a safe space for sharing experiences and offering mutual support.

3. **Mindfulness and Meditation Sessions:** Host regular sessions to teach relaxation and stress reduction techniques.

4. **Mental Health Fairs:** Organise community events where local therapists, counsellors, and wellness coaches share information and services.

5. **Guest Speaker Series:** Invite speakers with personal experience of mental health challenges or those working in the field to share their insights.

6. **Community Art Projects:** Encourage expression and healing through creative activities such as painting, sculpture, or collaborative murals with a mental health theme.

7. **Book Clubs:** Create a mental health-themed book club focusing on relevant literature, followed by group discussions.

8. **Nature Walks or Gardening Clubs:** Promote mental wellness through outdoor activities such as nature walks or community gardening, providing a calm space for open conversation.

9. **Parenting Workshops:** Offer sessions to help parents understand and support their children's mental health.

10. **Youth and Teen Counselling:** Provide dedicated counselling services or workshops addressing issues faced by young people.

11. **Educational Film Screenings:** Show films or documentaries about mental health, followed by discussions or a panel with professionals.

12. **Wellness Retreats:** Organise day-long or weekend retreats focused on mental and spiritual well-being, including activities such as yoga, meditation, and group discussions.

13. **Panel Discussions:** Host panels featuring mental health professionals, community leaders, and church members with lived experience.

14. **Interactive Webinars:** Offer virtual sessions for those who prefer to participate from home.

These activities encourage valuable conversations about mental health while building a supportive and understanding community that fosters inclusivity and acceptance.

The role of the church in facilitating a national conversation on faith and mental well-being and how to involve the public

The church can play a pivotal role in facilitating a national conversation on faith and mental well-being by using its community influence, moral authority, and existing support structures.

1. **Create Safe Spaces:** Establish non-judgemental environments where people feel comfortable sharing their mental health struggles. This could include support groups, counselling sessions, or workshops that integrate faith and mental well-being.

2. **Educational Programmes:** Organise seminars and discussions linking faith with mental health awareness to help destigmatise mental illness. These can feature both mental health professionals and faith leaders.

3. **Training Leaders:** Educate clergy and church leaders about mental health issues so they can recognise warning signs and direct individuals towards professional help.

4. **Partnerships with Mental Health Professionals:** Collaborate with mental health organisations and practitioners to enhance support, such as hosting workshops or offering on-site counselling.

5. **Involving the Community:** Hold public events focused on mental health to raise awareness and demonstrate the church's commitment. Activities could include talks, relaxation exercises, and stress-reduction techniques.

6. **Harnessing Media and Technology:** Use social media, podcasts, and digital platforms to share faith-based mental health content and engage a wider audience.

7. **Testimonies and Storytelling:** Encourage those who have managed mental health challenges with the help of their faith to share their stories, offering hope and encouragement.

8. **Resource Development:** Produce reading materials, pamphlets, and online resources that combine practical mental health advice with spiritual guidance.

9. **National Events and Campaigns:** Lead or participate in national mental health campaigns in partnership with other organisations.

To involve the public effectively:

- **Community Surveys and Feedback:** Ask community members which mental health topics matter most to them or which services they find useful. Use this feedback to shape programmes.

- **Inviting Diverse Voices:** Ensure inclusivity by involving people from different backgrounds and experiences.

- **Regular Updates and Engagement:** Keep the public informed about initiatives through newsletters, bulletins, or social media.

By integrating faith with mental health support, the church can be a source of hope and healing, fostering a more compassionate society and promoting overall well-being.

Mental Health First Aid

Mental Health First Aid (MHFA) is a training programme designed to teach people how to identify, understand, and respond to signs of mental illnesses and substance use disorders. Here are some key components of Mental Health First Aid:

1. **Early Recognition:** Learning to recognise the early warning signs and symptoms of mental health issues, such as changes in mood, behaviour, or physical health.

2. **Risk Assessment:** Understanding how to assess the risk of harm to the individual, including the potential for self-harm or harm to others.

3. **Providing Support:** Knowing how to provide initial support in a non-judgemental and empathetic way.

4. **Listening Skills:** Developing active listening skills, showing empathy, and maintaining confidentiality while addressing someone's concerns.

5. **Encouraging Professional Help:** Guiding individuals towards appropriate professional help and resources, such as counselling, therapy, or medical treatment.

6. **Self-care for the Helper:** Emphasising the importance of self-care for those providing support and understanding one's own boundaries and limits.

7. **Action Plan:** Usually includes a specific action plan to guide the helper in offering assistance in a structured and effective way.

8. **Building Community Understanding:** Increasing overall community awareness and understanding of mental health to reduce stigma and encourage supportive environments.

Mental Health First Aid can be highly beneficial in various settings, including workplaces, schools, and community groups. It equips individuals with the skills and confidence to help someone experiencing a mental health problem or crisis.

How to Become Certified in Mental Health First Aid?

To become certified in Mental Health First Aid, you generally need to complete a structured training programme offered by certified instructors. Here's how you can typically pursue certification:

1. **Find a Course:** Look for Mental Health First Aid courses in your area. Check local community health organisations, mental health associations, or educational institutions. Many countries have dedicated MHFA websites listing available courses.

2. **Choose the Right Type:** There are various MHFA courses, such as those focused on adults, youth, veterans, or workplace settings. Select a course that best suits your interests or needs.

3. **Register for the Course:** Once you've chosen a suitable course, register online or contact the provider directly to secure your place.

4. **Attend the Training:** The training usually involves a combination of in-person and online sessions, lasting around 8–12 hours in total. It covers topics such as recognising signs of mental health issues, providing initial help, and understanding crisis situations.

5. **Participate Actively:** Engage in discussions, group activities, and practice scenarios to build your understanding and skills. This practical experience is crucial to becoming an effective Mental Health First Aider.

6. **Complete Assessments:** Some courses may include quizzes or practical assessments to ensure you understand the material and can apply it in real-life situations.

7. **Receive Certification:** After successfully completing the course, you'll receive a Mental Health First Aid certificate,

typically valid for a set period (e.g., three years). Refresher courses may be required to maintain certification.

8. **Stay Informed:** Continue learning about mental health through additional resources and training to keep your knowledge up to date.

Always verify the credentials of the course providers and trainers to ensure they are officially recognised by the relevant national or international mental health organisations.

Opportunity for future co-location of mental health services in community settings and possible role of faith communities

The co-location of mental health services within community settings presents a valuable opportunity, and faith communities can play a significant role in this integration.

1. Safe and welcoming spaces

- Faith communities often have available space that can host mental health services, providing a non-stigmatising environment for those seeking help.
- Dedicated areas within religious centres could be used for counselling and therapy sessions.

2. Community trust and familiarity

- Leveraging established trust and rapport with the community can encourage individuals to seek mental health support.
- Faith leaders can act as advocates, reducing stigma and promoting mental wellness.

3. Holistic approach to wellness

- Integrating spiritual and mental health support encourages a more holistic approach to well-being.
- Offering programmes that combine spiritual practices with mental health care, such as meditation, prayer, and mindfulness sessions.

4. Support networks

- Facilitating peer support groups and outreach programmes led by trained community members.
- Encouraging mentorship schemes where community members support those experiencing mental health challenges.

5. Education and awareness

- Hosting workshops and seminars on mental health topics to educate the community and reduce stigma.
- Providing resources and materials that promote mental health awareness and understanding.

6. Access and affordability

- Ensuring mental health services are accessible and affordable by partnering with local health organisations.
- Offering sliding scale payment options or free services through grants and donations.

7. Crisis intervention

- Training faith leaders and volunteers in crisis intervention techniques and mental health first aid.

- Establishing emergency response teams within the community to provide immediate support.

8. Collaboration with mental health professionals

- Partnering with mental health professionals to provide regular counselling services.
- Creating referral systems for specialised mental health care when needed.

By embracing these roles, faith communities can play a crucial part in integrating mental health services into community settings, fostering a supportive environment that promotes overall well-being.

Integrating Mental Health Services into Faith Communities

Integrating mental health services into faith communities can be a transformative way to support the well-being of individuals. Here are some specific services that can be incorporated:

1. Counselling and therapy

- Individual and group therapy sessions tailored to the community's needs.
- Family counselling services to address collective issues within households.

2. Support groups

- Peer-led groups focusing on specific mental health challenges such as depression, anxiety, addiction, or grief.
- Spiritual support groups for those wishing to incorporate faith into their healing process.

3. Workshops and seminars

- Educational workshops on topics such as stress management, coping strategies, and emotional resilience.
- Seminars addressing the intersection of faith and mental health, helping individuals navigate their spiritual and psychological journeys.

4. Crisis intervention services

- On-site crisis intervention and emergency support for individuals experiencing acute mental health episodes.
- Establishing a hotline or emergency contact system for immediate help.

5. Mindfulness and relaxation programmes

- Meditation, yoga, and mindfulness classes that promote mental relaxation and stress reduction.
- Breathing exercises and relaxation techniques integrated into religious practices or offered as standalone sessions.

6. Youth and adolescent programmes

- Mental health initiatives designed for young people, addressing issues such as bullying, self-esteem, and peer pressure.
- Peer mentorship and after-school support activities.

7. Training for faith leaders

- Workshops for clergy and community leaders on mental health awareness and basic counselling skills.

- Training to recognise mental health symptoms and make appropriate referrals.

8. Community outreach and education

- Initiatives to raise mental health awareness within the community through events, newsletters, and social media.
- Partnerships with local schools and organisations to extend mental health education and resources.

9. Resource and referral services

- Providing information on local mental health resources, including clinics, hotlines, and online support.
- Developing a referral network with mental health professionals for specialist care.

10. Spiritual and pastoral counselling

- Offering counselling that incorporates spiritual beliefs and practices, tailored to those seeking faith-based guidance alongside psychological support.

By integrating these services, faith communities can become key resources in promoting mental health and bridging the gap between spiritual well-being and psychological care.

How Spirituality Enhances Mental Health Treatment?

Applying spirituality to mental health treatment is beneficial because it is often a significant part of who we are. "People's beliefs and convictions are interconnected with their mental health and social lives," said June. "If a person's beliefs are incongruent with the way they're behaving, we try to help the person heal by addressing that."

Some of the most important ways spirituality enhances mental health treatment include the following:

- **It provides a sense of purpose.** Having a strong sense of purpose is often linked with better mental health and overall well-being. Faith can help you focus on the bigger picture, alleviate stress, improve symptoms of depression, and increase confidence. "I have the honour to watch people grow in their faith and get a sense of belonging, purpose, and meaning," said June. "That convinces me that it's very valuable."

- **It gives you hope.** Many people who are struggling with their mental health experience a sense of hopelessness about their lives and the future. Faith can help us actively work towards our goals for mental wellness. "Faith is what keeps you going in the journey of life, especially when the road gets rocky," said Reverend Tim.

- **It helps you feel peace.** If you have anxiety, depression, or another mental health issue, you may struggle with low moods, anger, intense worry, and other life-disrupting symptoms. Faith-based treatment encourages self-care and focuses on spiritual activities that reduce stress and promote relaxation. "I see people finding more peace and having more confidence," said June. "I feel honoured to be walking with them in their journey and seeing their improvement in their personal spirituality."

- **It encourages community.** Being part of something larger than yourself can help you find a sense of community and support during times of crisis. People with depression or anxiety may lose connection with their faith community and wish to re-engage with it or connect with something new. Faith integration in treatment can help rebuild these connections and offer comfort and security for healing.

- **It offers effective coping methods.** Praying, meditating, or reading religious or spiritual literature can help reduce symptoms by easing stress and worry, managing triggers, and boosting mood. "We can incorporate various coping methods that support your faith," said June. "Anything people in your faith like to do to relax or feel peaceful – whether it be read, meditate, chant, or spend time in nature – can be integrated into treatment. Anything that feeds the transcendent part of a person – let's see how we can work that into your recovery plan."

Faith-Based Treatment at LiveWell Counselling

If you are looking for compassionate mental health counselling that actively supports and integrates your faith or spirituality, LiveWell Counselling can help. Our knowledgeable and caring therapists provide talk therapy services that can incorporate any faith. To learn more, please call (201) 848-5800 or visit ChristianHealthNJ.info/LiveWellCounseling.

Examples of Faith-Based Mental Health Programmes

Faith-based mental health programmes often integrate spiritual practices and beliefs into care to provide holistic support. Examples include:

1. **Celebrate Recovery:** A Christ-centred programme that helps individuals overcome various forms of addiction and emotional distress through a structured, biblical recovery process.

2. **NAMI FaithNet:** Part of the National Alliance on Mental Illness, this network offers faith communities resources and guidance to support mental health with compassion and understanding.

3. **The Sanctuary Model:** A trauma-informed approach used in various faith-based settings to provide a supportive environment for healing, focusing on safety, emotional intelligence, and shared values.

4. **Jewish Community Services:** Many Jewish community organisations provide mental health services that integrate Jewish values and traditions, offering counselling and support groups tailored to cultural and religious needs.

5. **Muslim Mental Health:** Organisations such as the Institute for Muslim Mental Health provide culturally and religiously competent care, educate communities, and offer networks for mental health professionals within the Islamic faith.

6. **Buddhist Meditation and Mindfulness Programmes:** These incorporate mindfulness meditation practices to promote well-being, focusing on compassion, self-awareness, and emotional regulation.

Additional examples:

1. **Saddleback Church's Mental Health Ministry (California, USA):** Launched after the senior pastor's son died by suicide, this programme offers support groups, workshops, and conferences on mental health in a faith context, as well as leader training.

2. **Jewish Family and Children's Services (JFCS) – Shalom Bayit (California, USA):** Focuses on creating peaceful and healthy family environments, offering counselling, support groups, and education about mental health and domestic violence.

3. **Muslim Mental Health Consortium (USA):** A national network providing culturally and spiritually competent mental health services to Muslim communities, along with professional training and resources.

4. **Episcopal Mental Health Ministries (USA):** Provides education, support, and advocacy, integrating faith and spirituality into compassionate mental health care.

5. **The Sanctuary Mental Health Ministries (Canada):** Equips churches with resources and training to integrate Christian faith and mental health understanding, aiming to reduce stigma.

6. **Black Church's Initiative Mental Health Reform (USA):** A coalition of African-American churches providing mental health resources tailored to Black communities, with cultural sensitivity and professional connections.

7. **Mental Health First Aid Trainings by Churches (Global):** Churches around the world offering training to recognise mental health crises and provide initial support before professional help is sought.

8. **Bethel AME Church (Baltimore, USA):** Hosts annual Mental Health Awareness Sundays with educational resources, guest speakers, and links to local services.

These programmes show how faith communities can combine spirituality with evidence-based mental health practices to foster holistic well-being.

Navigating this area requires sensitivity, respect, and a collaborative approach. I often work closely with spiritual advisors, such as pastors or chaplains, to ensure patients feel supported in both their spiritual and mental health journeys. This collaboration helps create more comprehensive care plans that honour faith while addressing psychological needs.

A further challenge is addressing guilt or shame some patients may associate with mental illness. Some believe their condition reflects a lack of faith or is a punishment for wrongdoing. In these cases, it is essential to foster understanding and compassion, helping them see that mental illness is not a moral failing but a medical condition requiring care.

I also work to educate patients and families about the role of medication and therapy, emphasising that seeking medical help is not a lack of faith but a proactive step towards healing. Integrating faith-based practices with evidence-based treatment can be a powerful combination, enhancing recovery.

Ultimately, the intersection of faith and mental health is a delicate balance, but one that can be navigated with empathy, understanding, and open communication. Supporting patients in this dimension of their lives not only reinforces hope but can also lead to more meaningful and effective treatment outcomes. Through this process, I have witnessed the resilience and strength of the human spirit, shaped by both faith and the pursuit of mental wellness.

Incorporate Spirituality into Treatment Plans

Incorporating spirituality into treatment plans requires a thoughtful, sensitive approach that respects each patient's beliefs while aligning with their mental health needs. Here's how I typically approach it:

1. **Initial Assessment:** Begin by understanding the patient's spiritual beliefs through open-ended questions during the initial assessment. This helps identify the role spirituality plays in their life and their perception of mental health.

2. **Collaborative Treatment Planning:** Work with the patient to decide how they would like spirituality integrated into their treatment. This could include prayer, meditation, or discussions about faith during sessions.

3. **Work with Spiritual Advisors:** When appropriate, collaborate with trusted spiritual leaders or advisors. This can bridge gaps and provide a support network that respects both spiritual and medical perspectives.

4. **Incorporate Spiritual Practices:** Encourage practices such as mindfulness, meditation, or spiritual rituals that

align with the patient's beliefs. These can offer comfort and grounding alongside traditional therapeutic techniques.

5. **Therapeutic Techniques:** Use approaches that align well with spiritual themes, such as Acceptance and Commitment Therapy (ACT), which focuses on values and meaning, or narrative therapy, which can incorporate spiritual narratives.

6. **Cultural Competence:** Learn about the spiritual practices and beliefs common in your patient population. This knowledge can build trust and make treatment more effective.

7. **Education:** Provide information on how mental and spiritual health can coexist, ensuring patients understand that treatment need not conflict with their beliefs.

8. **Encourage Reflection:** Use journaling or reflection exercises that help patients explore how their spiritual beliefs intersect with their mental health journey.

9. **Build a Safe Space:** Create a non-judgemental environment where patients feel comfortable discussing spiritual concerns. This can strengthen the therapeutic alliance.

10. **Feedback and Adjustments:** Regularly ask for feedback on how the integration of spirituality is affecting treatment, and be ready to adjust based on what is or isn't working.

Incorporating spirituality respects the whole person — mind, body, and spirit — and can lead to more meaningful, comprehensive healing. The goal is to create a plan as unique as the individual.

How Do I Address a Patient's Spirituality if They Seem Hesitant to Discuss It?

If a patient refuses to discuss spirituality, it's essential to respect their decision and focus on other aspects of their care. Here are some steps:

1. **Respect Their Boundaries:** Acknowledge their choice and reassure them their preferences are respected. This helps maintain trust.

2. **Shift Focus:** Explore other areas of their life and treatment they are comfortable discussing. Well-being can be addressed without mentioning spirituality.

3. **Explore Other Sources of Support:** Ask about supportive resources such as family, friends, hobbies, or community activities.

4. **Discuss Coping Mechanisms:** Help them develop coping strategies aligned with their values and beliefs, even if these are not explicitly spiritual.

5. **Offer Flexibility:** Let them know they can bring up spirituality at any point in the future.

6. **Use Secular Language:** Sometimes the term "spirituality" itself creates discomfort. Discuss meaning, purpose, or connection in non-spiritual terms if this feels easier for them.

7. **Work on Building Trust:** Continue developing the therapeutic relationship. As trust grows, they may feel more comfortable raising the subject later.

8. **Focus on Overall Well-Being:** Address physical, emotional, and social health, ensuring a holistic approach without requiring spiritual discussion.

9. **Validate Their Experience:** Make sure they feel heard and supported in their choice not to engage with spirituality, reinforcing their autonomy in therapy.

Ultimately, the patient's comfort and autonomy take priority. They should lead on whether and how spirituality plays a role in their care.

10

Blending Mental Health Practices with Spiritual Care

A Christian faith-based mental health service can offer valuable support to the community, addressing both psychological and spiritual aspects of healing.

Engaging the Community: A Practical Guide

Here's how to get the community involved:

1. **Define a Clear Purpose**

    Communicate the project's goals, objectives, and expected community benefits clearly. When people know their involvement matters, they're more likely to engage.

2. **Build a Strong Online Presence**

    Use social media, newsletters, blogs, and websites to share updates, insights, and spark conversations. Choose platforms your target community uses most.

3. **Host Interactive Events**

    Organise workshops, webinars, and Q&A sessions. These can be virtual or in-person, encouraging direct interaction.

4. **Encourage Collaboration**

   Offer opportunities for community members to contribute ideas and collaborate. Open-source projects or community-driven initiatives work well.

5. **Provide Incentives**

   Recognise contributions with rewards, special content, or public acknowledgment to motivate participation.

6. **Solicit Feedback**

   Regularly seek feedback on the project's progress. It makes people feel valued and involved.

7. **Ensure Diversity and Inclusivity**

   Make sure the project welcomes diverse voices. Different perspectives enrich the project and broaden its appeal.

Building a Sense of Belonging

Create an environment where every community member feels welcome and valued.

9. **Utilise Community Champions**

   Engage local leaders or influencers who can advocate for your project and encourage broader involvement.

10. **Share Success Stories**

    Highlight testimonials and success stories to show the positive impact of the project.

11. **Be Transparent**

    Be honest about the project's progress, challenges, and decisions. Transparency builds trust.

12. **Create Easy Entry Points**

   Make it simple for newcomers to get involved without requiring a heavy initial commitment.

Spirituality and Mental Health: The Redbridge Experience

Focus Groups with Faith Leaders in a Religiously Diverse London Borough

By Roxanne Keynejad

Redbridge, an ethnically and religiously diverse borough, faces psychiatric inequalities. Spirituality plays a significant role in mental health and access to treatment, but it hasn't been explored in-depth in this region. This pilot project examines the mental health needs of community faith leaders and their roles in a borough reflecting much of modern British society's diversity.

The findings of qualitative focus groups with faith leaders suggest that integrating spirituality into psychiatric services is vital for engaging diverse communities. The report concludes with recommendations for collaboration between statutory services and community workers, ensuring the integration of cultural, spiritual, and religious needs in psychiatric care at all levels.

The Local Context

Redbridge is the ninth most ethnically diverse area in England and Wales (51.9% White, 16.9% Indian, 17.2% Other Asian, 11.3% Black), with a correspondingly diverse religious and spiritual population. Projections show growing percentages of ethnic minorities, leading to even greater religious and cultural diversity. Redbridge has the fourth-largest Hindu (7.8%), Jewish (6.2%), and Sikh (5.5%) populations in England and Wales, as well as the twelfth-largest Muslim (11.9%) population, and the tenth-lowest Christian (50.7%) population.

Religious communities interpret mental illness differently and have varying preferences for seeking help. To engage these communities with psychiatric services, spirituality must be acknowledged. An NHS audit in North East London found that few inpatients were asked about their spiritual needs, despite many wanting this consideration. Most felt the lack of space to explore their spirituality hindered recovery:

"If you talk about spirituality, they think you're mad... so we just say 'Don't talk too much.' It creates a barrier between staff and patients."

Mental Health Training for Faith Leaders

Training is recommended for faith leaders in spiritual groups to support mental health.

1. Handbook of Faith and Mental Health

- **Practical Focus**: Provides clear advice, tools, and methodologies, often structured with step-by-step guidance for real-world application.
- **Comprehensive Resource**: Covers a wide range of topics, offering actionable insights and strategies.
- **User-Friendly**: Well-organised, with sections or chapters focused on different aspects of faith and mental health.

2. Faith and Mental Health

- **Theoretical/Mixed Focus**: Likely blends theory and practice, discussing the relationship between faith and mental health, incorporating academic or theological perspectives.

- **Broader Exploration**: Covers wider themes, possibly with narratives or case studies, but with less emphasis on practical guidance.

In summary, the *Handbook of Faith and Mental Health* is a practical guide, while *Faith and Mental Health* offers a broader exploration of the connection between the two fields.

The future of faith and mental health over the next decade will likely see deeper integration, reflecting shifts in societal values and technological progress.

1. **Integration of Science and Spirituality**: We're likely to see a growing alignment between scientific understanding and spiritual practices. Mental health professionals could increasingly use mindfulness and meditation—practices rooted in religious traditions—as recognised therapeutic tools.

2. **Tech-Driven Spiritual Experiences**: Virtual reality (VR) and augmented reality (AR) could offer new ways for people to engage with their faith. These technologies might enable virtual pilgrimages or digitally enhanced sacred spaces.

3. **Digital Faith Communities**: Online platforms may become crucial spaces for faith communities, particularly for those with limited access to physical congregations. Social media and apps could provide spiritual guidance tailored to individual mental health needs.

4. **Holistic Mental Health Approaches**: Faith-based organisations may increasingly offer holistic mental health programmes, blending counselling, spiritual guidance, and community support to address a wide range of mental health challenges.

5. **Increased Dialogue and Tolerance**: As globalisation advances, interfaith dialogue could promote greater understanding and mental well-being, reducing religious intolerance and fostering inclusive communities that support diverse mental health needs.

6. **AI and Faith-Based Counselling**: AI-driven chatbots may offer immediate, faith-based counselling, delivering support aligned with personal spiritual beliefs while adapting to modern lifestyles.

7. **Focus on Youth and Mental Health**: There will likely be greater focus on addressing the mental health of young people within faith communities, tackling issues like anxiety and depression with a combination of traditional teachings and modern psychological approaches.

8. **More Research and Evidence-Based Practices**: Increasing research may bridge the gap between faith and mental health, fostering evidence-based practices that demonstrate the positive impact of spiritual beliefs on mental wellness.

9. **Crisis Response and Resilience Building**: Faith communities could play a vital role in crisis response, offering comfort and helping build resilience. Collaboration with mental health professionals could create comprehensive support networks during difficult times.

10. **Ethical and Privacy Concerns**: As digital spiritual support grows, ethical and privacy concerns will need addressing. Discussions around data protection and maintaining trust in virtual faith environments will become more prominent.

The next decade may see faith and mental health intertwine more deeply, offering innovative approaches to spiritual and psychological well-being. Faith communities and mental health professionals can collaborate to create environments that tackle complex individual and societal challenges.

The Role of Religious Leaders in Mental Health Support

Religious leaders can play a significant role in supporting mental health, blending spiritual and emotional guidance. Here's how they can help:

1. **Emotional Support**: Religious leaders provide a compassionate, listening ear, offering a safe space for individuals to express their struggles and reminding them they're not alone.

2. **Spiritual Guidance**: Drawing on religious texts and teachings, they help individuals find meaning and purpose, which can be essential for coping with mental health challenges.

3. **Community Connection**: Religious leaders foster a sense of belonging and support, which can be invaluable for individuals experiencing isolation or loneliness.

4. **Moral and Ethical Counselling**: They offer counsel on moral dilemmas, helping individuals navigate complex issues that affect their mental well-being.

5. **Stigma Reduction**: By openly discussing mental health, religious leaders can help reduce stigma, encouraging individuals to seek help without fear of judgement.

6. **Referrals**: Religious leaders can guide individuals to professional mental health services when necessary, bridging the gap between spiritual care and professional support.

7. **Practical Support**: Faith-based programmes may provide practical help, such as support groups, workshops, or retreats focused on mental health and well-being.

8. **Advocacy**: Religious leaders can advocate for mental health awareness within their communities, supporting initiatives that improve mental health care resources.

Religious leaders' involvement in mental health is shaped by their understanding of religious and cultural contexts, enabling them to approach mental health issues in a way that resonates with their communities' beliefs and values.

Examples of Religious Leaders Helping with Mental Health Cases

Here are a few examples of religious leaders' active involvement in mental health support:

1. **Faith-Based Support Groups**: Many religious leaders organise support groups where individuals can share personal struggles and receive community-based support.

2. **Counselling Services**: Religious leaders offer one-on-one counselling. For instance, a pastor or rabbi might meet with congregants to provide spiritual guidance aligned with faith.

3. **Workshops and Seminars**: Religious organisations host mental health workshops and seminars to educate communities on mental health issues, often featuring professionals for deeper discussion.

4. **Awareness Campaigns**: Religious leaders participate in campaigns to educate their communities on mental health, challenging myths and reducing stigma, which encourages more individuals to seek help.

5. **Crisis Intervention**: Religious leaders offer immediate emotional support during crises, providing spiritual comfort, organising prayers, and coordinating resources during events like natural disasters.

6. **Collaboration with Mental Health Professionals**: Many religious leaders work alongside mental health professionals, offering a holistic approach to care by referring individuals for therapy while continuing to provide spiritual support.

7. **Initiatives Addressing Social Issues**: In areas where issues like poverty and violence impact mental health, religious leaders often lead initiatives to address these root causes, improving overall well-being.

Faith Leaders as the Bridge

These examples highlight the proactive role religious leaders can play in mental health support, often bridging the gap between spiritual and professional care.

The Co-Location of Services in Church Settings

Co-locating services in church settings involves integrating various social and community services within the church environment. This approach can significantly enhance access to support. Here's how:

1. **Accessibility**: Offering multiple services in one location makes it easier for individuals to access the help they need, reducing barriers like transportation or unfamiliarity.

2. **Holistic Support**: Combining spiritual guidance with other services creates a more holistic care approach, addressing mental, physical, and spiritual well-being.

3. **Community Trust**: Churches often have strong community ties, making them a trusted environment where people are more likely to seek services.

4. **Resource Sharing**: Co-location enables resource sharing between services, improving efficiency and enhancing the overall quality of care provided.

5. **Increased Engagement**: Those attending one service, like a food pantry, may become aware of additional support services, leading to higher engagement with other community resources.

6. **Reduced Stigma**: Offering mental health support in a church setting can help normalise seeking help, reducing stigma and encouraging individuals to reach out.

7. **Enhanced Coordination**: Having multiple services under one roof improves coordination, creating more effective care plans for individuals.

8. **Convenience**: Providing various services in one place saves time, encouraging individuals to return for follow-up or engage in ongoing support.

In summary, co-locating services in church settings leverages the church's community role, enhancing access, trust, and the overall effectiveness of the services offered.

Colocation of mental services in churches can address stigma and inequalities

The colocation of mental health services in churches indeed help address stigma and inequalities associated with mental health care. Here's how:

1. Reducing Stigma: Society has always accepted and seen churches as places of support and healing. By offering mental health services within this trusted setting, churches can help normalise seeking mental health care. This normalisation can reduce the stigma often associated with mental health issues, making individuals feel more comfortable and accepted when they seek help.

2. Building Trust: Many people have established relationships with their church communities, which can foster trust and openness. This trust can encourage individuals to access mental health services without fear of judgment, promoting mental well-being as part of holistic health.

3. Increasing Accessibility: Churches are frequently more accessible and welcoming than traditional mental health facilities, especially in under-resourced areas. By co-locating services, churches can reach people who might otherwise face barriers such as transportation issues or lack of familiarity with mental health facilities.

4. Cultural Relevance: Churches often play significant roles within their communities and can provide services that are culturally relevant and sensitive. This can help ensure that mental health care is aligned with the values and beliefs of the community, which can be particularly important in diverse or underserved populations.

5. Addressing Inequality: By offering mental health services in locations that are accessible to all community members, regardless of socioeconomic status, churches can help bridge the gap in mental health care access. This can be especially important in areas where mental health resources are limited or difficult to access.

6. Creating Community Support Systems: Churches can foster community support systems that extend beyond traditional counselling, such as support groups, workshops, and peer support. This community-based approach can enhance the effectiveness of mental health interventions.

7. Coordinated Care: By integrating mental health services with other church-based support systems, individuals can receive more coordinated and comprehensive care, addressing various facets of their well-being.

Overall, the colocation of mental health services in churches can create a more accepting and supportive environment for individuals seeking help, reducing stigma and addressing inequalities in mental health care access.

Peer Support and Community:

Building a supportive community and finding peer support often attracts young people looking for understanding and acceptance.

Here are some examples of churches that have implemented mental health services:

1. Saddleback Church (Lake Forest, California, USA): Saddleback Church has a renowned mental health ministry that offers support groups, workshops, and resources for mental health education. They have been active in advocating for mental health awareness, hosting conferences, and providing training for other churches on how to start their own mental health ministries. Stateside.

2. The Potter's House (Dallas, Texas, USA): Led by Bishop T.D. Jakes, The Potter's House offers mental health services through its counselling centre. They provide a range of support services including individual and family counselling, workshops, and seminars addressing mental health topics.

3. First Baptist Church of Glenarden (Upper Marlboro, Maryland, USA): This church has a comprehensive counselling and mental health ministry that provides professional counselling services, support groups, and workshops to address various mental health issues.

4. The Church of England: Across the UK, many Church of England parishes have initiated mental health services and support programs. They work to create safe spaces for conversations about mental health, often collaborating with local mental health organizations.

5. St. Lydia's (Brooklyn, New York, USA): This progressive church incorporates mental health awareness into its community practices, offering group support and one-on-one counselling as part of its ministry. They emphasize creating safe and inclusive spaces for mental health dialogue.

6. Grace Cathedral (San Francisco, California, USA): Grace Cathedral has hosted various events and discussions focused on mental health, aiming to reduce stigma and promote understanding. They collaborate with mental health professionals to provide support to their community.

These examples illustrate how churches can integrate mental health services into their community support systems, promoting well-being, reducing stigma, and addressing mental health needs holistically.

Several churches have implemented mental health services to support their communities:

- St Marylebone Parish Church (London, UK): Hosts an NHS GP practice and a long-term counselling service in its crypt, offering drop-in mental health groups led by qualified therapists.

- Crossroads Church (Ohio, USA): Opened a mental health resource centre providing free materials, referrals, and awareness resources during worship services.

- First Plymouth Congregational Church (Denver, USA): Established FP WISE, a mental health ministry offering education, support groups, and stigma reduction through shared experiences.

- St Michael and Angels (Houghton-le-Spring, UK): Operates "Space 4," a drop-in centre addressing isolation and mental health needs.

Challenges that Churches will face when implementing mental health services:

- **Lack of Training**: Many clergy and church leaders will feel **ill-equipped** to address mental health issues due to inadequate training during ministerial education or professional development.

- **Stigma and Misunderstanding**: Mental health issues, especially conditions like schizophrenia or bipolar disorder, often remain stigmatised within churches. Over-spiritualised explanations can alienate those struggling.

- **Complex Needs**: Families affected by mental illness may feel unsupported and misunderstood by their faith communities, leading to reluctance in seeking help.

- **Barriers to Inclusion**: Assimilation processes, sensory environments, or lack of accommodations can discourage participation by individuals with mental health challenges.

Emerging Trends and My Predictions

Faith, Therapy, and Medical Treatment: Exploring the compatibility of faith with traditional mental health treatments, including counselling and medication.

These trends suggest a promising shift towards a more integrated and compassionate approach to mental health, where faith and spirituality are viewed as complementary elements that can enhance overall well-being. The next decade could see a world where mental health and faith work together to promote healing, peace, and resilience in individuals and communities.

The intersection of faith and mental health is drawing increasing attention as both fields evolve into the next decade. Here are some emerging trends and predictions:

1. **Integration of Faith and Therapy:** Mental health professionals are recognising more and more the role of spirituality in promoting psychological well-being. Therapists may incorporate spiritual practices and beliefs into treatment plans, considering a client's faith as an asset in the healing process.

2. **Holistic Approaches:** We may see a rise in holistic approaches that combine faith-based practices with psychological counselling. This could include meditation, prayer, and mindfulness, alongside therapeutic techniques to offer comprehensive care.

3. **Technology and Accessibility:** The use of technology in mental health services will expand, offering virtual therapy sessions and digital faith-based support groups. This increase in accessibility will help reach underserved communities that rely heavily on faith systems but lack mental health resources.

4. **Faith Leaders as Mental Health Advocates:** Religious leaders are expected to play a larger role in advocating for mental health awareness within their communities. Training in basic mental health knowledge could become part of religious education, equipping leaders to guide congregants towards professional help.

5. **Research and Evidence-Based Practices:** More research will be needed to explore the psychological benefits of faith, aiming to provide an evidence-based foundation for combining spirituality and mental health practices. This research could influence the development of new therapeutic modalities.

6. **Cultural Sensitivity:** There will be an improvement in the understanding of diverse cultural and religious backgrounds, ensuring mental health services are culturally sensitive and respectful of different faith traditions. This might involve personalised treatment plans that honour a person's spiritual beliefs.

7. **Public Discourse and De-stigmatisation:** As conversations around mental health become more open and inclusive, the stigma associated with seeking help will likely decrease. Faith communities could play a key role in supporting these discussions and fostering environments of acceptance and compassion.

8. **Education and Awareness:** Both religious institutions and educational systems might prioritise education about mental health, cultivating a deeper understanding among individuals about the importance of mental well-being alongside spiritual health.

Specific Faith-Based Practices that Can Help with Mental Health

Faith-based practices can offer valuable support for mental health by providing community, purpose, and a sense of tranquillity. Here are some traditional practices:

1. **Prayer:** Regular prayer can offer comfort and a sense of connection to a higher power, providing solace during difficult times and an opportunity for reflection and thanksgiving.

2. **Meditation:** Many faiths incorporate meditation practices, which can enhance mindfulness, reduce stress, and improve emotional regulation by promoting a calm and focused state of mind.

3. **Scripture Reading:** Reading and reflecting on sacred texts can provide guidance, inspiration, and a deeper understanding of life's challenges, helping individuals find meaning and purpose.

4. **Community Worship:** Participating in group worship services can foster a sense of belonging and community support, reducing feelings of isolation and loneliness.

5. **Service and Charity:** Engaging in acts of kindness and service can boost self-esteem and happiness, fostering a sense of fulfilment and connection to others.

6. **Rituals and Sacraments:** Engaging in religious rituals, such as communion, fasting, or rites of passage, can provide structure, stability, and a sense of spiritual continuity.

7. **Gratitude Practices:** Many faiths emphasise gratitude as a practice, encouraging individuals to focus on the positive aspects of their lives, which can enhance overall well-being and mental health.

8. **Spiritual Counselling:** Seeking guidance from a spiritual advisor or faith leader can provide support and clarity, helping individuals navigate life's challenges with a sense of faith and hope.

9. **Pilgrimage and Retreats:** Journeying to sacred places or participating in retreats can offer a break from daily life, facilitating reflection, renewal, and spiritual growth.

10. **Chanting or Singing:** Engaging in religious songs or chants can be uplifting and meditative, promoting relaxation and emotional wellness.

These faith-based practices can provide individuals with tools to manage stress, build resilience, and enhance their mental well-being while aligning with their spiritual beliefs.

How Community Worship Specifically Helps with Mental Health

These elements of community worship help individuals build supportive networks, find personal meaning, and enhance overall mental health through spiritual and social connection. Community worship can significantly benefit mental health through several mechanisms:

1. **Sense of Belonging:** Attending services fosters a feeling of belonging and acceptance. Being part of a community provides emotional support and reduces feelings of loneliness or isolation.

2. **Emotional Support:** Within a worship community, individuals often find support during life's challenges. Sharing experiences and empathising with others can foster resilience and emotional healing.

3. **Shared Purpose:** Gathering with like-minded individuals for a common spiritual goal instils a sense of purpose and meaning, crucial elements for mental well-being.

4. **Routine and Stability:** Regular services create a routine, offering structure and predictability that can be comforting. Knowing a set time to connect with the community can provide mental stability.

5. **Positive Social Interactions:** Engaging socially with fellow worshippers can enhance mood and boost self-esteem, facilitating positive interpersonal connections.

6. **Spiritual Reflection:** Being part of communal worship encourages spiritual reflection and growth, which can lead to personal insights and a deeper understanding of life's challenges.

7. **Participation in Faith-Based Rituals:** Active engagement in religious rituals fosters a sense of continuity and connection to tradition, promoting feelings of safety and grounding.

8. **Inspirational Content:** Listening to sermons or teachings during worship can offer new perspectives and solutions to problems, inspiring hope and positivity.

9. **Opportunities for Service:** Community worship often includes opportunities to volunteer or assist others, which can increase feelings of self-worth and reduce anxiety.

10. **Expression of Faith:** Worship allows individuals to express their faith openly, helping them maintain connection and communication with their spiritual beliefs, which can be deeply reassuring.

Mental Health Legislation into the Next Decade and Beyond

In the UK, the future of mental health legislation over the next decade and beyond will likely focus on enhancing accessibility, integration, and protection of mental health services. Here are some key trends and focus areas that might shape future legislation:

1. **Increased Funding and Resources:** The UK government might continue to allocate more resources to mental health services, aiming to reduce waiting times, improve treatment facilities, and ensure equitable access to care across the country.

2. **Integration with Physical Health:** Legislation is likely to support the integration of mental health services with physical health care, promoting collaboration between healthcare providers to treat patients holistically.

3. **Workplace Mental Health Support:** New laws may require businesses to implement mental health policies, provide training for staff, and ensure employees have access to mental health resources and support.

4. **Digital and Telehealth Services:** With the expansion of digital health services, legislation will likely address the regulation of telehealth platforms, ensuring they are secure, accessible, and offer parity with in-person services.

5. **Youth and School-Based Mental Health:** There may be increased focus on the mental health of children and adolescents, with potential legislation mandating mental health education and support services in schools.

6. **Research and Innovation:** Supporting research into new treatments and mental health technologies will continue to be a legislative priority, encouraging innovation and evidence-based practices.

7. **Crisis Intervention and Support:** Developing robust crisis intervention services and legislation to improve emergency mental health responses, possibly shifting towards more non-police involvement and community-centred support.

8. **Data Privacy and Security:** Ensuring the protection of personal mental health data will be a critical area of focus as digital services expand, with legislation potentially enforcing stringent privacy regulations.

9. **Anti-Stigma and Anti-Discrimination:** Strengthening laws to combat stigma and discrimination faced by

individuals with mental health conditions in employment, healthcare, and society.

10. **Community-Based Support Systems:** Emphasis on community-based care models may lead to legislative support for local mental health initiatives, encouraging grassroots participation and resource sharing.

11. **Global Trends and Cooperation:** The UK may work towards aligning its mental health policies with global standards, sharing best practices, and addressing mental health at an international level.

12. **Rights and Protections:** Expanding and reinforcing patient rights in mental health care settings, ensuring individuals are treated with dignity and respect, and can voice their care preferences.

These future legislative trends reflect a comprehensive approach to mental health in the UK, aiming to create a society where mental health is a priority and resources are accessible and equitable for all individuals.

Recent Changes in UK Mental Health Legislation

Recent updates in UK mental health law focus on modernising policies for better patient-centred care, safeguarding rights, and improving service access. Key developments include:

1. **Mental Health Act Reform:** The government has been reforming the Mental Health Act to emphasise patient autonomy and enhance safeguards. Proposed changes aim to give individuals more control over their treatment and reduce compulsory detention.

2. **Improved Community Support:** There's a push to strengthen community-based mental health services to

reduce hospital admissions. This includes more funding and the development of mental health hubs.

3. **Workforce Expansion:** Efforts to expand the mental health workforce aim to meet the rising demand for services.

4. **Access to Services:** Initiatives have been introduced to improve access to mental health services, particularly for young people and marginalised groups, via digital platforms and targeted programmes.

5. **Crisis Services Enhancement:** There's a focus on expanding 24/7 mental health crisis services, including helplines, to support those in acute distress.

These changes aim to create a more equitable, accessible, and effective mental health system in the UK.

Reform of the Mental Health Act: Key Aspects

The reform of the Mental Health Act centres on improving patient rights and ensuring care is more personalised and responsive. Key aspects include:

1. **Patient Autonomy:** The reform seeks to give patients greater control over their treatment decisions, including when and how they receive care.

2. **Criteria for Detention:** The reform aims to tighten the criteria for detention, ensuring it's used only when absolutely necessary, with conditions for sectioning being reassessed.

3. **Community Treatment Orders:** Changes to Community Treatment Orders (CTOs) would ensure they are used appropriately, with regular reviews of their duration and conditions.

4. **Role of Families and Caregivers:** The reform strengthens the role of families and caregivers, ensuring they're better informed and involved in decision-making.

5. **Reducing Disparities:** The reform addresses disparities in how the Act is applied, particularly aiming to reduce the disproportionate detention of Black and minority ethnic communities.

6. **Improved Access to Advocacy:** The reform ensures better access to independent advocates to help patients understand their rights and options.

7. **Advance Choice Documents:** The reform encourages the use of Advance Choice Documents, allowing patients to outline treatment preferences in case they are unable to decide in the future.

8. **Review Processes:** The reform includes more robust review processes to regularly assess the necessity of continued detention or treatment.

The goal is a more compassionate, fair, and effective mental health care system, centred on dignity and patient rights.

Addressing Racial Disparities in Mental Health Care

The reform aims to tackle racial disparities in mental health care with targeted measures:

1. **Data Collection and Monitoring:** Enhanced data collection on ethnicity and mental health interventions will help identify patterns and ensure accountability in addressing disparities.

2. **Cultural Competency Training:** Increased cultural competency training for mental health professionals aims to reduce bias and promote equitable care.

3. **Community Engagement:** Stronger engagement with diverse communities will help understand their unique needs and shape culturally responsive services.

4. **Review of Detention Practices:** The reform includes a review of detention criteria to ensure they do not disproportionately affect Black and minority ethnic individuals.

5. **Supporting Diverse Voices:** The reform encourages representation from diverse backgrounds in mental health decision-making to reflect the needs of all communities.

6. **Access to Culturally Appropriate Advocacy:** Ensuring people from minority ethnic backgrounds have access to advocacy services that respect cultural differences.

7. **Community-Specific Interventions:** Developing tailored interventions to address the unique barriers faced by different ethnic communities in accessing mental health care.

These measures aim to create a more equitable system and reduce racial disparities, leading to fairer outcomes for everyone.

Community and Faith Institutions in Mental Health Care

Community and faith institutions play a vital role in addressing racial disparities in mental health care. Here's how they can contribute:

1. **Building Trust:** Faith institutions are often deeply trusted within communities. Collaborating with them can help reduce stigma and encourage people to seek help.

2. **Cultural Sensitivity:** Faith leaders understand cultural values, ensuring that mental health services are culturally relevant and sensitive to community needs.

3. **Awareness and Education:** These institutions can raise awareness about mental health through sermons, workshops, and community events, helping to reduce stigma.

4. **Support Networks:** Faith and community institutions provide strong emotional and spiritual support, which is crucial during mental health challenges.

5. **Access Points:** Integrating mental health services within community and faith settings offers support in familiar, non-stigmatising environments.

6. **Advocacy and Representation:** Faith and community leaders can advocate for their communities, ensuring mental health reforms are inclusive and reflective of their needs.

7. **Collaboration with Mental Health Professionals:** Partnerships between mental health services and community organisations can provide professional support directly within the community.

Working with community and faith institutions helps to create more inclusive, culturally competent mental health services, ultimately reducing racial disparities in care.

11

Neurodivergence and Faith - ADHD, Autism

WITH MORE AWARENESS AROUND ADHD, YOUNG PEOPLE ARE INTERESTED IN LEARNING ABOUT MANAGING SYMPTOMS AND BREAKING DOWN STEREOTYPES

If you are reading this book and going on a mental wellness journey, you are not alone. And it is not your fault. Be reassured that you will come good. You will overcome. But you need to practise. This book is dedicated towards two groups: the unheard, and those struggling to make sense of what is going on with their emotions. You are sometimes disbelieved or even ignored possibly because of ethnicity. We doctors are guilty of not listening actively, because we follow definite lines of questioning in order to reach an accurate diagnosis. Doctors are not trained to incorporate faith into their assessment, and this book aims to put that right. Research tells us 50% develop mental health problems by age 15 and 75% by age 18. These statistics have to concern each of us.

Neurodiversity

Feeling excluded and invisible is typical for autistic people.

We are often infantilised or portrayed as unemotional (almost robotic) people who love tech.

Pop culture narratives make this worse.

Reducing us to stereotypes and "othering" us shapes how we are perceived by others and by ourselves. The result is an overwhelming number of autistic people who feel isolated, misunderstood, and discriminated against in life and at work.

Autistic people struggle with sensory painful work environments, with arbitrary social demands, with office politics, and with management.

Still, we have ways to take charge of our careers, through job matching, job crafting, and by working with others to support neurodiversity inclusion.

Religious faith

Religious faith refers to a strong belief or trust in something based on spiritual conviction rather than empirical evidence. It often involves believing in a particular religion or spiritual system's teachings, doctrines, or principles. Here are some key aspects of religious faith:

Faith and Autism

How it feels to have autism?

You experience the world in a unique way, perceiving details that others might miss. Sounds can be overwhelming; the hum of a refrigerator may feel like a full orchestra playing in your head. Social interactions are often confusing, like trying to decode an intricate puzzle without clear instructions. While conversations move quickly around you, comprehending the hidden meaning in others' words is like translating a foreign language in real time.

Routine and predictability are your sanctuary amidst the chaos of sensory input and social dynamics. When things change unexpectedly, it's as if the ground shifts beneath your feet. You thrive on knowing what comes next, finding peace in familiar patterns.

Your attention to detail allows you to see beauty and intricacy where others may not. A fallen leaf might captivate you for hours, its veins telling a story of life and growth. Deep dives into topics of interest are exhilarating; acquiring every detail about a subject makes you feel alive, like solving a complex but gratifying puzzle.

You are often aware of the gap between how you perceive the world and how others expect you to behave. But within this, there is a richness in your perspective. Emotions and thoughts are vast and profound, and while expressing them can be a challenge, their presence is deeply felt.

Feeling different can be isolating, but it can also be a gift. The world you navigate is filled with intensity and colour; though challenging, it is uniquely yours. You understand that your journey is about embracing who you are, finding comfort in your authenticity, and carving out a space where you can shine brightly.

Autistic People Do Have Strengths

Individuals with autism often have a range of strengths that can be impressive and valuable. Some common strengths include:

1. **Attention to Detail**: Many people with autism can notice fine details that others may overlook. This can make them excellent at tasks requiring precision and accuracy.

2. **Deep Focus**: When engaged with a topic or task of interest, individuals with autism can exhibit profound concentration and dedication, often leading to a deep understanding of the subject.

3. **Strong Memory**: Some individuals possess remarkable memory skills, particularly with regard to facts, dates, and

figures, making them adept at recalling detailed information accurately.

4. **Analytical Thinking**: Many people with autism have strong analytical and logical thinking abilities, enabling them to solve complex problems and identify patterns effectively.

5. **Honesty and Integrity**: Individuals with autism often value honesty and are known for their straightforward communication, which can be refreshing and build trust in relationships.

6. **Creativity and Innovation**: Some individuals exhibit unique creative skills, approaching problems and ideas from different angles and offering innovative solutions.

7. **Technical Skills**: A strong affinity for technology, mathematics, or programming is common, making many individuals with autism skilled in technical fields.

8. **Passion for Specialised Interests**: Deep enthusiasm for specific interests can lead to expertise in those areas, with individuals often becoming subject matter experts in their passions.

9. **Consistency and Reliability**: Their preference for routine and consistency can make them dependable in tasks that require regularity and adherence to schedules.

10. **Ability to Visualise**: Enhanced visual thinking skills can assist in various fields like design, architecture, or art, where visualising concepts is essential.

These strengths can vary widely from person to person, and not everyone with autism will have the same set of abilities. However, recognising and nurturing these strengths can be powerful for personal growth and success.

Examples of Careers that Leverage the Strengths of Autism

Here are some career paths that can make the most of the strengths often associated with autism:

1. **Data Analyst**: Uses attention to detail, strong memory, and analytical thinking to interpret complex datasets and draw meaningful insights.

2. **Software Developer**: Benefits from deep focus, technical skills, and problem-solving abilities to design and build software applications.

3. **Graphic Designer**: Makes use of creativity, visual thinking, and an eye for detail to create compelling visual content.

4. **Archivist or Librarian**: Relies on strong memory, consistency, and organisational skills to manage and keep information resources accessible.

5. **Engineer**: Applies analytical thinking, technical skills, and a passion for specialised interests to design and improve complex systems and structures.

6. **Research Scientist**: Leverages deep focus, strong memory, and passion for specialised interests to conduct experiments and expand knowledge in a specific field.

7. **Accountant**: Uses attention to detail, consistency, and integrity to manage financial records and ensure accuracy and compliance.

8. **Technical Writer**: Employs strong memory and analytical skills to produce clear and concise documentation for technical processes and products.

9. **Quality Assurance Specialist**: Relies on attention to detail and consistency to test products and ensure they meet required standards.

10. **Artistic Fields (e.g., Illustrator, Animator)**: Uses creativity, visual skills, and passion for specialised interests to produce imaginative and original artworks.

11. **Cybersecurity Specialist**: Utilises strong problem-solving skills and attention to detail to identify security threats and protect information systems.

12. **Statistician or Mathematician**: Applies analytical thinking, strong memory, and technical skills to solve mathematical problems and analyse numerical data.

These careers can provide fulfilling opportunities for individuals with autism to harness and develop their abilities. They offer environments where attention to detail, deep focus, creativity, or technical aptitude are highly valued. It's important to align career choices with personal interests and strengths to achieve the best outcomes.

Resources for Parents of Autistic Children

Here are some valuable resources for parents of children with autism:

1. **Autism Speaks**: Offers a wealth of information, including toolkits, advocacy resources, support networks, and access to local services. Website: Autism Speaks

2. **Autistic Self Advocacy Network (ASAN)**: Provides resources created by and for individuals on the autism spectrum, focusing on advocacy and empowerment. Website: ASAN

3. **National Autism Association**: Offers educational resources, a safety toolkit, and support for autistic families. Website: National Autism Association

4. **Centre for Parent Information and Resources**: Provides information on special education and services for children

with disabilities, including autism. Website: <u>Centre for Parent Information and Resources</u>

5. **The Autism Society**: Offers educational resources, advocacy information, support groups, and a helpline for parents and carers of autistic children. Website: <u>Autism Society</u>

6. **Family Voices**: Focuses on family-centred care for children with special health needs, including autism, and offers peer support and resources. Website: <u>Family Voices</u>

7. **Understood**: Provides resources to help parents navigate developmental differences, find supportive communities, and understand educational rights. Website: <u>Understood</u>

8. **First Signs**: Focuses on early identification and intervention for children with autism and other developmental disorders. Website: <u>First Signs</u>

9. **Sesame Street and Autism**: Offers free resources, activities, and videos designed to support families with autistic children. Website: <u>Sesame Street and Autism</u>

10. **Local Support Groups**: Connecting with local support groups or special interest organisations can provide community support, information, and shared experiences.

These resources cover a broad spectrum of support, ranging from advocacy and education to community connections and intervention strategies. Parents can use these platforms to access the help and information they need to support their children effectively.

Christian Faith and Autism

The Christian faith can provide support and guidance for parents of children with autism in several meaningful ways:

1. **Community Support**: Churches and religious communities can offer a supportive network where parents can connect with others who may be experiencing similar challenges. This sense of belonging can be crucial for emotional support and practical help.

2. **Faith and Encouragement**: Faith can offer comfort and encouragement during difficult times. Many Christians find strength in prayer, worship, and scripture, which can help them cope with the stresses and emotions involved in raising a child with autism.

3. **Moral and Ethical Guidance**: The teachings of Christianity often emphasise love, patience, and compassion, which can guide parents in their interactions with their child and in their journey through life's challenges.

4. **Purpose and Meaning**: Some parents find that their faith helps them see a greater purpose and meaning in their child's uniqueness and challenges, leading to a more positive and hopeful outlook.

5. **Resilience and Hope**: Faith can foster resilience, enabling parents to better handle adversity. The belief in a higher power and an ultimate plan can provide hope and peace amidst uncertainty or difficulties.

6. **Access to Faith-Based Resources**: Many faith-based organisations and churches offer resources, support groups, counselling, and activities specifically for families with children who have special needs.

7. **Opportunities for Service and Advocacy**: Christianity encourages acts of service and advocacy, providing parents with avenues to engage in their community and work towards greater inclusivity for children with autism.

If you're interested, connecting with a local church or faith-based support group might provide additional resources and community. Also, speaking with a pastor or spiritual adviser could offer personal guidance tailored to individual needs and circumstances.

Faith and the Challenge of Autism

The intersection of faith, autism, discrimination, and mental health involves a complex blend of social, emotional, and environmental factors. Here's a closer look:

1. **Faith and Autism**: Navigating religious practices can be challenging for individuals with autism, who may struggle with sensory overload or rigid thinking patterns. Autistic people need to be supported in those instances and for carers or people to have understanding.

2. **Discrimination**: People with autism may face discrimination in faith communities, exacerbated by misunderstandings about their behaviours or needs. This can be compounded by faith-based discrimination, making this overlap particularly challenging.

3. **Link to Autism**: Many individuals with autism experience co-occurring mental health challenges, such as anxiety or depression. Experiences of social exclusion or discrimination can magnify these issues.

4. **Impact on Faith**: If there is a lack of support or understanding, mental health struggles can affect one's ability to engage with faith communities, especially.

Creating Supportive Environments

1. Raising awareness about autism and mental health within faith communities reduces stigma and enhances acceptance, leading to better inclusion.

2. Developing inclusive practices, such as quiet spaces or flexible participation in rituals, allows individuals with autism to engage more comfortably with their faith community.

3. Providing access to mental health resources and support groups can aid individuals facing these intersecting issues.

4. Open discussions within faith communities about mental health, autism, and discrimination can cultivate empathy and foster a more inclusive environment.

5. Legal protections against discrimination based on disability and faith can aid in creating equitable spaces. Advocacy efforts can also lead to policy changes and better resources.

Breakout and Workshop Activities

- **Discuss Peer Pressure**: For example, vaping (or another relevant topic). Talk about the role of peer pressure and how to handle situations where they might be offered a vape. Role-playing scenarios can be helpful.

- **Encourage Questions**: Invite your adolescent to ask questions and be prepared to answer them. If you don't know the answer, commit to finding out together.

- **Set Clear Expectations**: Let your child know your stance on vaping and set clear rules and consequences, but also let them know you're willing to have ongoing discussions.

- **Stay Connected**: Regularly check in with your child about their day-to-day activities and friends to keep the lines of communication open.

- **Be a Role Model**: Set a positive example in your behaviour and lifestyle choices. If you use tobacco products, be honest about the struggles and encourage healthy habits.

- **Revisit the Conversation**: Make it an ongoing dialogue rather than a one-off talk. Regular discussions can help reinforce the message and provide support as your child navigates various situations.

By approaching this topic with understanding and openness, parents can help their children make informed and healthy choices regarding vaping.

Self-Esteem

Let's chat about self-esteem. It's like the secret superpower you didn't know you had.

1. What is Self-Esteem?

It's like your personal cheerleader—the way you talk to and about yourself. With high self-esteem, you're ready to take on anything.

2. Why It's Important:

Picture this: walking into a room like you own it—not out of ego, but because you genuinely believe in yourself. Self-esteem helps you handle life's challenges, whether that's exams, friendships, or trying something new.

3. Boosting Your Self-Esteem:

- **Positive vibes only:** Surround yourself with people who lift you up, not drag you down.

- **Be kind to yourself:** Would you say mean things to your best mate? Exactly. Treat yourself the same way.

- **Try new stuff:** Failed that skateboarding trick? No worries. Keep at it, and celebrate every bit of progress, however small.

4. Social Media Smarts:

Remember, everyone posts their highlights—not the behind-the-scenes bloopers. Don't compare. Just be you, because that's pretty amazing.

5. Cool Ways to Practise Self-Love:

- **Journalling:** Write down things you love about yourself.
- **Affirmations:** Start the day with affirmations. "I am awesome and ready to tackle anything."
- **Creative hobby:** Dive into something you love, whether it's playing guitar, painting, or gaming.

6. Ask for Help:

Feeling low? It's okay to have those days. Chat with someone you trust. Remember, superheroes have sidekicks for a reason.

Self-esteem is a journey, not a destination.

Group Formation:

- Form small, supportive groups (3–5 members) to ensure a safe space for open dialogue and creativity.

1. Role Assignment:

- Assign roles that portray different perspectives—individuals experiencing mental health challenges, supportive friends, family members, or mental health professionals.
- Encourage voluntary role choices to boost comfort and authenticity.

2. Scenario Development:

- Design realistic scenarios that reflect mental health struggles and coping strategies, appropriate to the group's age.

- Include moments of conflict and resolution to show the importance of seeking help and offering support.

3. Guidelines:

- Set clear rules to ensure sensitivity and respect.
- Focus on creating a safe environment where students feel encouraged to express themselves.

4. Time Management:

- Plan time for brainstorming, rehearsing, performing, and feedback. Balance preparation with room for natural expression.

5. Feedback and Reflection:

- Run a debrief to discuss insights gained—empathy, understanding, and awareness.
- Encourage personal reflections and connections to the scenarios.

6. Resources and Support:

- Provide information on mental health for further learning.
- Ensure access to professionals if students need more support.

Expected Outcomes:

- Greater awareness and understanding of mental health.
- Improved empathy, communication, and coping skills.
- A supportive community where mental health is openly discussed.

Materials Needed:

- Quiet, comfortable space for group activities.

- Props or costumes (optional) to make scenarios feel more real.

Art Therapy

Short brief for an art therapist to develop breakout group activities to raise mental health awareness in young people

Objective:

Develop breakout group activities using art therapy to raise mental health awareness among young people.

Steps to Implement:

1. **Theme Exploration:**
   - Choose themes like expressing emotions, building self-esteem, recognising stress, and fostering connections.
   - Highlight art's role in healing and self-expression.

2. **Group Organisation:**
   - Form small groups (3–5 members) for supportive interactions.
   - Keep groups diverse to encourage different perspectives.

3. **Activity Design:**
   - Plan art activities for self-expression: emotion-driven painting, mask-making to represent feelings, or collages about personal experiences.
   - Add mindfulness activities like mandala colouring or nature-inspired art for relaxation.

4. **Guidelines and Safety:**
    - Set ground rules for respect and confidentiality.
    - Reinforce non-judgement to create open expression.

5. **Time Management:**
    - Divide time for introduction, creation, sharing, and reflection.
    - Keep the pace balanced—space to create and time to talk.

6. **Sharing and Reflection:**
    - Invite participants to share their artwork and insights.
    - Use prompts to guide discussion, like describing emotions captured in the art.

7. **Support and Resources:**
    - Provide information on mental health for deeper understanding.
    - Be ready to connect participants with professionals if needed.

Expected Outcomes:

- Better awareness of mental health issues.
- Stronger emotional expression, empathy, and communication.
- Closer peer support through shared experiences.

Materials Needed:

- Art supplies: paper, paints, markers, clay, collage materials.
- A comfortable space for creativity and discussion.

Suggested Christian Faith-Based Art Therapy Activities

1. **Scripture-Inspired Painting:**
    - Pick a favourite Bible verse and paint what it means to you. Use colours and symbols that feel personal.

2. **Prayer Journals:**
    - Create personalised prayer journals. Decorate covers with drawings, collage, or calligraphy. Use them as a way to talk with God.

3. **Biblical Story Collages:**
    - In groups, make collages that show the lessons and characters of chosen Bible stories.

4. **Cross Crafts:**
    - Use wood, beads, or fabrics to make decorative crosses. Add personal touches, or gift them to someone in need of encouragement.

5. **Faith Quilts:**
    - Everyone creates a quilt square about their faith journey or a biblical theme. Combine them into a "faith quilt" for unity.

6. **Psalm Art:**
    - Pick a psalm and create artwork reflecting its mood and message with paints or pastels.

7. **Gratitude Mandalas:**
    - Design mandalas focusing on gratitude. Include words or symbols inspired by Christian values.

8. **Creation Reflection:**
    - Paint or draw scenes from the story of creation, reflecting on the beauty of God's world.

9. **Spiritual Vision Boards:**
    - Build vision boards of spiritual goals and inspirations with drawings, scripture, and cut-outs.

10. **Iconography Exploration:**
    - Learn about Christian icons, then create one of a saint or biblical figure, exploring symbolism in faith-based art.

These activities combine creativity and faith, giving young people space to express their beliefs while building community and deepening spiritual growth.

Christian Faith-Based Art Therapy Activities

Faith-centred art therapy can provide a meaningful way for participants to explore spirituality, emotions, and their relationship with God. The following activities are designed for group sessions and individual reflection.

1. Prayerful Painting

- Begin with a short time of silent prayer, seeking guidance or clarity.
- Create a painting that reflects the impressions received in prayer, using colour and form to express spiritual insight and emotion.

2. Blessing Stones

- Provide smooth stones and art materials for decoration with words of blessing, encouragement, or scripture.

- This practice can serve as both a meditative exercise and a tangible reminder of God's presence.

3. Biblical Character Journalling

- Invite participants to select a biblical figure with whom they identify.
- Encourage them to create a journal entry or artwork reflecting on that character's story, challenges, and faith.

4. Forgiveness Art

- Guide participants in creating an art piece symbolising forgiveness—whether asking for it, receiving it, or extending it.
- This process can aid in spiritual healing and emotional release.

5. Guided Imagery and Art

- Lead a short meditation centred on a biblical scene (e.g. Jesus calming the storm).
- Participants then create artwork depicting their personal experience and emotions during the meditation.

6. Psalm Meditation Collage

- Select a psalm that speaks to the participant's current state of mind or heart.
- Following a time of reflection, participants express insights by creating a collage.

7. Tree of Life Drawing

- Invite participants to draw a "Tree of Life," incorporating roots, branches, and fruit to represent their faith journey and personal growth.

8. Burdens Box

- Participants decorate a small box to symbolise the act of entrusting burdens to God.
- Written prayers or concerns may be placed inside as a gesture of release and trust.

9. Joy Journals

- Encourage the creation of journals dedicated to joy and gratitude.
- Participants may include drawings, written reflections, and scripture to reinforce hope and positive thinking.

10. Heart Mapping

- Ask participants to draw a heart filled with images or words representing relationships, values, and faith milestones that hold spiritual significance.

Scripture for the Forgiveness Art Project

The following passages provide biblical foundations for reflecting on forgiveness:

- **Ephesians 4:32** – "Be kind and compassionate to one another, forgiving each other, just as in Christ God forgave you."
- **Colossians 3:13** – "Bear with each other and forgive one another if any of you has a grievance against someone. Forgive as the Lord forgave you."
- **Matthew 6:14–15** – "For if you forgive other people when they sin against you, your heavenly Father will also forgive you. But if you do not forgive others their sins, your Father will not forgive your sins."

- **Luke 6:37** – "Do not judge, and you will not be judged. Do not condemn, and you will not be condemned. Forgive, and you will be forgiven."

- **1 John 1:9** – "If we confess our sins, he is faithful and just and will forgive us our sins and purify us from all unrighteousness."

- **Isaiah 1:18** – "Come now, let us settle the matter," says the Lord. "Though your sins are like scarlet, they shall be as white as snow; though they are red as crimson, they shall be like wool."

Colours and Materials Symbolising Forgiveness

Colours

- **Soft pastels**: calmness, peace, and healing.
- **White**: purity, renewal, and fresh beginnings.
- **Green**: growth, renewal, and restoration.
- **Light yellow**: warmth, optimism, and positivity.
- **Turquoise**: tranquillity and balance.

Materials

- **Watercolour**: gentleness and flow.
- **Canvas**: depth and layering, reflecting complexity.
- **Pastels**: softness and warmth.
- **Papier-mâché**: symbolic of layered healing.
- **Textiles**: comfort and care.
- **Acrylic or oils**: vibrancy and depth, representing transformation.

Spiritual Challenges in Integrating Faith with Mental Recovery

Bringing faith into one's mental health journey can present challenges such as:

1. **Crisis of faith** – Questioning beliefs during periods of struggle.

2. **Seeking meaning** – Understanding the role of spirituality in recovery.

3. **Conflicting emotions** – Wrestling with anger, guilt, or doubt.

4. **Balancing practices** – Integrating prayer, worship, and therapy.

5. **Isolation** – Experiencing disconnection from a faith community.

6. **Spiritual discipline** – Maintaining regular practices while unwell.

7. **Integration with therapy** – Navigating faith within clinical contexts.

8. **Expectation versus reality** – Managing hopes for spiritual healing.

9. **Inner conflict** – Reconciling faith-based and medical perspectives.

10. **Acceptance of vulnerability** – Recognising that faith does not remove human frailty.

Mental Health Engagement Activity: *Brain Dump & Share*

This activity provides a creative and light-hearted approach to discussing mental health.

1. **Writing** – Note down thoughts, worries, or ideas currently occupying the mind.

2. **Emoji summary** – Represent the content of the "brain dump" using three emojis.

3. **Sharing** – Exchange emojis with others and interpret one another's chosen symbols.

4. **Fact exchange** – Each participant shares one positive fact or tip related to mental wellbeing.

5. **Community connection** – Encourage use of the hashtag **#BrainBuddyChallenge** on social media to extend participation and reduce stigma around mental health conversations.

More ideas for the challenge?

Here are a few more creative twists for your "Brain Buddy Challenge" that will keep it fun and engaging:

1. Mood Playlist: Create a playlist that reflects how you're feeling today. Share it with friends and invite them to add their favourite tracks reflecting their mood. Music is a universal language!

2. Gratitude Graffiti: Draw, doodle or write ten things you're grateful for on a piece of paper or a whiteboard. Snap a picture and share it with your group chat. Gratitude boosts happiness, and creative expression can be a delight!

3. Self-Care Bingo: Create a bingo card with self-care activities like "15-minute walk," "drink water," "share a meme," "dance break" etc. Challenge each other to complete a row or column by the end of the week.

4. Mindful Minute: Take one minute to sit in silence, breathe deeply, and focus on the present moment. Once done, swap

experiences with friends or jot down any interesting reflections.

5. Visual Journal: Sketch your mood or current thoughts rather than writing them out. Share your art with friends and try to interpret each other's drawings (bonus for creative or hilariously off interpretations).

6. Compliment Chain: Start a chain reaction of positivity by sending your friend a genuine compliment. Encourage them to pass it on to someone else. Watch those smiles spread!

7. Meme Therapy: Share the funniest meme you've seen this week in your group chat. Laughter is a great stress reliever, and who doesn't love a good meme?

8. Daily Check-In: Start a daily check-in with friends using one phrase: "Today, I feel like..." and finish it with whatever comes to mind, silly or serious.

9. Creative Cooking: Cook or bake something new, and share a photo of your culinary creation. Cooking can be therapeutic, and tasting new flavours can be an adventure in itself!

10. Future Me Letter: Write a positive letter to your future self, then seal it up or save it in your notes. Decide when you'll read it, maybe a year from now or on a significant date.

11. Mindful Photo Walk: Grab your phone and take photos of five things that make you smile during a walk. Share these moments with friends and discuss what little things make life bright.

Feel free to mix and match these ideas, or modify them to fit your group's vibe. The key is creating an environment where mental health discussions are meaningful and full of laughter and creativity!

Here are some activities for self-care you might enjoy:

1. Mindful Meditation: Spend a few minutes focusing on your breath or using a guided meditation app.
2. Nature Walk: Take a stroll in a park or forest to enjoy the fresh air and calming scenery.
3. Journaling: Write down your thoughts, gratitude lists, or doodle your feelings.
4. Bubble Bath: Relax in a warm bath with soothing music and aromatic candles.
5. Digital Detox: Spend time away from screens and reconnect with the physical world.
6. Chat on digital detox and wellness
7. Sure, let us explore the concept of digital detox and wellness in a way that is engaging and relevant for young people:

Digital Detox As a Therapeutic Intervention

Ever feel like you are glued to your phone or computer? Whether it is the endless scroll of TikTok, meme hunting on Instagram, or gaming marathons, our digital world is highly exciting but can also be overwhelming. Here is how you can hit the refresh button on your mind and life!

1. Why Consider a Digital Detox?

- Mental Clarity & Focus: Ever tried studying or just relaxing but felt distracted? Putting down your devices helps you concentrate and enjoy the moment.
- Emotional Well-Being: Less screen time can mean less comparison and anxiety. Let us face it, FOMO is real, but you deserve a break.

- Better Sleep: Blue light can disrupt your sleep. Swapping screens for snooze time can make your mornings feel magical.

2. Fun Ways to Detox Digitally

- Screen-Free Challenges: Try a 24-hour challenge with friends to see who can stay off social media the longest. Who will win the ultimate bragging rights?

- Digital-Free Zones & Times: Set up tech-free zones in your room or at mealtimes. Connect with your family and friends, or simply enjoy your meal—the way grandma intended.

- Outdoor Adventures: Head outside, explore nature, or discover a new hobby (hello, skateboarding!) to break the digital cycle whilst having fun.

3. Balancing Tech Use

- Mindful Consumption: Use technology purposefully. That means consciously deciding when and why you're picking up devices.

- Curate Your Feeds: Unfollow accounts that drain you. Follow ones that inspire, educate, or genuinely make you smile.

4. Reconnecting with Yourself & Others

- Journaling & Meditation: Spend a few minutes writing down your thoughts or meditating. Free your mind from digital clutter.

- Face-to-Face Hangouts: Meet friends in person, not just in chat rooms. There is nothing like a laughter-filled coffee catch-up.

5. Wellness for the Win

- Emotional Check-Ins: Take time to ask yourself how you are feeling. Discuss with friends or family when you're comfortable.

- Physical Activity: Join a sport, or just dance like no one is watching in your room! Movement is a fantastic way to feel alive.

Switching off can sound daunting, but remember, it is all about balance and having fun whilst being present in your own life. Ready to take a mini-break from screens and reconnect with what truly matters?

Let us get this digital detox rolling! What is one thing you would like to try from this list, or is there something brilliant you have already done to unplug?

Social Media and Your Mental Wellbeing

How online platforms affect your mental wellbeing

1. Yoga: Engage in a gentle yoga session to stretch and calm your body and mind.

2. Read a Book: Escape into a novel or read inspiring non-fiction.

3. Art & Craft: Try painting, drawing, knitting, or any creative activity you enjoy.

4. Cook a New Recipe: Experiment with a new, wholesome recipe in the kitchen.

5. Dance: Put on your favourite music and dance like nobody is watching.

6. Tea/coffee Ritual: Make a cup of your favourite tea or coffee and sip it slowly.

7. Gardening: Spend time nurturing plants or start a small herb garden.

8. Listen to Music or Podcast: Choose something you love or discover something new.

9. Spa Day at Home: Do a facial mask, manicure, and foot soak.

10. Sleep/Rest: Allow yourself to take a nap or enjoy a restful activity.

11. Exercise: Go for a run, try a new workout, or just stretch.

12. Connect with Loved Ones: Spend time or have a call with family and friends.

13. Explore a Hobby: Make time for a hobby you love or want to learn.

14. Gratitude Practice: Write down or think about things you are grateful for.

15. Mindful Cooking: Prepare a meal mindfully, enjoying every step of the process.

Trying any of these activities can help replenish your energy and improve your well-being. Enjoy your self-care time!

Activities that can help relieve stress:

1. Deep Breathing Exercises: Practise slow, deep breaths to calm your nervous system.

2. Progressive Muscle Relaxation: Tense and relax each muscle group to reduce physical tension.

3. Tai Chi: Engage in this gentle form of martial arts focused on slow, flowing movements.

4. Guided Imagery: Visualise a peaceful scene or place to mentally escape stress.

5. Aromatherapy: To soothe your senses, use essential oils like lavender or eucalyptus.

6. Laughter Therapy: Watch a comedy or engage in activities that make you laugh.

7. Mindful Walking: Walk slowly and attentively, noticing each step and your surroundings.

8. Creative Writing: Channel your thoughts and feelings through writing short stories or poetry.

9. Sing or Play Music: Express yourself through singing or playing a musical instrument.

10. Visualisation Techniques: Imagine reaching your goals and living stress-free.

11. Pet Time: Spend time with pets or visit a nearby animal shelter to enjoy their calming presence.

12. Water Therapy: Swim or relax by water bodies to absorb their tranquilising effects.

13. Breath of Fire: Practise this yoga breathing technique for quick energy and reduced stress.

14. Stretching Routine: Stretch your body intentionally to release built-up tension.

15. Digital Art: Experiment with creating a digital art piece or illustration.

16. Volunteer Work: Help others, which can provide perspective and reduce stress.

17. Gardening Therapy: Digging in the soil can be grounding and therapeutic.

18. Acupuncture or Massage: Consider treatments that focus on relieving physical tension.

19. DIY Projects: Engage in crafting or building something with your hands.

20. Stress Ball: Use a stress ball to physically channel anxiety or stress.

These activities can help you manage and alleviate stress, enhancing your emotional and physical well-being. Find what works best for you and incorporate it into your routine!

Who are Gen Z?

Generation Z, also known as Gen Z or Zoomers, refers to individuals born between 1996 and 2012. They are currently the second-youngest generation, following Millennials and preceding Generation Alpha. Gen Z is characterised by several unique traits:

1. **Digital natives:** They are the first generation to grow up with widespread internet access and smartphones as part of daily life.

2. **Diversity:** Gen Z is the most diverse generation in U.S. history, with nearly 50% being racial and ethnic minorities.

3. **Social consciousness:** They are known for their idealism, advocating for climate change action, racial justice, and sustainability.

4. **Pragmatism:** Despite their idealism, Gen Zers tend to be more pragmatic about their future, expecting economic struggles whilst seeking personal career fulfilment.

5. **Mental health awareness:** They generally have lower levels of emotional and social well-being compared to older generations and prioritise mental health.

Gen Z's values and experiences have been shaped by events such as the Great Recession, the COVID-19 pandemic, and rapid technological advancements. As they enter the workforce and become consumers, their impact on society is expected to be significant and transformative.

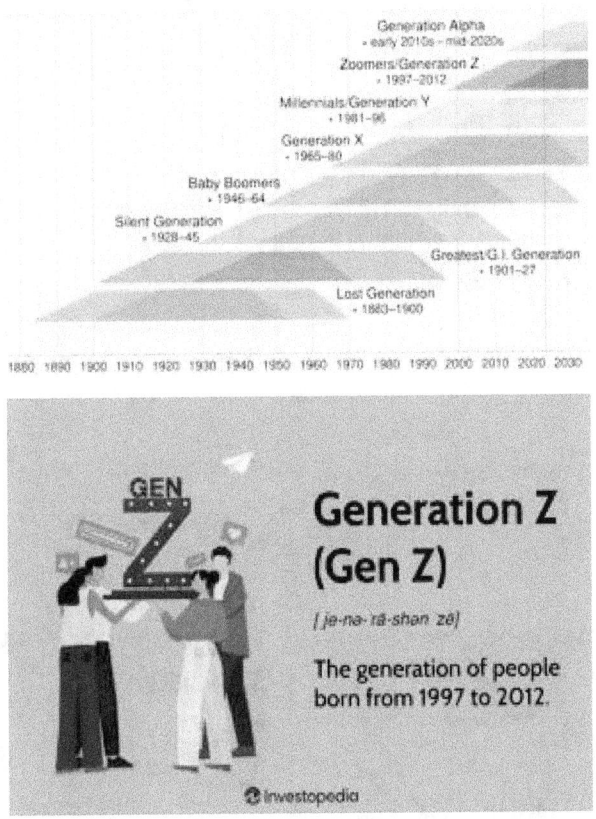

The generations defined

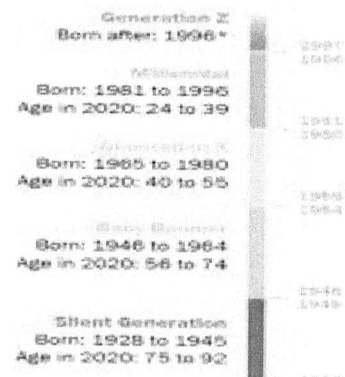

Generation Z
Born after: 1996*

Millennial
Born: 1981 to 1996
Age in 2020: 24 to 39

Generation X
Born: 1965 to 1980
Age in 2020: 40 to 55

Baby Boomer
Born: 1946 to 1964
Age in 2020: 56 to 74

Silent Generation
Born: 1928 to 1945
Age in 2020: 75 to 92

*No chronological endpoint has been set for this group.

"On the Cusp of Adulthood and Facing an Uncertain Future: What We Know About Generation Z So Far"

PEW RESEARCH CENTER

The generations defined

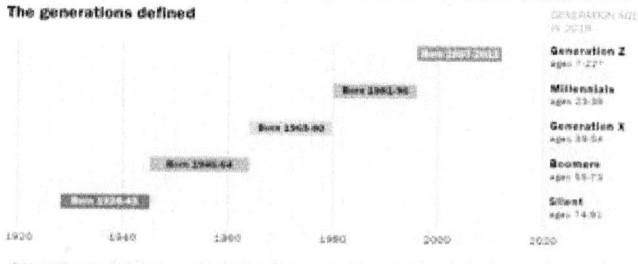

PEW RESEARCH CENTER

Generation Z

Gen Z constitutes 26% of the total population across the world. This means 2 billion people are in Gen Z. Generation Z is one of the most racially and ethnically diverse generations across the United States. Nearly 99% of Gen Zs either owns a smartphone or have access to one.

market.us

Key Differences between Generation Z and Millennials

Generation Z (born 1997–2012) and Millennials (born 1981–1996) differ in several key aspects:

1. **Outlook**: Generation Z tends to be more realistic, whilst Millennials are generally more optimistic. This is partly due to Generation Z growing up during economic challenges such as the Great Recession.

2. **Work ethic**: Generation Z values work–life balance and sets clear boundaries, whereas Millennials are more likely to embrace the "hustle" culture.

3. **Technology**: Generation Z are digital natives, born into a world of ubiquitous connectivity, whilst Millennials witnessed the rise of the internet and social media.

4. **Communication**: Generation Z prefers visual-based media and platforms such as TikTok, whereas Millennials favour text-based platforms.

5. **Career goals**: Generation Z emphasises finding their dream job, whilst Millennials prioritise stability.

6. **Financial attitudes**: Generation Z is more debt-averse and budget-minded compared to Millennials.

7. **Social consciousness**: Both generations are socially aware, but Generation Z tends to be more environmentally conscious and focused on social issues.

8. **Feedback preferences**: Generation Z prefers direct feedback, whilst Millennials respond better to positive, encouraging feedback.

These differences reflect the unique experiences and environments that shaped each generation, influencing their attitudes, behaviours, and expectations in various aspects of life.

Generation Z, also known as "Zoomers", refers to the generation born approximately between 1997 and 2012. This generation follows the Millennials and precedes Generation Alpha. Here are some key characteristics and defining aspects of Generation Z:

1. **Digital Natives**: Generation Z is the first generation to grow up with the internet and digital technology integral to daily life. They are highly proficient with smartphones, social media, and other digital communication tools.

2. **Diverse and Inclusive**: Generation Z is known for valuing diversity and inclusion, often advocating for equality across race, gender, and sexual orientation. They tend to be more accepting of different cultures and identities.

3. **Socially Conscious**: Many members of Generation Z are passionate about social issues such as climate change, racial justice, and mental health. They often engage in activism and use social media platforms to push for change.

4. **Entrepreneurial Spirit**: With access to vast information online, Generation Z tends to be entrepreneurial, seeking innovative ways to create opportunities and start ventures, whether online shops or content creation channels.

5. **Education and Career Focused**: Whilst valuing education, Generation Z also seeks alternative learning pathways and values practical skills. Career stability is important, but they often prioritise jobs that provide purpose and work–life balance.

6. **Mental Health Awareness**: Generation Z places significant importance on mental health, being open about discussing and seeking support for mental health issues.

7. **Preference for Digital Communication**: Often favouring texting and social media over face-to-face interaction, Generation Z communicates largely through digital platforms, creating online communities.

8. **Short Attention Span**: Raised in a fast-paced digital world with constant exposure to new content, Generation Z is accustomed to quickly consuming and moving on to new information.

Understanding Generation Z's unique characteristics helps in engaging with them effectively, whether in marketing, education, or community-building contexts.

Generation Z and Mental Health: The Faith Contribution

Generation Z faces a unique intersection of challenges impacting their mental health, but faith and spirituality can play a significant role in promoting well-being.

Mental Health Challenges

1. **Digital Revolution**: Constant exposure to social media and digital communication can lead to anxiety, depression, and loneliness due to comparison and cyberbullying.

2. **Academic and Career Pressure**: High academic achievement and career success expectations contribute to stress and anxiety.

3. **Social Issues**: Issues such as climate change, racism, and economic inequality create a sense of uncertainty and urgency, affecting mental health.

4. **Identity and Belonging**: Challenges surrounding identity, gender, and sexual orientation impact mental health, particularly for marginalised groups.

Generation Millennials, Faith, and Mental Health

"Generation Anxious" refers to the growing concern about mental health issues, such as anxiety and stress, particularly among younger generations. This term captures the societal, technological, and economic pressures that contribute to increased anxiety levels. Factors such as social media influence, job market unpredictability, academic pressures, and global issues such as climate change can heighten anxiety. Addressing these concerns involves promoting mental health awareness, providing access to supportive resources, and fostering open conversations about emotional well-being.

The relationship between Millennials, faith, and mental health is complex and multifaceted. Here are some insights into how these elements intersect:

1. **Seeking Meaning and Purpose**: Many Millennials explore faith or spirituality as a way to find deeper meaning and purpose in life. This search can positively impact mental health by providing a sense of identity and direction.

2. **Diverse Beliefs**: Millennials tend to have diverse beliefs and may not adhere to traditional religious practices. This generation often prioritises personal growth and well-being over organised religion, leading to a more eclectic spiritual lifestyle that can include meditation, yoga, and mindfulness.

3. **Community and Support**: For some Millennials, faith-based communities offer a sense of belonging and support that is beneficial for mental health. Participation in these

communities can reduce feelings of isolation and provide a network for sharing struggles and joys.

4. **Faith and Coping**: Faith can serve as a coping mechanism during difficult times, offering hope, comfort, and resilience. Many Millennials use faith-based practices or prayer as part of their mental health toolkit.

5. **Challenges with Religion**: Some Millennials experience conflict with traditional religious institutions, which can lead to stress or disillusionment. These challenges may stem from disagreements over social issues, religious dogma, or perceived hypocrisy within institutions.

6. **Stigma and Openness**: Millennials often advocate for open discussions about mental health, including in religious settings. There is a growing movement among faith communities to address mental health issues, reduce stigma, and integrate mental health support within congregations.

7. **Holistic Approaches**: This generation frequently embraces holistic well-being, combining faith, mental health practices, physical health, and emotional wellness to create a balanced lifestyle.

8. **Technological Connections**: With access to information online, Millennials explore a wide range of spiritual practices and mental health resources, often blending different traditions and modern psychology.

In summary, Millennials uniquely navigate the intersections of faith and mental health. Whilst some derive strength and guidance from traditional religious practices, others create personalised spiritual paths incorporating various faith and wellness practices. This generation's openness to discussing mental health has also sparked positive changes in how religious communities address and support mental well-being.

Common Mental Health Issues Faced by Millennials

Millennials face a variety of mental health challenges influenced by unique social, economic, and technological factors. Here are some common mental health issues affecting this generation:

1. **Anxiety**: High levels of anxiety are prevalent among Millennials, often fuelled by economic uncertainty, job instability, student debt, and societal pressures to succeed.

2. **Depression**: Depression is widespread, with factors such as loneliness, social media comparisons, and a lack of work–life balance contributing to the issue.

3. **Burnout**: Many Millennials experience burnout due to demanding work environments and constant pressure to be productive. The blurring of work–life boundaries in remote work settings has exacerbated this problem.

Integration into Mental Health Strategies

- *Interfaith Dialogues*: Encouraging openness and interfaith dialogues can help Generation Z find spiritual paths that resonate with their personal beliefs.

- *Spiritual Counselling*: Including spiritual counselling in mental health services can address both psychological and spiritual needs holistically.

- *Community Programmes*: Developing programmes within faith organisations to address mental health awareness and education can reduce stigma and promote support.

- *Digital Platforms for Faith*: Online faith communities can engage Generation Z in meaningful ways, providing support and guidance accessible to digital natives.

Incorporating faith and spirituality into mental health strategies can support Generation Z in managing their unique challenges, providing holistic well-being in a rapidly changing world.

Gender and Sex

Introduction: In opinion, as a lesbian, gay, bisexual or transgender person you are entitled to exactly the same standards of care as heterosexual people in the NHS.

It is a good idea to tell your doctor if you are gay, lesbian or bisexual. If your doctor knows about your sexuality or sexual preferences, it can be easier to discuss your life, relationships and health concerns. They can also keep an eye out for any health problems that might be relevant to you.

Methodology flaws: Studies have shown that lesbian, gay and bisexual people can feel reluctant to talk openly to their GP and may avoid appointments. This study has to be interpreted against this reluctance.

Either way, it is unacceptable and illegal. The law, the NHS and the General Medical Council, which regulates doctors, are clear that there should be no discrimination on the grounds of sexual orientation or gender identity.

The term 'trans' refers to a diverse community of people, including those who cross-dress (transvestites) and transgender people who have a strong desire to live as a person of the opposite sex.

In this study, transgender is defined as a person who believes he is a woman in a man's body or vice versa, and who has not undergone the necessary psychological evaluation. Like lesbian, gay and bisexual people, trans people may face prejudice, isolation and limited understanding of their lives.

The BBC is pushing the LGBTQ+ agenda onto children once again!

In another concerning step to incorporate adult sexuality and transgender ideology into family programming, the BBC is featuring drag queens in its flagship show, *Strictly Come Dancing*.

Recent episodes have featured drag queens in prominent roles; two drag queens have read the terms and conditions just a few episodes ago. The BBC has announced that the Christmas special will include *Drag Race UK* finalist Tayce as a contestant in the primetime Christmas Day slot.

Imagine the scene: families across the UK gather to watch Christmas television with their children, expecting age-appropriate entertainment from the BBC. What do they get? A man parading on the stage as a highly sexualised caricature of a woman.

'Drag' – characterised by men performing as exaggerated and hypersexualised caricatures of women – is an adult entertainment form. It is never appropriate for children! 'Drag queens' often have sexualised names, perform sexualised routines and are essentially a form of sexual entertainment aimed at gay men.

Tayce's drag persona is no different. It raises serious questions about how this is appropriate for a family audience. His social media features explicit content, including provocative poses and imagery such as him in a bikini covered in fake blood.

He is also a proponent of the infamous 'Drag Queen Story Hours', which he promotes, featuring in his drag persona on a documentary called *Striking with Pride: United at the Coalface*. In the documentary, he tells a group of children about Pride and the 'queer revolution' in Wales. Discussing the documentary, he said it was important to 'educate these little angels on Pride'.

Children should not be exposed to this kind of entertainment. It blurs the boundaries between men and women and exposes children to adult sexuality and concepts of gender identity, which they are too young to understand.

Exposing young children to transgenderism and adult sexuality increases their risk of becoming a victim of sexual abuse or engaging in underage sexual activity.

We have to protect our children from being exposed to these harmful concepts! We must protect childhood innocence wherever possible, and it is vital that child safeguarding is upheld. Our children deserve a safe childhood free from being sexualised at a young age.

We must hold the BBC accountable. You and I fund them! We have to stand together and show them that we will not stand by as they try to indoctrinate our children into the LGBTQ+ agenda.

The national broadcaster should not be using public money from licence-payers to fund its LGBTQ+ agenda in trying to normalise drag for children.

Urge the BBC to stop pushing radical ideologies and reconsider featuring a drag queen on its Christmas special. Ask the Director-General of the BBC, Tim Dave, and the Chief Content Officer of the BBC, Charlotte Moore, to act!

More information:

On Drag and the Loss of Safeguarding: Women's Rights Network:

https://www.womensrights.network/post/on-drag-and-the-loss-of-safeguarding

Drag Is Never Appropriate for Kids: *Newsweek*:

https://www.newsweek.com/drag-never-appropriate-kids-opinion-1807055

Why drag queen performances are not appropriate for children: *Washington Examiner*:

https://www.washingtonexaminer.com/news/2876760/

Faith, Co-Production And Mental Health

Faith, co-production, and mental health form a dynamic trio that can significantly enhance personal well-being and the effectiveness of mental health care services.

1. **Faith:** For many, faith provides a strong sense of community, purpose, and hope. It can offer comfort, help cope with stress, and foster resilience. Spiritual or religious beliefs can be a source of support, offering rituals and practices that promote positive mental health. Faith communities often provide a sense of belonging and acceptance, which is vital for emotional well-being.

2. **Co-production:** This approach involves collaboration between service users and providers, ensuring that mental health services are designed and delivered in a way that meets the real needs of individuals. By actively involving patients in designing and evaluating health services, co-production empowers individuals, respects their experiences, and promotes a more person-centred approach to treatment.

3. **Mental Health:** Mental health encompasses emotional, psychological, and social well-being. It is about how individuals think, feel, and behave, affecting their ability to handle stress, relate to others, and make choices. Mental health is essential at every stage of life, from childhood through adulthood. Effective mental health care involves recognising early signs, providing timely interventions, and ensuring ongoing support.

By integrating faith and co-production into mental health care, communities and healthcare providers can create more holistic and effective support systems. This integration acknowledges the whole person, respects individual experiences, and supports diverse pathways to recovery and well-being.

Exploring these concepts further can lead to innovative approaches that prioritise the person, enhance engagement, and improve mental health outcomes.

In Lambeth, there are several mental health services aimed at supporting young people. Here are some key services and initiatives:

1. **Children and Adolescent Mental Health Services (CAMHS):** Lambeth CAMHS provide mental health assessments and treatments for children and young people experiencing emotional, behavioural, or mental health difficulties. They offer a range of services including therapy and counselling.

2. **The Well Centre:** A health and well-being service for young people aged 13-20, offering mental health support, physical health assessments, and advice on a variety of issues. It is a confidential service where young people can speak to counsellors and healthcare professionals.

3. **Kooth:** An online counselling and emotional well-being platform accessible to young people in Lambeth. It offers anonymous support through an online community, live chat with professional counsellors, and engaging therapeutic articles.

4. **Off the Record (OTR):** Provides free and confidential services to young people aged 11-25. They focus on offering supportive counselling and resources to help young individuals cope with challenging feelings and situations.

5. **HeadStart Lambeth:** Aimed at 10-16-year-olds, this initiative works in schools and communities to promote emotional resilience and prevent mental health issues through workshops, mentoring, and peer support schemes.

6. **South London and Maudsley NHS Foundation Trust (SLaM):** Offers specialised mental health services for young people, including inpatient care. They provide help for serious mental health issues and work in conjunction with local authorities to offer comprehensive support.

7. **YoungMinds Helpline:** Although not specific to Lambeth, this national organisation offers a helpline for young people and parents to access information, advice, and support on mental health matters.

8. **Local Schools and Colleges:** Many educational institutions in Lambeth also provide access to counselling and support through trained staff and partnerships with local mental health organisations.

Each of these resources is designed to ensure that young people in Lambeth have access to the appropriate support and interventions they require for their mental well-being. Collaboration between families, schools, and healthcare providers is key to effectively addressing and supporting the mental health needs of young people.

Faith and Mental Health in Practice

Prayer and the Young Christian

Here is how these verses might help in practice for mental health:

The Bible offers numerous scriptures that emphasise peace of mind, highlighting the importance of trust in God and prayer. Key verses include:

- *Isaiah 26:3:* "You will keep in perfect peace those whose minds are steadfast because they trust in you."
- *Philippians 4:6-7:* "Do not be anxious about anything… and the peace of God, which transcends all understanding, will guard your hearts and minds."

- *John 14:27:* "Peace I leave with you; my peace I give you. Do not let your hearts be troubled."

These passages encourage reliance on God's promises for true peace amidst life's challenges.

The Fervent Prayer of a Righteous Man

Christian prayer is a way for believers to communicate with God. It is a spiritual practice where they express their thoughts, desires, gratitude, and requests to God. Prayer can involve praising God, confessing sins, seeking guidance, or asking for help for themselves and others. Christians often draw on examples from the Bible, such as the Lord's Prayer, as a guide for their own prayers. It is a personal, heartfelt conversation with God, guided by faith and the teachings of Christianity.

The Lord's Prayer

The Lord's Prayer is a central prayer in Christianity, taught by Jesus to His disciples. It is often recited in church services and personal prayer. Here is a simplified explanation of its key parts:

1. *Our Father who art in heaven:* Acknowledges God as a loving father and the divine being in heaven.

2. *Hallowed be thy name:* A declaration of holiness, giving honour and reverence to God's name.

3. *Thy kingdom come:* A request for God's rule and kingdom to manifest on Earth.

4. *Thy will be done on earth as it is in heaven:* A desire for God's desires and plans to be fulfilled on Earth, just like in heaven.

5. *Give us this day our daily bread:* A petition for God to provide for our daily needs.

6. *And forgive us our trespasses, as we forgive those who trespass against us:* Asking for forgiveness for sins and committing to forgive others.

7. *And lead us not into temptation:* A request for guidance away from sin and temptation.

8. *But deliver us from evil:* Asking for protection from harm and evil forces.

9. *For thine is the kingdom, and the power, and the glory, for ever:* Affirming God's eternal rule, power, and glory.

The prayer embodies reverence, humility, dependence on God, and commitment to living a life aligned with divine will.

How do people incorporate the Lord's Prayer in their daily life?

People incorporate the Lord's Prayer into their daily lives in various meaningful ways:

1. Daily Recitation: Many Christians start or end their day by reciting the Lord's Prayer, using it as a personal devotion to centre themselves spiritually.

2. Meditative Prayer: Some use it as a meditative framework, reflecting deeply on each phrase to cultivate mindfulness and spiritual insight.

3. In Church Services: It is frequently included in church services, where congregations recite it together, fostering a sense of community and shared faith.

4. Guided Prayer: Individuals use it as a guide, expanding on each line with personal thoughts and requests, allowing it to shape their discussions with God.

5. Teaching Tool: The prayer serves as an educational tool, helping new believers or children learn about important

aspects of faith such as forgiveness, reliance on God, and seeking His will.

6. In Times of Need: Many turn to the Lord's Prayer in moments of distress or decision-making, seeking comfort and guidance.

7. Family Prayer: Families may say the Lord's Prayer together, instilling shared spiritual practices and values.

8. Prayer Groups and Retreats: It can be used in group settings or retreats, encouraging communal reflection and unity.

By incorporating the Lord's Prayer into daily routines, individuals aim to align their lives with its teachings, strengthening their faith and connection with God.

Challenges of practising Christian faith for mentally unwell patients

As an experienced psychiatrist working with patients who are mentally unwell and practise the Christian faith, I have encountered a diverse array of experiences that highlight the complexities and challenges of integrating spirituality with mental health care. My journey with these patients is marked by a continuous learning process, as each individual's relationship with their faith is deeply personal and unique.

One of the primary challenges I have observed is finding the balance between respecting the patient's spiritual beliefs and addressing their mental health needs. Many patients find immense comfort and strength in their faith, using prayer, scripture, and fellowship as coping mechanisms. However, there are times when symptoms of their mental illness, such as delusions or hallucinations, become intertwined with religious themes, which can complicate their condition and potentially exacerbate their distress.

Self-Esteem and Confidence

LET US DISCUSS SELF-ESTEEM AND CONFIDENCE: YOUR ULTIMATE POWER-UP

Start Here: Self-esteem and confidence are like personal strengths. They are about how you see yourself and how you approach the world.

Dispelling Myths: Confidence is not about being the loudest in the room. It is about feeling good about who you are, even if you are a quiet individual.

Progress and Growth: See self-esteem like a progression. You gain points by achieving goals, embracing challenges, and learning new skills. Each "level-up" builds your confidence.

Mirror Talk: Your mind listens to what you say. Next time you are in front of the mirror, say something kind to yourself. It may sound unusual, but it works.

Overcoming Negativity: Everyone has that little voice of self-doubt. Challenge it. Replace "I cannot" with "I will try". Small steps can lead to significant progress.

Social Media: Remember, it is a highlight reel, not the whole story. Focus on your own journey, and celebrate your achievements.

Building Confidence: Starting with small tasks such as cooking a new recipe or speaking up in class can help build your confidence over time. Practice brings improvement.

Supportive Relationships: Surround yourself with people who support you, challenge you, and appreciate you for who you are.

Research Insight: Studies suggest that smiling can trick your brain into feeling happier and more confident.

The Journey: Confidence is a journey, not a destination. Be patient with yourself. Celebrate small victories and continue to grow.

For a new young Christian, prayer holds significant importance and serves various purposes in their spiritual journey. Here are some aspects highlighting the importance of prayer:

- Prayer is a fundamental way for young Christians to connect with God. It provides an opportunity to speak directly to Him, share their thoughts and feelings, and seek guidance.

- Through regular prayer, young Christians can grow spiritually. It helps them understand their faith better and builds a closer relationship with God.

- Prayer offers solace and peace, especially during challenging times. It can be a source of comfort, reassuring young Christians that they are not alone.

- By praying, young Christians can seek divine wisdom and guidance in their everyday decisions and life choices.

- Prayer encourages gratitude, allowing young Christians to reflect on their blessings and express thankfulness.

- Praying with others fosters a sense of community and unity among believers, reinforcing their shared faith journey.

- Regular prayer strengthens faith and trust in God's plans and timing, teaching young Christians patience and acceptance.

- Prayer can empower young Christians, giving them the strength to overcome personal struggles and face life's challenges with confidence.

Through these aspects, prayer becomes an integral part of their faith, nurturing their beliefs and supporting their spiritual journey.

I have personal experience of finding it hard to concentrate during prayer, and for a young Christian this can be a common challenge, but there are several strategies to help improve focus:

- **Set the Scene:** Create a quiet and comfortable environment for prayer. This could be a calm corner in your home or a peaceful spot outdoors.
- **Deep Breaths:** Begin your prayer by taking a few deep breaths to relax your mind and body. This can help you become more present and focused.

If necessary, write down your prayers.

Written Prayers: Preparing or reading written prayers can provide structure and help you maintain concentration throughout the prayer. Establish a regular prayer time. Consistent practice can gradually improve your ability to focus during these moments. Keep your prayers short and simple, especially if you find it hard to maintain focus for longer periods. Gradually increase the length as your concentration improves. Focus on Thankfulness. Start with expressing gratitude. Focusing on what you are thankful for can help direct your thoughts and set a positive tone for your prayer.

Guided Prayer or Meditation Apps. Consider using apps designed for prayer or meditation. They often provide guided sessions that can help maintain focus.

Start a Prayer Journal. Write down your prayers in a journal. This can help organise your thoughts and stay engaged throughout the prayer.

Use visual aids such as religious symbols, images, or candles that help you focus and remind you of the purpose of your prayer.

Mindful Listening: Listen to uplifting gospel music or nature sounds that promote calmness, especially if complete silence is distracting. It may help create a focus-friendly background. Pray for assistance in focusing. Sometimes simply acknowledging your difficulty and asking for help can bring peace and focus to your prayer.

Be Patient. Concentration can take practice. Be patient with yourself and remember that it is normal to have wandering thoughts.

Regular practice and the use of these techniques can gradually help improve your ability to concentrate during prayer.

Handling distractions during prayer can be challenging, but you can minimise their impact with a few strategies. Acknowledge the Distraction: Instead of fighting the distraction, acknowledge it. Recognise what is pulling your focus away, then gently guide your attention back to prayer.

Set an Intention: Begin your prayer by setting a clear intention or focus for what you want to achieve or meditate on. This gives your mind a clear path to follow.

Create a Quiet Space: Choose a specific area for prayer that is free from noise and distractions. Try to use this space consistently to associate it with a peaceful mindset.

Clear Your Mind First: Before starting to pray, take a moment to clear your mind through deep breathing or a brief meditation. This helps in calming your thoughts.

Use Physical Reminders: Holding a prayer bead, rosary, or other item can help keep your focus by providing a tactile reminder of your purpose.

Keep It Short: Start with shorter prayer sessions if you are easily distracted. As your focus improves, gradually increase the length of your prayers.

Limit Screen Time. Turn off or put away electronic devices before you begin, as screens can be a major source of distraction. It reduces your concentration.

Structured Prayer: Use a structured format for your prayer. Having a set order can help you stay on track and minimise mind-wandering. I start with Adoration, then follow this with Confession, then supplication, which is what I seek from God. I end my prayer with thanksgiving.

Musical or Nature Sounds: If silence is distracting for you, consider playing soft hymn or gospel background music that can help create a conducive environment.

Mindful Breathing: Incorporate breathing exercises into your prayer routine. Focusing on your breath can help anchor your mind.

Schedule Your Prayer: Choose a time when you are least likely to be interrupted or when you are naturally more focused, such as early morning or late evening. In between, it is good to say short prayers if you can while driving, on public transport, or when doing household chores.

Reflect After Prayer: Spend a moment reflecting on the distractions you experienced. Understanding them can help you better manage them in the future. Reflect also on the goodness of God and what He has done for you. Listen for a response from God.

By implementing these strategies and remaining patient with yourself, you can learn to better handle distractions during prayer and improve your focus over time.

The Lord's Prayer, also known as the Our Father Prayer

1. Our Father, who art in heaven: This opening line acknowledges God as a loving and spiritual Father, emphasising His divine presence and our relationship with Him.

2. Hallowed be thy name: This phrase expresses reverence and respect for God's holy and sacred name, recognising His holiness and the need to honour Him.

3. Thy Kingdom come: This reflects the desire for God's rule and guidance in our lives, hoping for the realisation of His divine kingdom on Earth.

4. Thy will be done, on earth as it is in heaven: It is a request for God's will and purpose to be fulfilled in our world just as they are in heaven, highlighting submission to His plans.

5. Give us this day our daily bread: This symbolises reliance on God for our daily needs and sustenance, both physical and spiritual.

6. And forgive us our trespasses, as we forgive those who trespass against us: It emphasises the importance of seeking God's forgiveness for our wrongdoings and, equally, forgiving others, fostering compassion and reconciliation.

7. And lead us not into temptation: A plea for guidance away from situations that may lead us into sin, asking for strength to resist temptations.

8. But deliver us from evil: This concludes the prayer with a request for protection from all forms of evil and harm.

The Lord's Prayer serves as a comprehensive model for prayer, encouraging a balance of adoration, petition, repentance, and submission to God's will. Many Christians use it during worship as it encapsulates key elements of faith and devotion.

A confession prayer that resonates with a teenager

"Dear God, I come to you to say I am sorry. I know I have made mistakes and done things I should not have. I have let things such as anger, jealousy, and fear get the best of me. Please forgive me for the times I have hurt others, or when I have ignored you in my life. Help me to do better, to choose kindness and love. Give me strength to make good choices and be a better friend, family member, and

person. Thank you for always being there and loving me no matter what. Amen."

This prayer acknowledges the challenges teenagers face and asks for guidance and forgiveness in a relatable way.

Christian Supplication Prayer

Christian supplication prayer is a request for God's help and blessings:

A prayer of supplication is a humble request to God for help or blessings, often reflecting a deep awareness of one's needs. It differs from intercession, which focuses on others.

Supplication emphasises humility and faith, recognising God's sovereignty while seeking His guidance and support in life's challenges.

Here are some examples of supplication prayers in the Bible:

Here are some notable examples of supplication prayers from the Bible:

- Hannah's Prayer for a Child: Hannah earnestly prayed for a son, promising to dedicate him to God (1 Samuel 1:11)
- 1 Samuel 1:11 NIV: And she made a vow, saying, "LORD Almighty, if you will only look on your servant's misery and remember me, and not forget your servant but give her a son, then I will give him to the LORD for all the days of his life, and no razor will ever be used on his head."
- David's Prayer for Mercy: In Psalm 51, David humbly asked for forgiveness and a clean heart after his sins with Bathsheba (Psalm 51:1-12)
- When the prophet Nathan came to him after David had committed adultery with Bathsheba.

Young People, Faith & Mental Challenges

1 Have mercy on me, O God,

according to your unfailing love;

according to your great compassion

blot out my transgressions.

2 Wash away all my iniquity

and cleanse me from my sin.

3 For I know my transgressions,

and my sin is always before me.

4 Against you, you only, have I sinned

and done what is evil in your sight;

so you are right in your verdict

and justified when you judge.

5 Surely I was sinful at birth,

sinful from the time my mother conceived me.

6 Yet you desired faithfulness even in the womb;

you taught me wisdom in that secret place.

7 Cleanse me with hyssop, and I will be clean;

wash me, and I will be whiter than snow.

8 Let me hear joy and gladness;

let the bones you have crushed rejoice.

9 Hide your face from my sins

and blot out all my iniquity.

10 Create in me a pure heart, O God,

and renew a steadfast spirit within me.

11 Do not cast me from your presence

or take your Holy Spirit from me.

12 Restore to me the joy of your salvation

and grant me a willing spirit, to sustain me.

Hezekiah's Prayer for Healing: Hezekiah pleaded with God to extend his life when he was gravely ill (2 Kings 20:2-3)

2 Kings 20:2-3

New International Version

2 Hezekiah turned his face to the wall and prayed to the Lord, 3 "Remember, Lord, how I have walked before you faithfully and with wholehearted devotion and have done what is good in your eyes." And Hezekiah wept bitterly.

Jesus in Gethsemane: Jesus prayed fervently for strength and submitted to God's will before His crucifixion (Luke 22:42-44)

Luke 22:42-44

New International Version

42 "Father, if you are willing, take this cup from me; yet not my will, but yours be done." 43 An angel from heaven appeared to him and strengthened him. 44 And being in anguish, he prayed more earnestly, and his sweat was like drops of blood falling to the ground.

Esther's Prayer for Deliverance: Esther sought God's help to save her people from destruction (Esther 4:15-16)

Esther 4:15-16

New International Version

15 Then Esther sent this reply to Mordecai: 16 "Go, gather together all the Jews who are in Susa, and fast for me. Do not eat or drink for three days, night or day. I and my attendants will fast as you do. When this is done, I will go to the king, even though it is against the law. And if I perish, I perish."

How can I incorporate the Lord's Prayer into my meditation practice?

Incorporating the Lord's Prayer into your meditation practice can be a beautiful way to deepen your spiritual experience. Here is a step-by-step guide to help you get started:

1. Create a Quiet Space: Find a peaceful spot where you can meditate without distractions. Consider lighting a candle or playing soft music to set the mood.

2. Begin with Breathing: Start by taking slow, deep breaths to calm your mind and body. Focus on your breath to become centred and present.

3. Recite the Prayer Slowly: Begin saying the Lord's Prayer, either aloud or silently. Take your time with each line, allowing the words to resonate deeply.

4. Reflect on Each Phrase: After each line, pause to reflect on its meaning. Consider how it applies to your life and what personal insights you can draw from it.

    - "Our Father in heaven, hallowed be your name": Reflect on your relationship with the divine and the reverence you feel.

    - "Your kingdom come, your will be done": Consider your hopes for the world and how you can contribute to a greater good.

    - "Give us today our daily bread": Think about gratitude and your daily needs.

- "Forgive us our debts, as we also have forgiven our debtors": Contemplate forgiveness—both giving and receiving.

- "And lead us not into temptation, but deliver us from evil": Focus on your moral and spiritual challenges and your desire for guidance.

5. Silent Meditation: After reflecting on each line, enter a period of silent meditation, allowing your mind to rest on the insights or emotions that have emerged.

6. Closing Affirmation: Conclude your meditation with a personal affirmation or short prayer, expressing gratitude for the experience.

7. Journaling: After your meditation, consider jotting down any significant thoughts or feelings in a journal. This can help solidify your insights and track your spiritual growth over time.

By integrating the Lord's Prayer into meditation, you can create a rich practice that supports both your spiritual journey and personal growth.

The Bible offers many verses that provide comfort, hope, and encouragement, which can be uplifting for individuals facing mental illness. Here are some verses:

1. Psalm 34:17-18 - "The righteous cry out, and the Lord hears them; he delivers them from all their troubles. The Lord is close to the broken-hearted and saves those who are crushed in spirit."

2. Philippians 4:6-7 - "Do not be anxious about anything, but in every situation, by prayer and petition, with thanksgiving, present your requests to God. And the peace of God, which

transcends all understanding, will guard your hearts and your minds in Christ Jesus."

3. Isaiah 41:10 - "So do not fear, for I am with you; do not be dismayed, for I am your God. I will strengthen you and help you; I will uphold you with my righteous right hand."

4. 2 Timothy 1:7 - "For God has not given us a spirit of fear, but of power and of love and of a sound mind."

5. Matthew 11:28-30 - "Come to me, all you who are weary and burdened, and I will give you rest. Take my yoke upon you and learn from me, for I am gentle and humble in heart, and you will find rest for your souls. For my yoke is easy and my burden is light."

6. Psalm 42:11 - "Why, my soul, are you downcast? Why so disturbed within me? Put your hope in God, for I will yet praise him, my Saviour and my God."

7. John 14:27 - "Peace I leave with you; my peace I give you. I do not give to you as the world gives. Do not let your hearts be troubled and do not be afraid."

8. 1 Peter 5:7 - "Cast all your anxiety on him because he cares for you."

9. Psalm 23:4 - "Even though I walk through the darkest valley, I will fear no evil, for you are with me; your rod and your staff, they comfort me."

10. Proverbs 3:5-6 - "Trust in the Lord with all your heart and lean not on your own understanding; in all your ways submit to him, and he will make your paths straight."

Warning: These verses are not a substitute for professional medical advice, but they can provide spiritual strength and support. If you or someone you know is experiencing mental illness, it is important to seek guidance from a healthcare professional.

Here are some Bible verses that can bring comfort and help when dealing with anxiety:

1. Philippians 4:6-7: "Do not be anxious about anything, but in every situation, by prayer and petition, with thanksgiving, present your requests to God. And the peace of God, which transcends all understanding, will guard your hearts and your minds in Christ Jesus."

2. 1 Peter 5:7: "Cast all your anxiety on him because he cares for you."

3. Matthew 6:34: "Therefore do not worry about tomorrow, for tomorrow will worry about itself. Each day has enough trouble of its own."

4. Psalm 34:4: "I sought the Lord, and he answered me; he delivered me from all my fears."

5. John 14:27: "Peace I leave with you; my peace I give you. I do not give to you as the world gives. Do not let your hearts be troubled and do not be afraid."

6. Isaiah 41:10: "So do not fear, for I am with you; do not be dismayed, for I am your God. I will strengthen you and help you; I will uphold you with my righteous right hand."

7. Psalm 55:22: "Cast your cares on the Lord and he will sustain you; he will never let the righteous be shaken."

8. Proverbs 12:25: "Anxiety weighs down the heart, but a kind word cheers it up."

9. Jeremiah 29:11: "For I know the plans I have for you," declares the Lord, "plans to prosper you and not to harm you, plans to give you hope and a future."

10. Matthew 11:28-30: "Come to me, all you who are weary and burdened, and I will give you rest. Take my yoke upon you

and learn from me, for I am gentle and humble in heart, and you will find rest for your souls. For my yoke is easy and my burden is light."

Meditating on these verses can help bring peace and remind you that you are never alone in your journey.

Here are some Bible verses that address fear and offer comfort and encouragement:

1. 2 Timothy 1:7: "For God has not given us a spirit of fear, but of power and of love and of a sound mind."

2. Isaiah 41:13: "For I am the Lord your God, who takes hold of your right hand and says to you, Do not fear; I will help you."

3. Psalm 23:4: "Even though I walk through the darkest valley, I will fear no evil, for you are with me; your rod and your staff, they comfort me."

4. Joshua 1:9: "Have I not commanded you? Be strong and courageous. Do not be afraid; do not be discouraged, for the Lord your God will be with you wherever you go."

5. Psalm 27:1: "The Lord is my light and my salvation— whom shall I fear? The Lord is the stronghold of my life— of whom shall I be afraid?"

6. Isaiah 43:1: "But now, this is what the Lord says—he who created you, Jacob, he who formed you, Israel: 'Do not fear, for I have redeemed you; I have summoned you by name; you are mine.'"

7. Deuteronomy 31:6: "Be strong and courageous. Do not be afraid or terrified because of them, for the Lord your God goes with you; he will never leave you nor forsake you."

8. Psalm 56:3: "When I am afraid, I put my trust in you."

9. Proverbs 3:25-26: "Do not be afraid of sudden terror or of the ruin of the wicked, when it comes, for the Lord will be your confidence and will keep your foot from being caught."

10. Romans 8:15: "The Spirit you received does not make you slaves, so that you live in fear again; rather, the Spirit you received brought about your adoption to sonship. And by him we cry, 'Abba, Father.'"

These verses remind us of God's constant presence and support, encouraging us to rely on His strength rather than fear.

Here are some additional Bible verses that focus on overcoming fear:

1. Philippians 4:6-7: "Do not be anxious about anything, but in every situation, by prayer and petition, with thanksgiving, present your requests to God. And the peace of God, which transcends all understanding, will guard your hearts and your minds in Christ Jesus."

2. 1 John 4:18: "There is no fear in love. But perfect love drives out fear, because fear has to do with punishment. The one who fears is not made perfect in love."

3. Psalm 34:4: "I sought the Lord, and he answered me; he delivered me from all my fears."

4. Matthew 6:34: "Therefore do not worry about tomorrow, for tomorrow will worry about itself. Each day has enough trouble of its own."

5. Psalm 118:6: "The Lord is with me; I will not be afraid. What can mere mortals do to me?"

6. Hebrews 13:6: "So we say with confidence, 'The Lord is my helper; I will not be afraid. What can mere mortals do to me?'"

7. Romans 8:31: "What, then, shall we say in response to these things? If God is for us, who can be against us?"

8. John 14:27: "Peace I leave with you; my peace I give you. I do not give to you as the world gives. Do not let your hearts be troubled and do not be afraid."

9. Psalm 91:5: "You will not fear the terror of night, nor the arrow that flies by day."

10. Zephaniah 3:17: "The Lord your God is with you, the Mighty Warrior who saves. He will take great delight in you; in his love, he will no longer rebuke you but will rejoice over you with singing."

These verses emphasise the power of faith, love, and God's presence in helping us overcome fear. They inspire confidence and trust in divine protection and guidance.

1. Psalm 34:17-18: "The righteous cry out, and the LORD hears them; he delivers them from all their troubles. The LORD is close to the broken-hearted and saves those who are crushed in spirit."

2. These verses remind us that God HEARS our cries and is always near, especially during difficult times.

WHAT DOES PSALM 34:17-18 VERSE MEAN TO THE FAITH-MENTAL HEALTH PRACTITIONER?

It helps in practice by encouraging individuals to seek God's presence and comfort when feeling broken-hearted or crushed in spirit.

2. Philippians 4:6-7: "Do not be anxious about anything, but in everything by prayer and supplication with thanksgiving let your requests be made known to God. 7 And the peace of God, which surpasses all understanding, will guard your hearts and your minds in Christ Jesus."

These verses ENCOURAGE turning anxiety over to prayer, offering a practical way to cope with anxious thoughts. By focusing on prayer and gratitude, one can experience God's peace, which provides a sense of calm and reassurance.

3. 2 Timothy 1:7: This passage reminds us of the spirit of power, love, and sound mind given by God. It can empower individuals to focus on cultivating courage and love, rather than succumbing to fear.

4. Matthew 11:28-30: Jesus invites those who are weary and burdened to find rest in Him. This can be practised by intentionally seeking rest through spiritual practices such as prayer, meditation, or reflection, trusting that He will provide relief.

5. Isaiah 41:10: This verse reassures us that God is with us and will uphold us through challenges. Practically, it encourages individuals to lean on faith and trust that they are not alone in their struggles, fostering resilience.

Each verse offers a reminder of divine support and guidance, which can be vital in maintaining mental and emotional wellbeing.

Scripture Verses when faced with Anxiety and Depression

1. **Matthew 11:28:** "Come to me, all you who are weary and burdened, and I will give you rest." This verse encourages those carrying heavy burdens to seek solace in God's promise of comfort and rest.

Faith-based merchandise

2. **Psalms 34:17-18:** "The righteous cry out, and the LORD hears them; He delivers them from all their troubles. The LORD is close to the broken-hearted and saves those who are crushed in spirit." These verses affirm God's compassion towards those experiencing emotional pain.

3. **1 Peter 5:7:** "Cast all your anxiety on him because he cares for you." Peter's words remind us that we can turn to God with our worries, secure in knowing He cares deeply for us.

Chorus: Cast your burdens onto Jesus, for He cares for you.

4. **Philippians 4:6-7:** "Do not be anxious about anything, but in every situation, by prayer and petition, with thanksgiving, present your requests to God. And the peace of God, which transcends all understanding, will guard your hearts and your minds in Christ Jesus." This passage provides a practical strategy for dealing with anxiety: bringing your concerns to God through prayer.

5. **Psalms 94:19:** "When anxiety was great within me, your consolation brought me joy." Here, the Psalmist testifies to God's ability to bring joy in the midst of anxiety.

6. **Psalms 143:7-8:** "Answer me quickly, LORD; my spirit fails. Do not hide your face from me or I will be like those who go down to the pit. Let the morning bring me word of your unfailing love, for I have put my trust in you. Show me the way I should go, for I entrust my life to you." This poignant plea encapsulates the experience of depression and the longing for divine guidance.

7. **Isaiah 41:10:** "So do not fear, for I am with you; do not be dismayed, for I am your God. I will strengthen you and help you; I will uphold you with my righteous right hand." This verse offers reassurance of God's constant presence and support in our lives.

8. **Jeremiah 29:11:** "For I know the plans I have for you," declares the LORD, "plans to prosper you and not to harm you, plans to give you hope and a future." This beloved verse reminds us of God's benevolent intentions for our lives.

9. **2 Timothy 1:7:** "For God has not given us a spirit of fear, but of power and of love and of a sound mind." Timothy's words inspire confidence and resilience by focusing on God's empowering gifts.

10. **Romans 8:38-39:** "For I am convinced that neither death nor life, neither angels nor demons, neither the present nor the future, nor any powers, neither height nor depth, nor anything else in all creation, will be able to separate us from the love of God that is in Christ Jesus our Lord." This passage emphasises the unconditional and inseparable nature of God's love.

11. **Proverbs 12:25:** "Anxiety weighs down the heart, but a kind word cheers it up." This verse acknowledges the impact of anxiety on the heart and the power of kind words to uplift it.

12. **John 14:27:** "Peace I leave with you; my peace I give you. I do not give to you as the world gives. Do not let your hearts be troubled and do not be afraid." In this verse, Jesus promises His peace, a peace that surpasses worldly understanding.

13. **Psalms 42:11:** "Why, my soul, are you downcast? Why so disturbed within me? Put your hope in God, for I will yet praise him, my Saviour and my God." Here, the Psalmist exhorts us to place our hope in God, even in the midst of deep emotional distress.

14. **Joshua 1:9:** "Have I not commanded you? Be strong and courageous. Do not be afraid; do not be discouraged, for the LORD your God will be with you wherever you go." This verse encourages strength and courage, affirming God's constant presence.

15. **Psalms 37:23-24:** "The LORD makes firm the steps of the one who delights in him; though he may stumble, he will not

fall, for the LORD upholds him with his hand." These verses offer assurance that God supports us even when we stumble.

16. **Psalms 30:5:** "Weeping may stay for the night, but rejoicing comes in the morning." This verse beautifully portrays the transitory nature of sorrow and the promise of joy to come.

17. **2 Corinthians 1:3-4:** "Blessed be the God and Father of our Lord Jesus Christ, the Father of mercies and God of all comfort, who comforts us in all our affliction, so that we may be able to comfort those who are in any affliction, with the comfort with which we ourselves are comforted by God." This passage recognises God as the ultimate source of comfort in all our afflictions.

18. **Isaiah 43:2:** "When you pass through the waters, I will be with you; and when you pass through the rivers, they will not sweep over you. When you walk through the fire, you will not be burned; the flames will not set you ablaze." This verse assures us of God's protection during life's most daunting challenges.

19. **Psalms 46:1-2:** "God is our refuge and strength, an ever-present help in trouble. Therefore we will not fear, though the earth give way and the mountains fall into the heart of the sea." These verses portray God as a reliable refuge and source of strength in times of trouble.

20. **Deuteronomy 31:8:** "The LORD himself goes before you and will be with you; He will never leave you nor forsake you. Do not be afraid; do not be discouraged." This final verse reaffirms the promise of God's steadfast presence, encouragement, and support.

The Bible's timeless wisdom provides countless verses offering solace and hope. When depression and anxiety take hold, these scriptures remind us of God's enduring love, presence, and the peace

He provides. Through these divine words, we can find the strength and courage to navigate life's most difficult moments.

Integrating these Bible verses into your daily routine

Integrating these Bible verses into your daily routine can provide spiritual strength and comfort. Here are some practical ways to do so:

1. **Morning Reflection:**

    Start your day by reading one of the verses and reflecting on its meaning. Write your thoughts in a journal, noting how you can apply the verse to your daily challenges.

2. **Prayer and Meditation:**

    Incorporate the verses into your prayer routine. Meditate on the words, asking for understanding and strength to live them out. Focus on feeling God's presence and peace.

3. **Daily Reminders:**

    Write the verses on sticky notes and place them around your home, workspace, or anywhere you frequently visit. These visual cues can serve as constant reminders throughout the day.

4. **Mindfulness Practice:**

    Use the verses during mindfulness exercises. Repeat a verse slowly, focusing on each word, and think about how it relates to your current thoughts and feelings.

5. **Verse Memorisation:**

    Commit the verses to memory by reciting them daily. This internalisation can make them readily accessible when you need encouragement or guidance during tough moments.

6. **Evening Reflection:**

   At the end of the day, revisit the verse and consider how it influenced your actions or thoughts. Reflect on any positive changes or new insights gained and give thanks or pray for continued guidance.

7. **Community Sharing:**

   Discuss the verses with friends, family, or a support group. Sharing interpretations and understanding with others can deepen your connection to the text and provide additional insights.

8. **Creative Expression:**

   Get creative by incorporating the verses into art, music, or writing. Expressing these ideas creatively can reinforce their meaning and help you internalise their messages.

Meaningful part of your daily life, offering comfort and perspective in times of need.

Christian Worship: The Art of Worship

If you are interested in the concept of praise, *Shabach* is a Hebrew term describing a form of loud, triumphant praise that involves shouting and declaring God's works. It emphasises passing faith between generations and expressing joy through vocal celebration.

Towdah: Expresses an extended hand, thanksgiving, and expectation, looking both backward at faithfulness and forward to promises fulfilled. An extension of the hand. Thanksgiving. A confession. A sacrifice of praise. Thanksgiving for things not yet received. A choir of worshippers. Expectant praise. This is the praise that extends a hand of gratitude. This is the praise that looks back on the faithfulness of God and forward in anticipation of everything He promised that He will be doing in the future and in eternity. The

Bible says, "In God have I put my trust: I will not be afraid. What man can do to me? Vows made to You are binding upon me, O God; I will render praises (towdah) to you." (Psalm 56:11-12, NIV)

Zamar: Involves making music, celebrating with song, and playing instruments as a form of worship. To make music. To celebrate in song or music. To touch the strings or parts of a musical instrument. Music opens and softens our hearts! The Bible says…"I will sing a new song to You, O God; On a harp of ten strings I will make music (zamar) to You." (Psalm 144:9, NIV)

Yadah: Depicts worship with extended hands, showing reverence and reaching out to God in dependency. To revere or worship with extended hands. To hold out the hands. To throw a stone or arrow. This is the act of reaching for God, physically and spiritually in an act of dependence. Like a child reaching for the parent, we reach to God in obedience and He reaches back. The Bible says…"May the peoples praise (yadah) You, O God; may all the peoples praise (yadah) You." (Psalm 67:3, NIV)

Barak: Represents kneeling in adoration, offering a quiet, humble form of praise.

Kneeling as Bodily Worship

These examples demonstrate how kneeling expresses worship through the body.

To the Biblical mind, there is hardly any other way to worship. The Hebrew word for worship, *shaha*, has the physical meaning of bowing down. And so, when we see worship in the Bible, it is frequently associated with a physical act of humility and reverence. Alongside kneeling, there are the frequent actions of bowing down from the waist or lying prostrate on the ground.

"At the name of Jesus every knee should bow, in heaven and on earth and under the earth, and every tongue confess that Jesus Christ is Lord, to the glory of God the Father" (Philippians 2:10-11).

"O come, let us worship and bow down, let us kneel before the Lord, our Maker!" – Psalm 95:6

To bless God as an act of adoration. To salute. To thank. This is the quiet praise that humbly kneels in the presence of God. This is a grateful posture that goes low, with lifted eyes to see God's grace and majesty. The Bible says, "I will bless (barak) the LORD at all times; His praise (tehillah) shall continually be in my mouth." (Psalm 34:1, NKJV)

Tehillah: Stands for hymns and spontaneous songs of praise, emphasising the greatness of God. A song of praise. A new song. A spontaneous song. This is the praise that just bubbles out of you. These are the soul songs that are solely focused on applauding the greatness of God. The Bible says, "Yet you are enthroned as the Holy One; you are the one Israel praises (tehillah)." (Psalm 22:3, NIV)

In a world where faith and understanding of mental health often tread separate paths, this enlightening exploration seeks to unite them. *Faith and Mental Health* delves into the profound connection between spiritual beliefs and the human psyche, offering a fresh perspective on healing and resilience.

Through captivating narratives and expert insights, this book journeys through the experiences of individuals who have navigated their mental health challenges with the guiding light of faith. It raises poignant questions: How can spiritual practices contribute to emotional well-being? Can belief systems offer solace where traditional therapy treads?

With testimonies from mental health professionals and spiritual leaders, discover the untapped synergy between these domains. Uncover strategies to harness the power of faith as a tool for mental health recovery and growth.

Step into a groundbreaking dialogue with *Faith and Mental Health*, where spiritual paths lead to new horizons of healing and hope.

The Role of Faith Leaders in Promoting Mental Health

Engaging faith leaders in mental health education can make them effective allies in providing support and guidance to individuals and families.

Promoting understanding and acceptance across these areas allows individuals to thrive not only within their faith communities but also in all aspects of life, contributing to a healthier and more inclusive society.

Teenage Pregnancy, Faith and Mental Health

Addressing the intersection of teenage pregnancy, faith, and mental health requires a nuanced approach that respects individuals' beliefs while providing comprehensive support. Here are some considerations and strategies: By integrating faith, education, mental health support, and community involvement, we can create a compassionate and effective framework for supporting teenagers navigating pregnancy, mental health challenges, and faith-based considerations.

1. **Holistic Support Systems:** Develop support programmes that consider the mental, emotional, and spiritual needs of pregnant teenagers. Collaborate with mental health professionals, faith leaders, and social workers to provide a well-rounded support network.

2. **Access to Counselling:** Ensure that teenagers have access to counselling services that respect their faith backgrounds while addressing mental health concerns. Culturally sensitive counsellors can provide guidance that aligns with the individual's beliefs.

3. **Faith-Based Support Groups:** Encourage faith communities to create supportive environments for pregnant teenagers. These groups can offer acceptance and understanding while discouraging stigma and judgement.

4. **Education and Awareness:** Educate teenagers about sexual and reproductive health, mental health, and the potential challenges of early pregnancy in a way that respects their faith values. This includes sharing information that helps them make informed choices.

5. **Confidentiality and Trust:** Foster environments where teenagers feel safe sharing their experiences without fear of judgement. Maintaining confidentiality is crucial for building trust and encouraging open communication.

6. **Partnerships with Faith Organisations:** Work with faith organisations to create outreach programmes that focus on education, support, and the destigmatisation of teenage pregnancy and mental health issues.

7. **Parent and Family Involvement:** Engage parents and families in the conversation, providing them with resources to support their children emotionally, spiritually, and practically during and after pregnancy.

8. **Crisis Intervention:** Establish crisis intervention services for teenagers experiencing acute mental health crises or facing challenges related to pregnancy and parenthood. Prompt support can prevent long-term negative outcomes.

9. **Training for Faith Leaders:** Offer training for faith leaders on how to support teenagers dealing with pregnancy and mental health issues effectively. Faith leaders can play a key role in guiding their communities towards compassion and understanding.

10. **Peer Support Programmes:** Develop peer support programmes where teenagers can connect with others who have had similar experiences. These programmes can reduce feelings of isolation and build resilience.

Black, Asian and Minority Ethnic (BAME) Communities

This content mentions discrimination or discriminatory violence (such as homophobia, racism, sexism and ableism), suicide or suicidal thoughts, self-harm, trauma, depression and anxiety. Please read with care. There are details of where to find help at the bottom of this page.

We recognise that not everyone likes the term BAME. It covers a wide range of people with diverse needs, and placing all those people into a single group can be problematic. However, it can be useful to show that people who are not White British can face specific issues and challenges because of their ethnicity. We use BAME here as a shorthand term but acknowledge people can find it unsatisfactory or prefer to use a different term to describe themselves.

Contents

- Are rates of mental ill-health different for people from a BAME background?
- What can affect the mental health of people from BAME communities?
- What barriers can BAME people face when getting support?

Are rates of mental ill-health different for people from a BAME background?

Rates of mental health problems can be higher for some BAME groups than for White people. For example:

- Black men are more likely to have experienced a psychotic disorder in the last year than White men.
- Black people are four times more likely to be detained under the Mental Health Act than White people.
- Older South Asian women are an at-risk group for suicide.
- Refugees and asylum seekers are more likely to experience mental health problems than the general population, including higher rates of depression, anxiety, and PTSD.

Some groups have better mental health. For example:

- Suicidal thoughts and self-harm were less common in Asian people than in White people.
- Mental ill-health is lower among Chinese people than among White people.

With all these statistics, it is important to note that they may not reflect the true extent of mental health problems among BAME groups. This is because not much data is available and also because BAME people may be less likely to report mental health problems.

What can affect the mental health of people from BAME communities?

As well as the factors that can affect everyone's mental health, people from BAME communities may also contend with racism, inequality, and mental health stigma.

Racism and discrimination

Racism can range from micro-aggressions (subtle but offensive comments) to explicit hurtful words, to verbal or physical aggression. Experiencing racism can be very stressful and negatively affect overall health and mental health.

Exposure to racism may increase the likelihood of experiencing mental health problems such as psychosis and depression.

If you have experienced racism, read our page on stigma and discrimination. While the page is about mental health, the tips on making a complaint are relevant to all discrimination cases. There is also a list of organisations that can help and advise you.

Social and economic inequalities

People from BAME communities often face disadvantages in society which can increase the risk of developing mental health problems.

Mental health stigma

Different communities understand and talk about mental health in different ways.

In some communities, mental health problems are rarely recognised or spoken about. They may be seen as shameful or embarrassing. This can discourage people from talking about their mental health or seeing their GP for help.

What barriers can BAME people face when getting support?

People from BAME backgrounds have the same right as everyone else to access mental treatment and services. But research shows BAME people can face barriers to getting help, including:

- Not recognising they have a mental illness because mental health was stigmatised or never talked about in their community.
- Not knowing that help is available or where to go to get it.
- Language barriers.

- Turning to family or friends rather than professional support, especially for people who do not trust formal healthcare services.

- Financial barriers, such as paying for private counselling.

- Not feeling listened to or understood by healthcare professionals.

- White professionals who do not understand their experiences of racism or discrimination.

Navigating Your Way to Good Mental Health

Imagine you are on a journey towards better mental health, and here is how you might navigate it:

Trouble is always round the corner

1. First, recognise that there is a challenge. It is like identifying a roadblock on your path. This awareness and acknowledgement is the first, crucial step.

2. Reach Out. You decide to reach out for help. This could be talking to a friend, family member, or a mental health professional. Imagine it as consulting a map or seeking guidance to ensure you are heading in the right direction.

3. Understand your feelings. With support from professionals such as therapists or counsellors, you gain a better understanding of your feelings and thoughts. It is similar to understanding the terrain or layout of a journey; knowing when and where the path might become rough.

4. Acquire new skills. You learn new coping skills through therapy (such as CBT, DBT, or MBT). These skills help you handle obstacles more effectively, much like learning to navigate using a compass or GPS.

5. Practise Self-Care. Incorporate self-care into your routine. This involves activities that promote physical and mental well-being, such as ensuring your vehicle has fuel, or the electric vehicle battery is charged, in readiness for the journey.

6. Surround yourself with supportive people who uplift and encourage you. It is akin to having fellow travellers or guides who assist you on your way.

7. Set small, achievable goals on your journey to track progress. Each goal achieved is like reaching a milestone marker, giving a sense of accomplishment.

8. Practise mindfulness, staying present and aware, reducing stress, and improving focus on your journey, much like enjoying the scenery along the way.

9. Adapt and Overcome. Challenges are part of the process. When setbacks occur, you learn to adapt and overcome them, similar to navigating through unexpected detours with patience and resilience.

10. Celebrate Progress. You celebrate even the small victories. Acknowledging how far you have come fuels motivation, much like savouring each completed stage of your journey.

Let's Talk Cannabis

Whilst cannabis offers therapeutic benefits and recreational enjoyment for many, its effects are varied, and it poses certain risks, particularly related to mental health.

Uses of Cannabis

1. **Medical Use:**
    - Treats symptoms such as chronic pain, nausea (especially from chemotherapy), muscle spasms from conditions like multiple sclerosis, and more.
    - Often used as a part of palliative care for terminal illnesses.

2. **Recreational Use:**
    - Consumed for its psychoactive effects, typically leading to relaxation, altered perceptions, and euphoria.

Effects of Cannabis

1. **Short-term Effects:**
    - Euphoria, altered senses (e.g., seeing brighter colours), altered sense of time, relaxation, and increased appetite.
    - Potential negative effects include impaired memory, altered judgement, and coordination issues.

2. **Long-term Effects:**
    - Possible development of Cannabis Use Disorder.
    - Potential impact on brain development, especially in young users.

Risks of Cannabis

1. **Mental Health Risks:**
    - Prolonged use can lead to or aggravate mental health issues such as anxiety, depression, or psychosis,

particularly in individuals predisposed to these conditions.

- Higher THC concentrations may increase the risk of psychosis or schizophrenia.

2. **Physical Health Risks:**
    - Respiratory issues from smoked cannabis.
    - Increased heart rate may pose risks for those with heart conditions.

3. **Addiction Risk:**
    - Approximately 9% of users may become dependent, with increased risk in those who start using at a young age or use frequently.

4. **Legal and Safety Risks:**
    - Legal issues depending on geographic location.
    - Impairment risks, especially when driving or operating machinery.

Cannabis and Mental Health

1. **Anxiety and Depression:**
    - Whilst some use cannabis to ease symptoms of anxiety or depression, excessive use might worsen these conditions.

2. **Psychosis and Schizophrenia:**
    - Strong association between cannabis use, particularly in adolescents, and the onset of psychotic disorders.

- Individuals with a family history of such disorders should exercise caution.

3. **Medication Interactions:**
    - Cannabis can interact with psychiatric medications, altering their efficacy or increasing side effects.

Cannabis Use Disorder

Cannabis Use Disorder (CUD) is a condition characterised by the problematic use of cannabis, leading to significant impairment or distress. It is recognised as a diagnosable condition often classified by its severity: mild, moderate, or severe. Here are the key symptoms and features:

1. **Increased Tolerance:**
    - Needing to use more cannabis to achieve the desired effect or experiencing diminished effects with the same amount.

2. **Withdrawal Symptoms:**
    - Experiencing symptoms such as irritability, sleep difficulties, decreased appetite, anxiety, or cravings when not using the substance.

3. **Cravings:**
    - Having a strong desire or urge to use cannabis.

4. **Loss of Control:**
    - Consuming more cannabis than intended, or over a longer period than planned.

5. **Unsuccessful Control Efforts:**
    - Repeated attempts to cut down or control the use of cannabis without success.

6. **Time Consumption:**
    - Spending a considerable amount of time obtaining, using, or recovering from the effects of cannabis.

7. **Neglecting Responsibilities:**
    - Failing to fulfil major role obligations at work, school, or home due to cannabis use.

8. **Social and Interpersonal Problems:**
    - Continuing cannabis use despite persistent social or interpersonal problems caused or exacerbated by its effects.

9. **Reduction in Activities:**
    - Giving up or reducing important social, occupational, or recreational activities because of cannabis use.

10. **Use in Risky Situations:**
    - Recurrent cannabis use in situations where it is physically hazardous, such as driving.

11. **Continued Use Despite Problems:**
    - Continuing to use cannabis despite knowing it is causing or worsening a physical or psychological issue.

Recognising the signs of Cannabis Use Disorder can be crucial for seeking appropriate help and treatment, which may include behavioural therapies, support groups, or, in some cases, medication.

Cannabis and Young People

Cannabis Use Disorder (CUD) is a medical condition characterised by problematic cannabis use that significantly impairs daily life. It includes habitual consumption even when it causes harm, difficulty stopping despite wanting to quit, and experiencing withdrawal symptoms when not using.

Key Features:

- **Craving and Dependence:** A strong urge to use cannabis, leading to frequent use and increasing tolerance.
- **Withdrawal Symptoms:** Irritability, mood swings, and sleep disturbances upon stopping.
- **Impact on Daily Life:** Neglecting personal or professional responsibilities, social withdrawal, or engaging in risky behaviours due to use.

Treatment Options:

- **Behavioural Therapies:** Cognitive Behavioural Therapy (CBT) and motivational enhancement can be effective.
- **Support Groups:** Joining groups such as Marijuana Anonymous can provide shared experiences and support.
- **Medication:** Though not widely used, some medications might help manage withdrawal symptoms or reduce cravings.

Signs of Cannabis Use Disorder (CUD) can vary, but common indicators include:

1. Increased Tolerance: Needing more cannabis to achieve the same effects.
2. Withdrawal Symptoms: Experiencing irritability, anxiety, sleep disturbances, or appetite changes when not using.

3. **Unsuccessful Attempts to Quit:** Trying to cut down or stop using cannabis but failing repeatedly.

4. **Loss of Control:** Using cannabis in larger amounts or over a longer period than intended.

5. **Neglecting Responsibilities:** Failing to fulfil obligations at work, school, or home due to cannabis use.

6. **Significant Time Spent:** Spending a lot of time obtaining, using, or recovering from cannabis.

7. **Reduced Activities:** Giving up or reducing social, occupational, or recreational activities due to cannabis use.

8. **Continued Use Despite Problems:** Persisting in use despite knowing it causes or worsens physical, social, or psychological issues.

9. **Cravings:** Having strong urges or desires to use cannabis.

Recognising these signs early is important for seeking help and managing the disorder effectively.

How you will know you have it? Cannabis addiction

Here is how you might recognise if you are experiencing cannabis use disorder:

1. **Noticing a Higher Tolerance:** You find that you are using more cannabis to feel the effects that you used to get with less.

2. **Experiencing Discomfort When Not Using:** When you stop or reduce your use, you might feel more irritable, anxious, or have trouble sleeping and eating.

3. **Difficulty Quitting:** You have tried to cut back or quit using cannabis, but it has not gone as planned.

4. **Using More Than Intended:** Every so often, you might find yourself using more cannabis than you meant to or using it for a longer time.

5. **Neglecting Responsibilities:** Your use may be affecting your job, studies, or duties at home.

6. **Spending a Lot of Time on Cannabis:** A significant amount of your time might revolve around obtaining, using, or recovering from cannabis.

7. **Skipping Activities:** You stop participating in hobbies or social events because of cannabis use.

8. **Continued Use Despite Knowing It Causes Issues:** You recognise that cannabis use is causing problems in your life, but you continue using it.

9. **Feeling Cravings:** There is a strong desire or urge to use cannabis that is hard to resist.

If you notice these signs in yourself, talking to a professional for more guidance might be helpful.

Effective Ways to Reduce Cannabis Use

Reducing cannabis use can be a positive step towards improved health and well-being. Here are some effective strategies you may wish to consider:

1. **Set Clear Goals**: Decide how much you want to reduce your use or whether you want to quit entirely. Having clear goals can help guide your efforts.

2. **Understand Your Triggers**: Pay attention to situations, emotions, or environments that encourage you to use cannabis. Once you know your triggers, you can try to avoid or manage them.

3. **Develop New Routines**: Finding alternative activities to replace cannabis use can be helpful. Engage in hobbies, exercise, or take up activities you enjoy.

4. **Seek Support**: Talk to friends, family, or mentors who support your decision. Joining a support group or seeking professional help can also be highly beneficial.

5. **Practise Mindfulness and Relaxation**: Techniques such as meditation, yoga, or deep breathing can help reduce stress and the urge to use cannabis.

6. **Track Your Progress**: Keep a journal or use an app to monitor your usage and celebrate your milestones. Seeing your progress can motivate you to continue.

7. **Gradual Reduction**: If quitting abruptly seems challenging, consider gradually reducing the amount you use over time.

8. **Healthy Lifestyle Choices**: Focus on a balanced diet, regular exercise, and sufficient sleep to improve your overall well-being.

9. **Educate Yourself**: Learn about the effects of cannabis and how it impacts your mind and body. Knowledge can reinforce your decision to cut back.

10. **Seek Professional Help**: If self-help strategies are not enough, a counsellor or therapist specialising in addiction can provide guidance tailored to your needs.

Remember, it is acceptable to have setbacks. What is important is staying committed to your goal and reaching out for help when required.

Faith and Cannabis Use

Deliverance ministry is a Christian spiritual practice focused on freeing individuals from negative influences or spiritual oppression.

In relation to addressing cannabis use disorder, deliverance ministry might be considered by some as a spiritual approach to supplement conventional treatment methods. Here are a few ways it might work alongside efforts to reduce cannabis use:

1. **Spiritual Guidance and Support**: Practitioners of deliverance ministry provide spiritual guidance, helping individuals strengthen their faith and find spiritual resources to overcome addiction.

2. **Prayers and Healing Sessions**: Deliverance ministers may engage in prayer and healing sessions aimed at providing spiritual comfort and encouragement to those struggling with cannabis use disorder.

3. **Addressing Spiritual Roots**: The ministry might focus on uncovering and addressing any spiritual or emotional factors believed to contribute to substance use.

4. **Community and Fellowship**: Churches or spiritual communities that practise deliverance ministry can offer a supportive network, creating a sense of belonging and accountability.

5. **Integrating Faith into Recovery**: Encouraging individuals to integrate their faith and spiritual practices into their recovery journey may help them find strength and hope.

It is important to note that while spiritual practices can be supportive, they should not replace evidence-based treatments for cannabis use disorder. Combining spiritual support with traditional therapies, such as counselling and medical treatment, can provide a more comprehensive approach to recovery. Always consider consulting healthcare professionals to develop a balanced treatment plan.

Limitations of the Effectiveness of Deliverance Ministry for Addiction

The effectiveness of deliverance ministry for addiction is a complex topic, as it largely depends on individual beliefs, the specific approach of the ministry, and the context in which it is applied. Here are some points to consider:

1. **Spiritual and Emotional Support**: For those with strong faith, deliverance ministry can offer significant spiritual and emotional support. This can enhance motivation and provide hope, which are valuable in the recovery process.

2. **Community and Accountability**: Being part of a faith-based community can foster a sense of belonging and accountability. This support network can be crucial in maintaining motivation and preventing relapse.

3. **Holistic Approach**: Deliverance ministry may address not only the physical aspects of addiction, but also spiritual and emotional factors, making it a holistic approach for some individuals.

4. **Varied Outcomes**: The effectiveness can vary greatly among individuals. Some may find substantial benefit from incorporating spiritual practices into their recovery, whilst others may not experience the same impact.

5. **Lack of Scientific Evidence**: There is limited scientific research on the efficacy of deliverance ministry specifically for addiction treatment. Traditional medical and psychological approaches such as therapy and medication have more empirical support.

6. **Integration with Conventional Treatments**: When combined with conventional treatment methods such as counselling, behavioural therapy, or medication, deliverance

ministry might enhance overall well-being and recovery outcomes for some individuals.

7. **Potential for Misinterpretation**: It is important that deliverance ministry does not discourage individuals from seeking necessary medical or psychological treatment. It should be considered complementary rather than a replacement for professional care.

Overall, deliverance ministry can benefit some individuals in their journey to overcome addiction, particularly those who strongly value spiritual practices. However, it is most effective when used in conjunction with evidence-based treatments and professional guidance. Each person's experience with addiction and recovery is unique, so a personalised approach that considers all aspects of an individual's life is often the most effective strategy.

Faith and Cannabis Use Disorder

Faith can play a significant role in addressing cannabis use disorder, providing both challenges and opportunities for individuals seeking recovery. Here is how faith intersects with this issue:

1. **Moral and Ethical Framework**: For some, faith provides a moral or ethical framework that discourages substance use, including cannabis. This can serve as a strong motivator for those trying to overcome their addiction.

2. **Community Support**: Faith communities often offer a supportive environment that can help individuals struggling with cannabis use disorder. These communities can provide emotional support, accountability, and a sense of belonging.

3. **Spiritual Practices**: Engaging in spiritual practices, such as prayer or meditation, can offer comfort and a means of coping with cravings or stress associated with recovery. Such practices can help individuals find peace and strengthen their resolve.

4. **Role of Clergy and Faith Leaders**: Clergy and faith leaders can play a pivotal role in counselling individuals, offering guidance and spiritual support. They can also help individuals connect with resources and support groups.

5. **Integration with Treatment**: While faith can be a powerful component of recovery, it is often most effective when integrated with professional treatment options. Combining faith-based approaches with conventional therapies can provide a comprehensive strategy for recovery.

6. **Challenges**: It is important to recognise that some individuals may struggle if they perceive their substance use as a failure of faith. Encouragement and reassurance from the faith community can help in overcoming feelings of guilt or shame.

7. **Faith-Based Programmes**: Some recovery programmes are specifically tailored to individuals of faith, incorporating spiritual teachings and values into their approach. These programmes can resonate more with individuals seeking a faith-aligned recovery process.

In summary, faith can be a vital element in recovery from cannabis use disorder for many individuals, offering motivation, support, and guidance. However, it should complement rather than replace evidence-based treatments, ensuring a holistic approach to recovery. Each person's journey is unique, and blending faith with professional care can often lead to the best outcomes.

Faith-Based Recovery Programmes for Cannabis Use Disorder

Several faith-based recovery programmes can support individuals dealing with cannabis use disorder. These programmes integrate spiritual teachings and community support as central components of their approach. Here are a few notable ones:

1. **Celebrate Recovery**: A Christian-based programme that helps individuals overcome a variety of addictions, including cannabis use disorder. It focuses on healing through the power of Christ and community support.

2. **Alcoholics Anonymous (AA) and Narcotics Anonymous (NA)**: Whilst not exclusively Christian, these programmes incorporate spiritual elements and belief in a higher power, which can appeal to individuals seeking a faith-based approach. Many groups hold meetings in churches and have a spiritual foundation.

3. **SMART Recovery with a Faith-Based Approach**: Some SMART Recovery groups provide a secular, evidence-based approach to recovery that can be adapted to include a faith component, depending on the preferences of participants.

4. **Jewish Alcoholics, Chemically Dependent Persons, and Significant Others (JACS)**: A programme specifically for Jewish individuals, offering a supportive community and resources for those dealing with addiction within a cultural and faith-based context.

5. **Islamic Recovery Programmes**: These programmes focus on Islamic teachings and principles to provide support for individuals struggling with addiction, emphasising community and faith in Allah as part of the healing process.

6. **12-Step Programmes with Religious Affiliations**: Many 12-step programmes are hosted by various religious organisations, allowing participants to incorporate their specific faith traditions into the recovery process.

7. **Latter-day Saint (Mormon) Addiction Recovery Programme**: This programme uses a 12-step model aligned with LDS beliefs, offering support for members of the church dealing with addictions.

These programmes provide a blend of spiritual guidance, community support, and practical tools for recovery. It is important for individuals to find a programme that resonates with their personal beliefs and recovery needs to enhance effectiveness.

Common Side Effects of Antipsychotic Drugs

Barriers to Treatment Engagement: Erectile Dysfunction and Antipsychotics

Erectile dysfunction (ED) can indeed be a challenging side effect of antipsychotic medications. Here is a brief guide on how to manage and communicate about this concern:

1. **Understand the Connection**:
    - Some antipsychotics can impact sexual function by affecting neurotransmitters in the brain. It is important to recognise that this is a known side effect for many, and you are not alone in experiencing it.

2. **Actively Communicate**:
    - Share specifics about your symptoms with your healthcare provider, such as when they began, their severity, and their impact on your daily life.

3. **Consider Medication Adjustments**:
    - *Alternative Medications*: Discuss the possibility of switching to another antipsychotic with a potentially lower impact on sexual function.
    - *Dosage Changes*: Sometimes adjusting the dosage under medical guidance can help reduce side effects without compromising effectiveness.

4. **Explore Additional Treatments:**

    o *ED Medications*: Ask if medications such as sildenafil (Viagra) or tadalafil (Cialis) could be safely added to manage erectile dysfunction.

    o *Therapy and Counselling*: Sometimes, addressing psychological aspects can also provide relief.

5. **Lifestyle Measures:**

    o Exercise and diet can impact overall health and may contribute to improving sexual function.

    o Reducing alcohol consumption and quitting smoking can also positively affect erectile dysfunction.

6. **Seek Specialist Advice:**

    o Consider consulting a specialist, such as an endocrinologist or urologist, who can offer targeted advice and treatment options.

7. **Empower Yourself with Information:**

    o Gaining a deeper understanding of your medication and its side effects can help you make informed decisions about your treatment plan.

Approaching this issue with openness and a collaborative mindset can help you and your healthcare provider find a viable solution.

Cosmetic side effects: Enlarged breast and lactation in men following antipsychotics. A cause of stigma

Enlarged breasts (gynaecomastia) and lactation (galactorrhoea) in men can be distressing side effects of certain antipsychotic medications, and they can indeed carry a stigma. Here is a closer look at what causes these side effects and how to address them:

Causes

1. **Hormonal Changes:**
    - Antipsychotics can increase levels of prolactin, a hormone typically involved in milk production in women. Elevated prolactin can lead to breast enlargement and, occasionally, lactation in men.

2. **Medication Impact:**
    - Some antipsychotics, particularly first-generation ones and certain second-generation ones such as risperidone, are more likely to influence prolactin levels.

Addressing the Stigma

1. **Education and Awareness:**
    - Understanding that these are medical side effects can help reduce the stigma. It is a biological response to medication, not a reflection of masculinity or personal choice.

2. **Open Conversations:**
    - Discuss openly with healthcare providers and consider conversations with supportive friends or family. Normalising these discussions can help mitigate feelings of embarrassment or isolation.

Management Strategies

1. **Medication Review:**
    - Talk to your doctor about switching to an antipsychotic with a lower risk of causing hormonal changes. There might be alternatives that work better for you without these side effects.

2. **Potential Treatments:**
   - Hormonal treatments or medications to reduce prolactin levels may be an option. Your healthcare provider can discuss these with you.

3. **Support Groups:**
   - Connecting with others who experience similar side effects can provide support and reduce feelings of isolation.

4. **Lifestyle Considerations:**
   - Focus on healthy lifestyle choices, such as regular exercise and a balanced diet, which can help manage some side effects.

5. **Professional Counselling:**
   - Psychological support or counselling can assist in dealing with any emotional distress or social anxiety associated with these side effects.

The common antipsychotics that cause gynaecomastia

What is gynaecomastia?

Some antipsychotic medications are more commonly associated with causing gynaecomastia due to their effects on prolactin levels. Here are a few of them:

1. **Risperidone (Risperdal):**
   - Known for potentially raising prolactin levels significantly, leading to gynaecomastia and, in some cases, galactorrhoea.

2. **Haloperidol (Haldol):**
   - A first-generation antipsychotic that can also elevate prolactin levels.

3. **Paliperidone (Invega):**
   - Similar to risperidone, it can cause an increase in prolactin and may result in gynaecomastia.

4. **Chlorpromazine (Thorazine):**
   - Another first-generation antipsychotic associated with prolactin elevation.

5. **Fluphenazine (Prolixin):**
   - Also linked to increased prolactin levels, potentially causing gynaecomastia.

It is important to note that individual responses can vary, and not everyone taking these medications will experience these side effects. If you or someone you know is dealing with these effects, consulting with a healthcare provider for a review of the medication and potential alternatives is recommended.

The Future – trailblazers into the next decade

I am In Me

"I AM IN ME" is a charitable organisation focused on supporting young people, particularly from disadvantaged backgrounds, to achieve their full potential. The charity emphasises social mobility, promoting the idea that individuals can transcend their circumstances through empowerment and opportunity. They offer guidance and resources to help young people develop their purpose, passion, and identity, fostering sustainable futures. The organisation encourages partnerships to expand its impact and assist communities in need. The charity has a close working relationship with the church and has an impactful presence in the London Borough of Lambeth. The founder and CEO of the charity "I AM IN ME" is Sasha Gay Smith, is a personal development specialist with a BA in Business with Psychology, a teaching qualification, and experience as a mentor and coach. Sasha leads the charity, which specialises in holistic and bespoke personal development training and career services for young people, particularly those from disadvantaged background

Through these initiatives, the New Testament Church of God, Brixton, is committed to creating a supportive and nurturing environment that prioritises mental health as a critical component of overall well-being.

Types of therapies that work best in conjunction with faith

When integrating faith into mental health recovery, several types of therapies can work well in conjunction with an individual's spiritual beliefs:

1. **Cognitive Behavioural Therapy (CBT):** Focuses on identifying and challenging negative thought patterns. It pairs well with faith by encouraging individuals to replace negative thoughts with positive, faith-based affirmations.

2. **Mindfulness-Based Therapy:** This includes practices such as mindfulness-based stress reduction (MBSR) and mindfulness-based cognitive therapy (MBCT). These therapies can integrate meditation and mindfulness practices that align with many spiritual traditions.

3. **Acceptance and Commitment Therapy (ACT):** ACT encourages individuals to accept their thoughts and feelings and commit to actions that reflect their values. This aligns well with spiritual practices that emphasise acceptance and values-driven living.

4. **Narrative Therapy:** This therapy allows individuals to reshape their personal stories. Faith narratives can provide new perspectives, helping individuals find meaning and purpose through their religious beliefs.

5. **Pastoral Counselling:** Provided by trained counsellors who incorporate spiritual guidance, this type of therapy honours the client's faith perspective while addressing psychological and emotional issues.

6. **Existential Therapy:** Focuses on life's big questions, purpose, and meaning, aligning well with spiritual beliefs that address existential concerns.

7. **Art and Music Therapy:** These can incorporate religious or spiritual themes, allowing individuals to express their faith creatively as part of the healing process.

Each type of therapy can be tailored to respect and incorporate an individual's faith or spiritual beliefs, creating a more personalised and meaningful treatment experience. Individuals need to discuss their faith and spiritual preferences with their therapist to ensure the approach is both respectful and effective.

Faith in Action

Narrative therapy can be adapted to include religious beliefs in several meaningful ways:

1. **Incorporating Religious Texts:** Clients can explore stories from their religious texts that resonate with their personal narratives. These stories often provide insights or alternative perspectives that can be healing or empowering.

2. **Identifying Faith-Based Themes:** Utilising themes from religious beliefs, such as redemption, grace, and forgiveness,

can help reshape personal narratives. Clients can reflect on how these themes influence their lives and personal stories.

3. **Creating Parallels with Spiritual Journeys:** Encourage clients to see their life as a spiritual journey or pilgrimage. This perspective allows them to frame their experiences as part of a larger, meaningful path aligned with their faith.

4. **Using Religious Imagery and Metaphors:** Religious imagery can be powerful in helping clients understand and reframe their experiences. Metaphors such as "crossing the Red Sea" or "finding inner peace" can make abstract concepts more tangible.

5. **Exploring Values and Morals:** Clients can be guided to explore how their faith-based values influence their life decisions and relationships. This can provide clarity and direction in rewriting their narrative.

6. **Prayer and Spiritual Reflection:** Encourage prayer or spiritual reflection moments during sessions. This integrates a client's spiritual practice into the therapeutic process, offering them comfort and guidance.

7. **Highlighting Community and Support:** Emphasise the role of religious communities in the client's narrative. These communities can provide support, companionship, and shared faith, which can be crucial in healing.

By honouring and incorporating a client's faith into narrative therapy, therapists can help them construct a story that is both empowering and deeply connected to their spiritual beliefs. It is important for therapists to remain sensitive and respectful to each individual's unique religious views and practices.

Some effective questions to ask clients about their spiritual beliefs

Exploring a client's spiritual beliefs can provide deep insights into their values, motivations, and coping mechanisms. Here are some effective questions to facilitate this exploration:

1. Can you describe your spiritual or religious beliefs?

    o This open-ended question invites clients to share what is most important to them in their spiritual life.

2. How do your beliefs influence your everyday life and decisions?

    o It helps them understand the practical role of spirituality in their daily experiences.

3. Do you find particular stories or teachings from your faith especially meaningful?

    o This can reveal sources of inspiration or guidance for the client.

4. How does your spiritual journey impact your current situation or challenges?

    o This question encourages clients to connect their spiritual path with their present circumstances.

5. What role does prayer or meditation play in your life?

    o Understanding their spiritual practices can offer insights into their coping strategies and sources of comfort.

6. In what ways do you feel supported by your spiritual or religious community?

- Exploring the community aspect can highlight external support systems.

7. Have there been times when your beliefs have been challenged or strengthened?
    - Discussing these moments can reveal personal growth and how clients navigate conflict or adversity within their faith.

8. What spiritual goals or aspirations do you have?
    - This helps them understand their hopes and how spirituality ties into their future vision.

9. How do you incorporate spirituality into your healing process or mental well-being?
    - Exploring this can guide therapeutic approaches that align with their spiritual views.

10. Are any rituals or traditions particularly important to you?
    - Identifying meaningful rituals can be significant for understanding a client's cultural and spiritual identity.

These questions are designed to open up meaningful dialogue, allowing clients to express their spiritual identity and how it relates to their broader life narrative.

How to approach a client about their spiritual beliefs?

Approaching a client about their spiritual beliefs requires sensitivity, respect, and an open mind. Here is how you can create a safe and supportive environment for this conversation:

1. **Establish Trust:**
    - Build a solid foundation of trust with your client. Ensure that they feel safe and respected in your professional relationship before delving into personal topics such as spirituality.

2. **Create an Open Environment:**
    - Assure your client that this is a judgement-free zone. Encourage them to share as much or as little as they feel comfortable with, emphasising that their beliefs are valuable and respected.

3. **Use Open-Ended Questions:**
    - Begin with broad, open-ended questions that allow clients to share at their own pace. For example, "Would you like to share any aspects of your spiritual beliefs with me?"

4. **Be Respectful and Nonjudgemental:**
    - Approach the topic with curiosity and respect. Avoid making assumptions or judgements about their beliefs. Show genuine interest in understanding their perspective.

5. **Acknowledge Diversity:**
    - Recognise and respect the diversity of spiritual beliefs. Understand that spirituality can mean different things to different people, from religious practices to personal philosophies.

6. **Integrate When Relevant:**
    - Introduce the topic when it is relevant to the client's goals or challenges. You might say, "Some people

find their spiritual beliefs helpful in navigating situations like this. Is this something that resonates with you?"

7. **Be Mindful of Timing:**
   - Choose an appropriate time to discuss spirituality, such as when the conversation naturally leads in that direction. Ensure the client is receptive and in a good place to engage with this subject.

8. **Encourage Reflection:**
   - Encourage clients to reflect on how their beliefs align with their values and life choices. Ask questions such as, "How do your spiritual beliefs guide you in your life?"

9. **Offer Continual Support:**
   - Let clients know that they can revisit discussions about spirituality at any time. Their comfort and willingness to share may evolve over time.

10. **Seek Consent:**
    - Always seek permission before exploring spiritual beliefs. A simple, "Would you like to explore how your spiritual beliefs relate to this topic?" is respectful and empowering.

By approaching this conversation with empathy, respect, and an open mind, you create a safe space for clients to explore and discuss their spirituality as part of their personal and professional journey.

Examples of open-ended questions to ask clients

Here are some open-ended questions that you can ask clients to encourage deeper discussion and reflection:

1. "Can you tell me more about what brings you joy and fulfilment in your life?"
2. "How do you typically approach challenges or difficult situations?"
3. "What are some of your core values, and how do they manifest in your daily life?"
4. "In what ways do you find meaning or purpose in your work?"
5. "How do you envision your ideal future, and what steps do you see yourself taking to get there?"
6. "What are some experiences that have significantly shaped who you are today?"
7. "How do you define success for yourself, both personally and professionally?"
8. "What role do your relationships play in your overall happiness and well-being?"
9. "How do you balance different aspects of your life, such as work, family, and personal interests?"
10. "What are some goals you have for yourself over the next few months or years?"

These questions are designed to encourage conversation and insight, allowing clients to explore their thoughts, feelings, and aspirations more deeply.

Young carers – People whose parents have mental disorders

Supporting young carers whose parents have mental disorders is crucial for their well-being and development. Here are some strategies to help them:

1. **Provide Information and Education:** Educate young carers about their parent's mental health condition in an age-appropriate way. Understanding the situation can help reduce anxiety and confusion.

2. **Emotional Support:** Offer a safe space for young carers to express their feelings. Encourage them to talk about their experiences, fears, and emotions with a trusted adult or counsellor.

3. **Connect with Support Groups:** Introduce them to support groups or networks where they can meet others in similar situations. Sharing experiences with peers can reduce feelings of isolation.

4. **Access to Counselling:** Ensure they can access professional counselling or therapy. Mental health services can provide coping strategies and emotional resilience.

5. **Build Life Skills:** Help young carers develop practical life skills, such as time management and problem-solving, which can ease the burden of their responsibilities.

6. **Encourage Education:** Support their education by communicating with teachers and school counsellors. Ensure they receive any necessary accommodations or support in school.

7. **Respite Care:** Arrange for regular breaks or respite care to relieve them of their caregiving duties, allowing them time to engage in social activities and personal interests.

8. **Involve Other Family Members:** Involve extended family in caregiving duties if possible, to help distribute responsibilities and provide relief to the young carer.

9. **Ensure Safety:** Guarantee that they know how to access emergency support if the situation with their parent becomes unsafe or unmanageable.

10. **Promote Self-Care:** Encourage young carers to prioritise their own health and well-being. Regular physical activity, hobbies, and relaxation are vital for maintaining balance.

By providing comprehensive support, we can help young carers navigate their challenging roles while ensuring their own needs are met.

Caregivers – Parents whose children have mental disorders

The shock of watching your child change suddenly in front of your eyes and being sectioned is something that cannot be described. In those moments you have no words to pray with; someone else has to do it for you. And there comes the issue: a diagnosis of mental health is like none other. The stigma attached to it, the shame you feel that you have somehow failed as a parent prevents you from seeking help from family or friends.

In my case I continued to work a few yards away from where my son was sectioned. It was a bank holiday and I felt I could not call in and ask for leave. Interestingly no one took me off the shift and I continued right up to the point where he was sectioned. I will never forget the psychiatrist who took my hands in hers and reassured me after she had sectioned him.

Kindness that touches you sometimes comes from the most unexpected quarters.

In the ensuing days, witnessing his rage, tears, and vulnerability was different every day. We never knew what to expect. Then, you share small portions of what is happening with family, leaving aside the main story. You might say that your child is going through some difficulties without specifying what they are. People who love you will sustain you in their prayers without asking for details.

In my case I could not find the words but some dear friends supported and sustained. My husband was a revelation, his stoic calmness as our child's mood fluctuated during every painful visit, his patience whilst watching his paranoid outbursts, the love for our child shown in so many ways, visiting him daily when I could not.

Life seemed suspended during those long days and painful nights as I continued to work. You believe that your child will get better but every visit tests your faith. It is a dark place that I hope no parent has to visit. We had a wonderful psychiatrist who firmly believed in our child's recovery and went to great lengths to help him. In a way his calm confidence helped us too.

In the ensuing months, life continued to fluctuate. There were good days and then very bad days. One day you would feel a glimmer of hope and the next day there would be another violent outburst that left you frightened and helpless.

I prayed on some days, I could not on others.

When we thought we were finally getting somewhere, I lost my father, someone my child was very close to. We were back to square one as he suffered a relapse whilst we were thousands of miles away. It took several months for recovery.

In those dark days what kept me functioning was the realisation that I needed to be there for my child now more so than ever, the calm patience and the love of my husband, the understanding of a few friends who listened to understand and not reply.

We are in a better place now. There is always the watchful waiting, the realisation that life will never be the same again, the careful monitoring of his activities to prevent another crisis. In faith we walk and look forward to a new tomorrow where we will all be whole again – his father, his sister and I. No one goes untouched.

A mother's heartfelt journey.

A mother's story of navigating the complexities and challenges of supporting a loved one with psychosis is incredibly touching and powerful. The resilience, hope, and love that her family has shown are both inspiring and deeply moving.

Her determination to remain present for her child, no matter what, even in the face of immense challenges, speaks volumes about her strength and dedication as a mother. It is truly heart-warming for me as a psychiatrist, and it is wonderful to hear that she had a supportive psychiatrist whose belief in her child's recovery offered some comfort and reassurance during such a turbulent time.

Experiencing grief and loss while already managing the emotional rollercoaster of mental health challenges adds an unimaginable layer of complexity, and yet she has proven resilient and unwavering. The support system you describe — from her husband to understanding friends — plays a crucial role in providing strength and solidarity when she needed it most.

I was moved to hear that she is in a better place now, although I understand that the journey is ongoing. The "watchful waiting" and vigilance she speaks of are common feelings among parents and caregivers in similar situations. It is evident that faith, love, and resilience fuel her hope for healing and wholeness one day.

Her story serves as an important reminder of the impact of understanding and support, emphasising the notion that no one truly remains untouched by mental illness. Each step forward, each moment of hope, no matter how small, is a testament to her courage and love.

I am reminded that seeking continued support is equally essential. Whether through counselling, support groups, or simply nurturing her own well-being, taking care of her emotional health allows her to remain strong for her family.

Suggested Coping Strategies for Caregivers

Caring for someone with a mental illness can be both rewarding and challenging. Here are some coping strategies that might help:

1. **Educate Yourself:** Understanding the condition can help you feel more in control and reduce anxiety. Learn about symptoms, treatment options, and potential challenges.

2. **Set Realistic Goals:** Recognise what you can and cannot control. Set achievable goals for yourself and the person you are caring for.

3. **Seek Support:** Join a support group for caregivers. Sharing experiences with others who understand can be comforting and provide new perspectives.

4. **Take Breaks:** Regularly take time for yourself. Whether it is a short walk, reading, or another activity you enjoy, make sure to recharge.

5. **Establish Boundaries:** It is important to set limits on your availability and what you can do. This helps prevent burnout and maintains a healthier relationship.

6. **Focus on Communication:** Open, honest, and compassionate communication can help resolve conflicts and improve understanding between you and your loved one.

7. **Practise Self-Care:** Ensure you care for your physical and mental health. This might include exercise, a healthy diet,

regular sleep, and relaxation techniques such as meditation or deep-breathing exercises.

8. **Manage Stress:** Utilise stress management techniques such as mindfulness, yoga, or journaling to help manage your stress levels.

9. **Stay Organised:** Keep medical information, appointments, and care plans well organised. This can help reduce stress and provide a greater sense of control.

10. **Seek Professional Help:** Do not hesitate to reach out to a therapist or counsellor for emotional support or guidance specifically for caregivers.

Remember: seeking help is a sign of strength and an essential part of being an effective caregiver. It is not a weakness. If you ever feel overwhelmed, reaching out for professional help can be incredibly beneficial.

How to Identify Signs of Caregiver Burnout

Caregiver burnout can creep up slowly, and recognising the early signs is crucial to addressing it effectively. Here are some common indicators:

1. **Physical Exhaustion:** Feeling constantly tired regardless of how much rest you get.

2. **Emotional Overwhelm:** Feeling as though your emotions are out of control, experiencing frequent mood swings, or heightened irritability.

3. **Withdrawal from Activities:** Losing interest in activities and hobbies you once enjoyed, and withdrawing from friends and family.

4. **Changes in Appetite or Sleep:** Experiencing significant changes in eating or sleeping patterns, such as insomnia or overeating.

5. **Increased Illness:** Getting sick more often than usual due to a weakened immune response.

6. **Feelings of Helplessness or Hopelessness:** Feeling trapped or hopeless about your situation, and seeing no way out of the stress you are experiencing.

7. **Neglecting Personal Needs:** Prioritising caregiving over your own needs consistently, and possibly neglecting your health or well-being.

8. **Cognitive Overload:** Difficulty concentrating, forgetfulness, or feeling mentally overloaded.

9. **Escape Fantasies:** Frequently daydreaming about leaving your caregiving situation or considering drastic changes.

10. **Increased Anger or Irritability:** Feeling resentment towards the situation or the person you are caring for, and finding it difficult to maintain patience.

11. **Substance Use:** Using alcohol, drugs, or food as a way to cope with stress or escape negative emotions.

If you notice several of these signs in yourself, it is important to take them seriously and seek support. Consulting a mental health professional, joining a support group, or simply talking to a trusted friend or family member can provide much-needed relief. Remember, taking care of yourself is just as important as taking care of others.

Reimagining Mental Health for Black People

Reimagining mental health for Black people involves addressing systemic barriers and integrating culturally informed practices. Initiatives such as the Young Changemakers programme in the UK emphasise involving young Black people in designing mental health services to tackle racism and improve support.

Culturally informed approaches, such as healing circles and storytelling, are also vital, as they resonate with African-centred values and help counter systemic racism.

Organisations such as Black Minds Matter connect individuals with Black therapists, aiming to make mental health services more accessible and relevant for the Black community.

The Success Rates of Mentorship Programmes

The success rates of mentorship programmes can vary based on the programme's focus, resources, and the metrics used to measure success. However, some general successes associated with these programmes include:

1. **Improved Educational Outcomes:** Programmes such as iMentor and Black Girls Code often report higher high school graduation and university enrolment rates among participants compared to their peers.

2. **Career Advancement:** Initiatives such as The Hidden Genius Project and the LEAD Programme often see participants entering STEM fields and securing internships and job placements through networking and skill development.

3. **Personal Development:** Organisations such as Brotherhood-Sister Sol and Young Black Leadership Alliance highlight improvements in leadership skills, self-esteem, and community involvement among their mentees.

4. **Reduced Dropout Rates:** Programmes such as My Brother's Keeper and 100 Black Men of America are known to help decrease dropout rates by providing strong support systems and academic guidance.

5. **Increased STEM Participation:** Black Girls Code and StreetCode Academy have significantly contributed to increasing the representation of Black youth in technology and entrepreneurship sectors.

Specific statistics depend on individual programmes and their evaluation methods. Some programmes conduct longitudinal studies to track participants' progress over time, while others may use surveys, focus groups, and performance metrics to assess impact.

Cultural and Spiritual Sensitivity

Dive into the World of Culture and Spirituality: Discover Your Unique Identity

What is it about? Culture and spirituality are the values and beliefs that make people, places, and communities unique. They are the foundations of history, traditions, and inner peace.

Cultural Exploration: Culture can be seen as the backdrop of life's narrative. It includes music, art, food, language, and more. Every culture tells a story—what does yours say?

Spirituality Simplified: It is not solely about religion; it is about connecting with something greater than yourself, finding inner peace, and understanding who you are at your core.

Create Your Own Mix: You can explore different cultures through travel, literature, cuisine, and meeting new people. Combine experiences to create a cultural identity that suits you.

Seek Your Spiritual Path: Whether through meditation, nature, or art, find what resonates with you. Spirituality acts as a compass guiding you towards well-being.

Cultural Fusion: Imagine fusion cuisine, but with ideas and traditions. Embrace diversity, and experience the enrichment it brings.

Reflect and Connect: Engage with world music or spiritual discussions. Let rhythm and words inspire you, and feel the connection to a wider world.

Unique Identity: Your cultural background and spiritual beliefs are integral to who you are. Embrace, explore, and share your story.

Grounding Techniques: Use practices such as deep breathing or journaling to centre yourself. This can act as a pause in the midst of life's demands.

Global Community: The world is full of diverse people, and everyone's journey is unique. Respect, learn, and grow from those around you.

Unlock the Powers of Cultural and Spiritual Sensitivity

What is Cultural and Spiritual Sensitivity? It is the ability to be empathetic, respectful, and open-minded towards people with different backgrounds and beliefs. It is about seeing the world through someone else's eyes.

Why it Matters: By practising cultural and spiritual sensitivity, you are not only learning about others; you are promoting understanding, peace, and unity.

Walk in Their Shoes: Imagine approaching different perspectives as you would a new challenge. Every culture has its own story, strengths, and challenges. Embracing these makes life richer.

Travel Without Moving: Explore documentaries, books, or new friendships. This allows you to experience the world's variety without leaving home.

Respect as a Principle: Whether someone prays, dances, or meditates, respecting their traditions and beliefs demonstrates that you value them.

Curiosity over Judgement: Ask questions before making assumptions. Understanding the 'why' behind traditions can be enlightening.

Conversation Starter: "What is something unique about your culture or spiritual practice that you would like to share?" This opens the door to meaningful exchanges.

Build Bridges, Not Walls: Strong relationships are based on understanding and acceptance. Be the bridge that connects diverse ideas and people.

Celebrate Diversity: Engage with multicultural events, such as food festivals, and experience diversity first-hand.

Promote Peace and Understanding: Practising cultural and spiritual sensitivity helps spread peace and compassion.

Challenge Yourself: Step outside your comfort zone. Learn a new language or participate in cultural practices to gain greater insight.

1. Representation: Young Black people often feel a lack of representation in media, education, and leadership roles, which can affect their engagement and trust.

2. Trust Issues: Historical and systemic inequalities have led to distrust in institutions and authority figures, making it crucial to build authentic relationships.

3. Language and Communication: Different generational slang and communication styles can create misunderstandings if not approached with openness and willingness to understand.

4. Social Issues: Addressing concerns related to racial discrimination, economic disparities, and educational opportunities is vital to demonstrate understanding and support.

5. Community Involvement: Engaging in community activities and showing genuine interest in their lives helps build strong relationships.

6. Access to Resources: Inequities in access to education, technology, and other resources can hinder opportunities for connection and advancement.

A connection can be more effectively established by actively listening, showing empathy, and making concerted efforts to understand and address these challenges.

Building trust with young Black people requires genuine effort, empathy, and understanding. Here are some strategies to consider:

1. Active Listening: Pay close attention to their thoughts, feelings, and concerns without interrupting or making assumptions. Show them that their voices are valued.

2. Educate Yourself: Take the initiative to learn about Black history, culture, and current issues affecting young Black communities. Knowledge shows respect and reduces unintentional harm.

3. Authenticity: Be genuine in your interactions. Avoid using popular slang or expressions artificially; honesty is more appreciated than forced participation in cultural trends.

4. Representation and Role Models: Highlight and support Black role models in various fields, showing young Black people that their dreams and aspirations are attainable.

5. Community Engagement: Participate in or support community initiatives that focus on uplifting young Black

individuals. Being present in the community shows commitment.

6. Mentorship Opportunities: Offer mentoring or skill-building opportunities that acknowledge individual talents and aspirations. Demonstrating personal investment in their growth fosters trust.

7. Collaborative Approaches: Involve young Black people in decision-making processes, particularly in matters affecting their communities, allowing them to have a direct impact.

8. Addressing Bias and Prejudices: Be aware of your biases and work actively to overcome them. Conversations about race and privilege should be approached with sensitivity and openness.

9. Consistent Support: Be there consistently, showing reliable and unwavering support for their issues, interests, and aspirations.

10. Feedback and Adaptation: Welcome constructive feedback and be willing to adjust your approaches accordingly. This demonstrates flexibility and respect for their perspectives.

Building trust is a continuous process that requires time and effort, but these strategies can help foster meaningful connections.

Some examples of community initiatives that can support young Black people:

1. Mentorship Programmes: Connect young Black individuals with mentors in various fields, such as business, arts, science, or technology. These programmes provide guidance, support, and networking opportunities.

2. Youth Leadership Workshops: Organise workshops to develop leadership skills, focusing on public speaking, project management, and community organising.

3. Educational Scholarships: Offer scholarships or financial aid for young Black students to pursue education in their desired fields, reducing financial barriers.

4. Cultural and Heritage Programmes: Create programmes that celebrate and educate about Black history, culture, and achievements. Activities could include film screenings, art exhibitions, and cultural festivals.

5. STEM Camps and Competitions: Host camps or competitions focusing on science, technology, engineering, and mathematics to inspire interest and participation in these fields.

6. Art and Music Initiatives: Provide platforms for young Black artists and musicians to showcase their talents. This could include community concerts, art galleries, or recording opportunities.

7. Health and Wellness Workshops: Offer workshops on mental and physical health, addressing specific challenges young Black communities face, such as healthcare access or dealing with stress and discrimination.

8. Entrepreneurship Incubators: Set up programmes that offer resources, funding, and mentorship for young Black entrepreneurs looking to start or expand businesses.

9. Safe Spaces and Support Groups: Establish safe spaces where young Black individuals can discuss their experiences, challenges, and aspirations, providing peer support and solidarity.

10. Civic Engagement and Advocacy Training: Educate young people on political processes and advocacy, empowering them to participate actively in their communities and on issues that matter to them.

11. Environmental and Sustainability Projects: Involve young people in projects that improve the environment and promote sustainability, offering hands-on experience and community impact.

These initiatives, tailored to young Black people's specific needs and interests, can foster empowerment, growth, and community cohesion.

Here are a few examples of successful mentorship programmes specifically designed for young Black people:

1. My Brother's Keeper Alliance: Initiated by President Obama, this programme aims to address opportunity gaps young men of colour face through mentoring and support networks.

2. iMentor: This programme partners with public schools to match students with mentors who help guide them from secondary school through university completion, providing support, resources, and encouragement.

3. Big Brothers Big Sisters of America: While not exclusively for Black youth, this programme has specific initiatives aimed at supporting young Black individuals through one-to-one mentoring relationships.

4. The Young Black Leadership Alliance (YBLA): Focused on developing young Black leaders, YBLA provides mentorship, leadership development, career readiness, and community service opportunities.

5. 100 Black Men of America: This organisation's mentoring model addresses health and wellness, economic empowerment, education, and leadership development, offering guidance at local and national levels.

6. Black Girls Code: Although focused on technology, this programme mentors young Black girls by teaching them coding and computer programming skills, preparing them for futures in STEM fields.

7. StreetCode Academy: This platform offers mentorship in technology, entrepreneurship, and community building, aimed at equipping Black youth with skills to succeed in a digital world.

8. Brotherhood-Sister Sol: Located in Harlem, New York, this youth development organisation provides comprehensive, holistic support, including mentoring, to help young people define their identity and build leadership skills.

9. LEAD Programme: Through partnerships with leading colleges and universities, this programme offers business and STEM-focused education, while pairing students with mentors in these fields.

10. The Hidden Genius Project: Focused on Black male youth, this initiative mentors and trains participants in technology creation, entrepreneurship, and leadership skills.

These programmes have successfully created supportive environments that foster personal and professional growth among young Black people. By providing mentors who can relate to their unique experiences and challenges, these initiatives help bridge gaps and open doors to new opportunities.

Best Mentorship Programmes for Young Adults

Several highly regarded mentorship programmes for young adults focus on different areas such as education, career development, and personal growth. Here are some of the best known:

1. **iMentor**: Focused on building one-to-one mentoring relationships to empower students from disadvantaged

communities to graduate from secondary school, succeed in higher education, and achieve their ambitions.

2. **Big Brothers Big Sisters**: One of the oldest and largest youth mentoring organisations in the United States, providing one-to-one mentoring to empower young people to achieve their full potential.

3. **Year Up**: Offers an intensive training programme that provides young adults with hands-on skills development, coursework eligible for university credits, corporate placements, and wraparound support from mentors.

4. **The Hidden Genius Project**: Concentrates on unlocking the potential of black male youth by providing them with mentorship and intensive training in technology creation, entrepreneurship, and leadership skills.

5. **CareerVillage.org**: A platform where students can obtain career advice directly from professionals, offering mentorship and guidance to help young adults explore career paths.

6. **Code2040**: Aims to activate, connect, and mobilise the largest racial equity community in technology to dismantle the structural barriers that prevent the full participation and leadership of Black and Latinx people in the innovation economy.

7. **Brothers, Sons, Selves Coalition**: Engages young men of colour in community campaigns for positive change, through mentorship that includes self-esteem and leadership skill development.

8. **MentorClub**: Provides mentoring for aspiring entrepreneurs and professionals aiming to develop their skills and accelerate their careers.

9. **Upward Bound**: Part of the TRIO programmes, it provides support to participants in their preparation for university entrance, with a strong emphasis on mentoring.

These programmes offer various forms of mentoring, whether in person or virtually, and often provide resources that extend beyond traditional mentoring, including workshops, networking opportunities, placements, and more. Each programme serves different needs and communities, so exploring which one aligns best with an individual's specific goals and interests can be beneficial.

ADHD

Living with ADHD may feel as though your mind is a whirlwind, constantly buzzing with thoughts and ideas. You may experience:

1. **Being Easily Distracted**: You might find it difficult to focus on a single task because everything around you can capture your attention. A structured environment with fewer distractions can help you concentrate more effectively.

2. **Hyperactivity and Restlessness**: At times, it may feel as though there is a motor running inside you, urging you to move and fidget. Regular breaks for movement can be beneficial.

3. **Impulsivity**: You might speak or act without forethought, which can lead to unintended situations. Gentle reminders to pause and reflect can help you manage impulsive tendencies.

4. **Difficulty with Time Management**: Managing time may be challenging, as you can lose track of it or prioritise tasks differently. Visual schedules or timers can assist you in organising your day.

5. **Intense Focus on Interests**: While some tasks are difficult to start, others may capture your focus entirely—time seems

to disappear when you are deeply engaged. Celebrating these moments of focus can be empowering.

6. **Forgetfulness**: You may easily forget tasks or misplace items. Checklists or alarms can be useful for remembering important details.

7. **Emotional Sensitivity**: Emotions may feel particularly intense and swift. Having supportive people around you who understand your emotional landscape can be reassuring.

To assist, one can:

- Be understanding: Recognise that your attention may shift unpredictably, and patience in these moments can be reassuring.

- Provide structure: Create a structured environment with clear instructions, which may be easier to navigate.

- Encourage breaks: Allow time for movement, particularly during tasks requiring prolonged concentration.

- Use tools: Employ organisational tools such as planners, applications, or timers to manage tasks and deadlines.

- Exercise patience in communication: If you speak out of turn or quickly, gentle reminders can aid in communication.

Having someone who understands these experiences makes navigating life with ADHD more manageable and enjoyable. Empathy and support can serve as a powerful anchor.

What a Person with Anxiety Experiences

Living with anxiety may feel like being constantly on high alert, as if your body and mind are preparing for a threat that never comes. You may experience:

1. **Persistent Worry**: Thoughts may be filled with concern about both large and small matters, making it difficult to focus on anything else. Grounding techniques, such as deep breathing, can help to calm these thoughts.

2. **Physical Symptoms**: The body may react with a racing heart, perspiration, or tightness in the chest. Relaxation exercises can ease these physical symptoms.

3. **Restlessness**: Sitting still may feel almost impossible, as the body mirrors the unease of the mind. Activities such as yoga or walking can help release restlessness.

4. **Overthinking**: You may find yourself trapped in a cycle of repetitive thoughts, analysing every detail. Journaling can provide an outlet for these ruminations.

5. **Avoidance**: Certain places, situations, or people that trigger anxiety may be avoided, even when they pose no actual threat. Gradual exposure, with support, can slowly rebuild confidence in facing such situations.

6. **Sleep Difficulties**: Falling asleep may be a nightly struggle, with racing thoughts preventing rest. A calming bedtime routine can make it easier to unwind.

7. **Hypervigilance**: It may feel as though danger is ever-present, even in safe environments. Mindfulness exercises can help you remain present and recognise your safety in the moment.

Recognising these feelings and symptoms is important. Coping strategies, combined with support from others, can greatly improve the ability to manage anxiety.

What a Person with Social Phobia Experiences

Living with social phobia can make interactions feel overwhelmingly daunting, as if every encounter is a high-stakes performance. You may experience:

1. **Intense Fear of Judgement**: Entering a room, you may feel as though others are scrutinising and judging you, even when they are not. Reminding yourself of previous successful interactions can be reassuring.

2. **Avoidance of Social Situations**: You might avoid gatherings, conversations, or public speaking, rationalising your absence to avoid anticipated anxiety. Gradual exposure, beginning with smaller steps, can build confidence.

3. **Physical Symptoms**: The body may react with trembling, blushing, or perspiration in social settings, creating fears that others will notice your discomfort. Controlled breathing can help regulate these responses.

4. **Overwhelming Self-Consciousness**: It may feel as though all eyes are upon you, analysing your every move. Grounding techniques can help you refocus and ease the intensity of this perception.

5. **Difficulty in Conversations**: Finding the right words may be a struggle, accompanied by fears of saying something foolish or being misunderstood. Preparing topics or questions in advance can reduce pressure.

6. **After-Event Analysis**: Hours later, you may replay interactions in your mind, scrutinising what you said or did. Acknowledging these thoughts, then consciously redirecting focus, can lessen their grip.

7. **Avoidance of New Opportunities**: You may shy away from trying new activities or pursuing interests if they involve

meeting new people or group settings. Taking gradual steps towards less intimidating situations can expand your comfort zone.

Awareness and understanding of social phobia are crucial. Confronting these fears gradually—possibly with professional support or cognitive-behavioural strategies—can help you navigate social situations with greater ease.

Mindfulness Techniques

What is Mindfulness?

Mindfulness simplified

Mindfulness is essentially about being fully present and engaged in the moment. It does not require elaborate skills or actions; instead, it involves cultivating an open awareness of whatever is happening right now. Here is a breakdown of the concept:

1. **Natural State**: Being mindful is rooted in our natural ability as humans to be aware and attentive. It is about tapping into our innate capacity to be present.

2. **Simple Practice**: Mindfulness does not demand complex techniques despite its profound effects. A little practice helps you to connect more deeply with the present moment, creating a sense of ease and natural engagement.

3. **Tuning Inward**: Mindfulness involves tuning inward, paying attention to your thoughts, feelings, bodily sensations, and the surrounding environment without judgement or distraction. It is about creating a still space within yourself.

4. **Non-Doing**: You do not need to do anything specific; it is more about being. Mindfulness is a state of acceptance

where you allow experiences and thoughts to come and go freely.

5. **Awareness of the Present**: The focus is purely on the present moment—right here, right now. It is about observing what is happening without getting lost in thoughts about the past or worries about the future.

6. **Observation and Acceptance**: Part of mindfulness is observing whatever arises in your consciousness—a thought, an emotion, a sensation—and letting it pass naturally without clinging to it or pushing it away.

7. **Ease and Effortlessness**: Mindfulness is considered simple since all that is required is to be aware and open. With time, it becomes a more natural part of your life.

Mindfulness practices, such as meditation or simple exercises like deep breathing and mindful walking, often help enhance this natural ability, allowing you to experience life more fully and clearly. Embracing mindfulness can lead to increased emotional balance, clarity, and a greater sense of peace.

You have pinpointed two significant challenges that many face when cultivating mindfulness: the active mind and forgetfulness. Let us delve into these obstacles and explore some strategies to tackle them:

1. The Overactive Mind

Challenge: Our minds are naturally prone to chatter and activity. They leap from thought to thought, making it difficult to find calm.

Strategies:

- **Mindful Meditation**: Incorporate short meditation sessions where you focus on your breath. If your mind wanders, gently return to your breathing.

- **Labelling Thoughts**: When thoughts arise, practise labelling them (e.g., "planning," "worrying"). Recognising thought patterns can help detach you from them.
- **Set Intentions**: Begin your day with a mindful intention. Remind yourself of the benefits of mindfulness, reinforcing your commitment.

2. Forgetfulness

Challenge: Life's busyness often makes us forget to be mindful until we are too tired.

Strategies:

- **Mindfulness Cues**: Use everyday activities as reminders. For example, whenever you drink water or touch a door handle, take a moment to be present.
- **Mindfulness Apps/Reminders**: Set reminders to pause and breathe or use an app with guided mindfulness exercises.
- **Align with Daily Habits**: Incorporate mindfulness into activities you already do, like brushing your teeth or having a meal. Focus fully on these activities.

Additional Tips

- **Consistency over Duration**: Even a few minutes of mindfulness daily can significantly impact your well-being.
- **Compassionate Approach**: Be kind to yourself when your mind wanders or you forget to be mindful. Recognise that this is part of the journey.

Mindfulness is about progress, not perfection. Addressing these obstacles with patience and persistence can slowly transform your relationship with the present moment, making it a natural part of your life.

Here are some handy tips to help you remember to be mindful throughout your day:

1. **Mindfulness Cues**: Choose common activities as reminders, like drinking water, brushing your teeth, or opening doors. Each time you do these activities, pause and focus on the present moment.

2. **Visual Reminders**: Place sticky notes or artwork with mindfulness quotes or symbols around your home or workspace. These serve as gentle nudges to practise mindfulness.

3. **Set Reminders**: Use your phone or a mindfulness app to set daily reminders or alarms. These can remind you to take a moment for deep breathing or a quick mindfulness exercise.

4. **Mindful Breathing Breaks**: Schedule brief breathing breaks throughout your day. Even a minute of attentive breathing can help you reset and reconnect with the present.

5. **Anchor to Daily Routines**: Attach mindfulness to routines you already have, such as during your commute, morning coffee, or before bed. Use these moments to practise being present.

6. **Mindfulness Journal**: Keep a journal to jot down your experiences, reflections, or reminders about mindfulness. Writing can reinforce your commitment and awareness.

7. **Partner Practice**: Team up with a friend or family member interested in mindfulness. You can remind each other and even practise together.

8. **Wear a Reminder**: Consider wearing a bracelet or ring you associate with mindfulness. When you notice it, take a moment to pause and be present.

9. **Mindful Listening**: Choose a sound in your environment, like a phone ring or bird song, as a cue to bring yourself back to mindfulness.

10. **Gratitude Practice**: Regularly practise gratitude in the morning or evening. Reflecting on what you are thankful for can centre you and enhance mindfulness.

By integrating these tips, you can create a more mindful day-to-day experience, making mindfulness a natural and easy part of your life.

Mindfulness at Work

Incorporating mindfulness into your workday can enhance focus, productivity, and overall well-being. Here are some practical ways to weave mindfulness into your work routine:

1. **Start with Intention**: Begin your day by setting a mindful intention. Take a few moments to decide how you want to approach your work and interactions.

2. **Mindful Breathing**: Take short breaks to breathe deeply and mindfully. Even a minute of focused breathing between tasks can refresh your mind.

3. **Unplug Breaks**: Step away from screens during breaks. Focus on something non-digital, like stretching, looking out of a window, or simply closing your eyes for a moment.

4. **Mindful Eating**: If you have lunch or snacks at your desk, eat mindfully. Pay attention to flavours and textures, and avoid multitasking during meals.

5. **Stretch and Move**: Schedule brief periods to stand up, stretch, or take a quick walk. Moving your body can help release tension and refocus your mind.

6. **Focused Tasks**: Practise single-tasking by giving your full attention to one task at a time. This reduces stress and improves the quality of your work.

7. **Mindful Listening**: During meetings or conversations, focus wholly on what is being said without immediately planning your response. This can enhance understanding and empathy.

8. **Digital Mindfulness**: Set specific times to check emails and messages, rather than reacting to each notification. This keeps distractions at bay and enhances focus.

9. **Breathing Cues**: Use sounds, such as phone rings or email alerts, as cues to engage in a quick deep-breathing exercise.

10. **End-of-Day Reflection**: Take a few minutes to reflect on your day. Note any accomplishments and decide how you can approach tomorrow with mindfulness.

Integrating these practices into your workday does not require significant time but provides great benefits by helping you become more present, calm, and productive.

Mindfulness Techniques

1. **Body Scan Meditation**: Focus your attention on each part of your body, from head to toe, noticing any sensations without judgement.

2. **Five Senses Exercise**: Engage each of your five senses individually to ground yourself in the present moment.

3. **Mindful Listening**: Listen to music or sounds in your environment, noting the different elements without labelling or analysis.

4. **Mindful Eating**: Eat slowly and deliberately, savouring each bite and paying attention to the flavours, textures, and aromas.

5. **Box Breathing**: Inhale for four counts, hold for four, exhale for four, and hold again for four. Repeat this cycle.

6. **Observational Walk**: Take a walk and notice shapes, colours, and textures around you, paying close attention to your surroundings.

7. **Loving-Kindness Meditation**: Focus on extending kindness and well-wishes to yourself and others, using phrases like "May I be happy and healthy."

8. **Journalling**: Write about your thoughts and feelings in a non-judgemental way to process your emotions mindfully.

9. **Gratitude Practice**: Reflect on things you are grateful for and write them down daily, fostering a positive mindset.

10. **Breathing Anchor**: Focus solely on your breath as a point of concentration. When your mind wanders, gently bring it back to your breath.

11. **Appreciative Inquiry**: Focus on positive aspects of your life and ask reflective questions about them to enhance mindfulness.

12. **Mindful Colouring**: Use adult colouring books to focus your mind on the act of colouring and the intricate designs.

13. **Guided Meditation Apps**: Use apps like Headspace or Calm for structured mindfulness practices.

14. **Mindful Pausing**: Take short pauses throughout your day to reset your mind, breathing deeply and observing your thoughts.

15. **Mindful Observation**: Choose a natural object and observe it intently for a few minutes, noticing every detail as if you are seeing it for the first time.

Incorporating these techniques into your daily routine can enhance your mindfulness practice and improve your mental clarity and emotional well-being. Choose the ones that resonate with you and adapt them to fit your lifestyle.

12

SUICIDE

Dear friend,

Times can be difficult.

I would like to have a brief conversation about something extremely important: mental health and managing difficult periods in life. At times, life can feel overwhelming, and it is not always easy to discuss such feelings. However, it is crucial to understand that you are not alone.

If you have ever felt hopeless or as though there is no way forward, please know that while it is natural to feel this way, it is also vital to reach out for support. There are many people who care about you and wish to help—whether that is friends, family, or a professional counsellor.

Here are a few points to keep in mind:

1. **Talking Helps:** Speaking with someone you trust can be a great relief. It may feel daunting, but sharing your experience can be the first step towards feeling better.

2. **You Matter:** Even when life feels dark, your existence is important. You make a difference in the world simply by being yourself.

3. **Help is Available:** There are resources and helplines where you can speak with trained individuals who understand your situation. They are there to listen and provide support without judgement.

4. **Finding Joy:** Engaging in small activities that bring comfort—whether music, art, sport, or spending time with a pet—can provide moments of peace.

5. **You Are Stronger Than You Realise:** Even if it does not feel like it, you possess great inner strength to overcome challenges. Taking small steps towards healing is perfectly acceptable.

Stay connected, reach out when needed, and remember that your story is important. There will always be someone ready to listen and support you.

Take care of yourself.

Coping with Feeling Overwhelmed

When life feels overwhelming, there are several approaches that may help:

1. **Talk to Someone:** Contact a trusted friend, family member, or mentor. Sharing your feelings can lighten the burden and provide perspective.

2. **Take a Break:** Step away briefly from sources of stress. Deep breathing, a short walk, or listening to calming music can help.

3. **Prioritise Tasks:** Create a list and tackle one thing at a time. Breaking tasks into smaller steps makes them more manageable.

4. **Practise Self-Care:** Engage in activities that make you feel positive, such as exercise, reading, or spending time outdoors.

5. **Set Boundaries:** Learn to say no if you feel overextended. It is entirely acceptable to prioritise your own wellbeing.

6. **Seek Professional Help:** If feelings of being overwhelmed persist, consider speaking with a mental health professional.

7. **Mindfulness or Meditation:** Simple practices can calm the mind and bring focus to the present moment.

8. **Limit Stressors:** Reduce exposure to sources of stress, such as social media, news, or difficult environments.

9. **Stay Nourished and Hydrated:** Basic needs like food and water can have a large effect on mood and resilience.

10. **Practise Gratitude:** Reflecting on positive aspects of life can bring relief and perspective.

Feeling overwhelmed is a natural human experience. Seeking support and taking proactive steps demonstrates strength and self-awareness.

Self-Care Activities

Here are some enjoyable and effective self-care activities you may wish to try:

1. **Exercise:** Walking, yoga, sport, or even dancing at home can boost energy and mood.

2. **Meditation & Mindfulness:** Spend a few minutes in stillness; many guides and apps are available.

3. **Reading:** Books provide a relaxing escape.

4. **Art & Crafting:** Drawing, painting, or knitting can be therapeutic.

5. **Cooking or Baking:** Experiment with recipes or enjoy preparing favourite meals.

6. **Journalling:** Writing thoughts or feelings can help process emotions.

7. **Nature Walks:** Time outdoors can lift the spirits.

8. **Bath or Spa Time:** A warm bath with salts or oils can be deeply relaxing.

9. **Listening to Music or Podcasts:** Choose uplifting or thought-provoking material.

10. **Gardening:** Caring for plants, even indoors, can be grounding.

11. **Puzzles or Games:** Mental stimulation through puzzles or games can be satisfying.

12. **Decluttering and Organising:** A tidy space encourages calmness.

13. **Planning a Day Out:** Museums, parks, cafés, or new places can refresh the mind.

14. **Watching a Film or Series:** Entertainment can be restorative.

15. **Mindful Breathing:** Slow, deliberate breathing exercises are simple yet powerful.

Experiment with what feels right for you. Self-care is personal, and making time for it regularly is essential for balance.

Knife Crime in the UK

The Law

The United Kingdom has some of the strictest knife laws globally. Carrying a knife can result in a permanent criminal record and serious legal consequences.

The Reality

Carrying a knife may feel like self-protection, but in truth, it often increases the risk of harm. Safety is about being sensible and aware, not armed. Experts confirm that the likelihood of injury is greater when knives are involved.

Influence

Films and games sometimes portray knives as impressive, but reality is very different. Carrying one can damage your reputation, instil fear in others, and negatively affect how you are perceived.

Safer Alternatives

If you are concerned for your safety, there are far better options: self-defence classes, personal safety smartphone apps, or even personal alarms. These provide reassurance without the legal and personal risks.

Long-Term Consequences

A conviction for carrying a knife can restrict future opportunities, such as employment or higher education. Many young people underestimate how much this can affect their future.

Support

If you ever feel compelled to carry a knife, speak to someone you trust. Teachers, community leaders, and support organisations can provide guidance and help.

Alternatives to Carrying Knives

If you have friends who feel unsafe, here are some safer options to suggest:

1. **Self-Defence Classes:** Build confidence and safety skills without weapons.
2. **Buddy System:** Walking in groups is far safer than being alone.
3. **Safety Apps:** Apps such as *bSafe* or *Noonlight* alert trusted contacts quickly in emergencies.
4. **Personal Alarms:** Compact devices that emit a loud sound to draw attention.
5. **Knowledge of Risks:** Awareness of unsafe areas and situations can prevent danger.
6. **Community Programmes:** Local initiatives encourage positive alternatives and safety.
7. **Public Transport Awareness:** Choose well-lit, busier routes or use reliable transport.
8. **Communication:** Share your location and arrival times with someone you trust.
9. **Confidence:** Walking with assurance and good posture can deter threats.
10. **Local Support Services:** Many services provide advice and assistance tailored to young people's needs.

The most important message is that there is no shame in seeking help. Safety and wellbeing are priorities, and they can be maintained without carrying weapons. Building a safer community is a shared responsibility.

Creating a safety plan with your friends is a proactive way to ensure everyone feels secure and supported. Here is a step-by-step guide to help you craft an effective plan:

1. **Identify Concerns:**
    - Begin a conversation about the specific situations or areas where they feel unsafe. Understanding these concerns is the foundation of a good plan.

2. **Set Communication Protocols:**
    - Choose a method of communication, such as a group chat or application, where everyone can quickly reach out if they require assistance.
    - Establish code words or phrases for discreetly communicating if one feels unsafe.

3. **Agree on Check-In Times:**
    - Schedule regular check-ins, particularly during times or in concerning areas. These can be via call or text to ensure everyone is safe.

4. **Map Out Safe Zones:**
    - Identify places that provide safety, such as the homes of trusted individuals, public spots like police stations, or community centres that can be accessed quickly.

5. **Plan Safe Routes:**
    - Encourage the use of well-lit, busy roads rather than isolated shortcuts. Identifying these routes in advance ensures a safer travelling experience.

6. **Outline Emergency Contacts:**
   - Compile a list of emergency contacts, including family, friends, and local authorities. Ensure each person has this list easily accessible.

7. **Equip with Essential Tools:**
   - Share information about personal safety devices such as alarms or applications that can alert others during an emergency.

8. **Mock Drills:**
   - Practise scenarios and responses to ensure everyone knows what to do if something concerning arises.

9. **Encourage Open Discussions:**
   - Make it routine to discuss new concerns, experiences, and strategies. Keeping communication open ensures everyone feels heard and supported.

10. **Review and Update Regularly:**
    - Ensure that the safety plan remains relevant, updating it according to changing needs or circumstances.

By building this safety plan collaboratively, friends increase their sense of security and strengthen their support network. Prioritising each other's safety encourages a safer community for everyone.

Examples of Code Words

Code words are a discreet and effective way to communicate, particularly when someone feels unsafe. Here are some examples:

1. **Fruit or Vegetable Names:**
   - "Pineapple": Indicates the need for immediate help.

- "Cucumber": Suggests feeling uncomfortable or needing an escape.

2. **Animal Names:**
    - "Elephant": Used to express a sense of being overwhelmed or trapped.
    - "Hedgehog": States that someone nearby is causing unease.

3. **Colours:**
    - "Blue": Represents feeling sad or in need of emotional support.
    - "Red": Signals an immediate need for assistance.

4. **Random Words:**
    - "Umbrella": Suggests a desire to leave or evacuate.
    - "Notebook": Signifies a need for a diversion or distraction.

5. **Simple Phrases:**
    - "Let's grab coffee": Indicates wanting to talk in private or leave the area.
    - "Forgot my keys": Suggests an urgent reason to exit a situation.

6. **Food Items:**
    - "Pizza": Represents the need to check in or stay close.
    - "Ice Cream": Indicates a desire for reassurance or comfort.

7. **Historical Figures:**
    - "Einstein": Signals the need for logical thinking or decision-making support.
    - "Cleopatra": Suggests feeling out of place or wanting to regroup.

These code words should be chosen based on what feels natural for your group to remember and use in conversation. They should also be easy enough to introduce without drawing attention in a social setting.

Highest Suicide Rates

- Greenland: 59.62 per 100,000 people, the highest globally.
- Lesotho: 87.48 per 100,000 (2019 data), the highest in Africa.
- Other countries with high rates include Guyana (40.85), Eswatini (40.46), and Kiribati (30.56).

Lowest Suicide Rates

- Palestine: 0.78 per 100,000, the lowest globally.
- Other countries with very low rates include Syria (0.89), Lebanon (0.94), and Egypt (1.01).

Global Trends

- Around 720,000 people die by suicide annually, with 73% occurring in low- and middle-income countries.
- Men are more likely to die by suicide than women globally, with male rates often double or more than female rates.
- Suicide is the third leading cause of death among individuals aged 15–29 years.

Regional Highlights

- The African region has the highest average suicide rate at 11.2 per 100,000, compared to the global average of 9.0 per 100,000.

- In OECD countries, South Korea and Lithuania report particularly high male suicide rates (34.9 and 33.1 per 100,000).

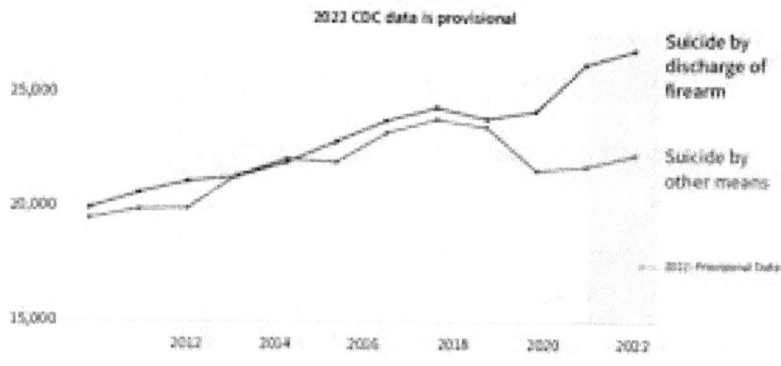

Young People, Faith & Mental Challenges

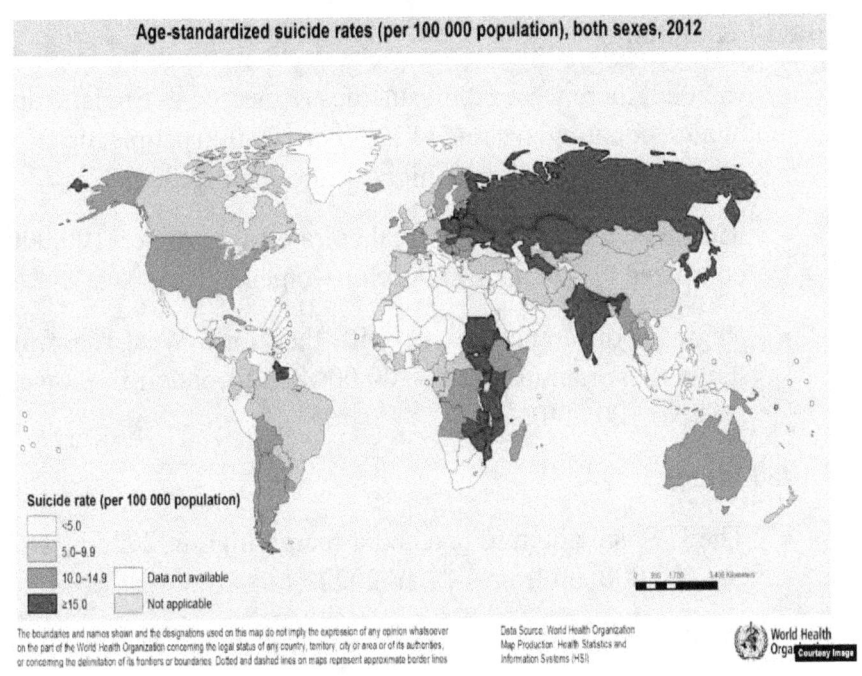

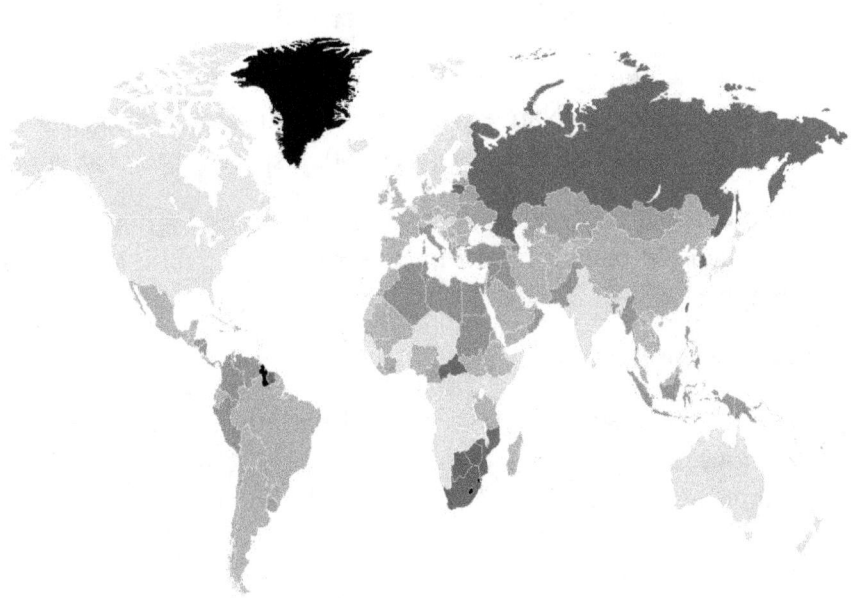

Suicide Rates in the UK and USA (2025)

United Kingdom

- In 2023, there were 6,069 suicides registered in England and Wales, equating to a rate of 11.4 per 100,000 people, up from 10.7 in 2022. This is the highest rate since 1999.
- Men had a significantly higher rate at 17.4 per 100,000, compared to 5.7 per 100,000 for women.
- Regional differences exist, with the North-West reporting the highest rate (14.7 per 100,000) and London the lowest (7.3 per 100,000).

United States

- The U.S. suicide rate reached a record high in 2025 at 14.7 per 100,000, up from 14.2 in 2022.
- In 2024, over 49,300 deaths were attributed to suicide.
- Men accounted for nearly 80% of suicides, with a rate of 23 per 100,000, compared to 5.9 per 100,000 for women.
- The elderly (85+) and non-Hispanic American Indian/Alaska Native populations had the highest rates at 23 per 100,000 and 27.1 per 100,000, respectively.

Both countries are experiencing rising suicide rates, highlighting the urgent need for mental health interventions and public awareness campaigns.

Suicide in the Bible

The Bible addresses suicide in several narratives and theological discussions, though it does not explicitly label it as a sin. Here are key points:

Examples of Suicide in the Bible

1. King Saul and his armour-bearer: Saul, mortally wounded, fell on his sword to avoid capture, and his armour-bearer followed suit (1 Samuel 31:4–5).

2. Ahithophel: After his counsel was rejected, he hanged himself (2 Samuel 17:23).

3. Zimri: Burned himself alive after his city was overtaken (1 Kings 16:18).

4. Judas Iscariot: Betrayed Jesus and later hanged himself in remorse (Matthew 27:5).

5. Samson: Brought down a temple on himself and others, though this is often seen as an act of sacrifice rather than suicide (Judges 16:26–31).

Theological Interpretations

- Suicide is often considered a sin because it violates the Sixth Commandment, "You shall not murder," as it is viewed as self-murder (Exodus 20:13).

- However, some argue that God's forgiveness extends even to those who die by suicide if they are believers (Romans 8:38–39).

Mental Health and Compassion

The Bible acknowledges despair in figures like Jonah (Jonah 4:3) and Paul (2 Corinthians 1:8), who expressed a desire to die but ultimately found hope in God. Modern interpretations emphasise understanding the mental health struggles that often lead to suicide.

Suicide in the Qur'an

In Islam, suicide is strictly prohibited and considered a major sin. The Qur'an explicitly states: *"And do not kill yourselves. Surely,*

Allah is Most Merciful to you" (Qur'an 4:29). Life is viewed as a sacred trust from God, and only He has the authority to give and take it. The Hadith further emphasises the gravity of suicide. The Prophet Muhammad (peace be upon him) warned that those who commit suicide will face punishment in the afterlife using the means by which they ended their lives (Sahih al-Bukhari and Sahih Muslim). However, scholars note that God's mercy may apply in cases where mental illness or extreme distress diminishes accountability. Islam encourages patience during hardships, reminding believers that trials are temporary and can lead to spiritual growth and forgiveness of sins.

Muslims cope with suicidal thoughts and depression through a combination of faith-based practices, community support, and professional mental health care. Here are key approaches:

1. Faith-Based Coping

- **Prayer and Supplication:** Muslims are encouraged to turn to Allah through prayer (Salah) and supplication (Dua) for strength and guidance during hardships.

- **Qur'anic Reflection:** Verses such as *"And do not kill yourselves. Surely, Allah is Most Merciful to you"* (Qur'an 4:29) remind believers of the sanctity of life and Allah's mercy.

- **Hope in Allah's Mercy:** Islam emphasises that hardships are temporary and that patience (*Sabr*) leads to spiritual growth and reward.

2. Community Support

- **Open Discussions:** Increasingly, Muslim communities are addressing suicide openly to reduce stigma, with Imams and leaders being trained to provide guidance.

- **Mosque Support:** Visiting local mosques for emotional support, advice from Imams, or group prayers can help individuals feel less isolated.

3. Professional Help

- **Therapy:** Muslims are encouraged to seek mental health professionals while understanding that faith complements therapy, not replaces it.
- **Crisis Resources:** Communities are working to provide access to suicide hotlines and trained counsellors.

4. Combating Stigma

Efforts are ongoing to reduce the stigma surrounding mental health in Muslim societies, encouraging individuals to seek help without fear of judgement.

How Christians Cope with Suicidal Thoughts and Depression

Christians cope with suicidal thoughts and depression by combining faith-based practices, community support, and professional mental health care. Here are key approaches:

1. Faith-Based Practices

- **Prayer:** Christians are encouraged to pour out their struggles to God in prayer, seeking His peace and guidance (Philippians 4:6–7).
- **Scripture Meditation:** Immersing in Bible verses such as Psalm 34:18 (*"The Lord is close to the brokenhearted"*) offers comfort and hope.
- **Trust in God's Grace:** Remembering that God's love is unconditional and that He understands human suffering provides reassurance during dark times.

2. Community Support

- **Church and Fellowship:** Engaging with a supportive Christian community through church services, Bible studies, or prayer groups helps combat isolation (Hebrews 10:23–25).

- **Mentorship and Accountability:** Building relationships with Christian mentors or friends who provide encouragement and prayer is vital.

3. Professional Help

- **Therapy and Counselling:** Seeking help from mental health professionals, including Christian counsellors, is emphasised as a sign of strength, not weakness.

- **Crisis Resources:** Utilising hotlines such as 111 or organisations like Samaritans for immediate support is recommended.

4. Holistic Self-Care

- **Physical Health:** Maintaining sleep, exercise, and a healthy diet supports emotional well-being.

- **Perspective Shift:** Viewing depression as an opportunity for spiritual growth can help reframe the struggle positively (James 1:2–4).

Christians are reminded that healing takes time and that God's presence remains constant even in their darkest moments.

Christian Faith, Self-Harm, and Suicide

Church Ministers who Committed Suicide

Several church ministers have tragically taken their own lives, highlighting the mental health challenges faced within ministry.

- **Iain D. Campbell:** A former Moderator of the Free Church of Scotland, he died by suicide in January 2017 amid revelations of multiple affairs.

- **Jarrid Wilson:** A California megachurch pastor and mental health advocate, he died by suicide in September 2019 at the age of 30, despite his efforts to help others with similar struggles.

- **Andrew Stoecklein:** Lead pastor at Inland Hills Church, he died by suicide in August 2018 after openly discussing his battles with mental illness.

These cases underscore the importance of mental health awareness in religious communities.

The suicides of pastors such as Jarrid Wilson, Andrew Stoecklein, and Darrin Patrick can be attributed to several interconnected factors:

- **Mental Health Issues:** Many pastors struggle with depression, anxiety, and loneliness, often exacerbated by the pressures of ministry. There can be no overstating the burden and pressures of leading a congregation and the reality of burnout.

- **Isolation:** A significant number report feeling isolated, lacking close friendships, and facing burnout.

- **Stigma:** There is often a cultural stigma within churches that discourages open discussions about mental health struggles.

- **Professional Pressure:** The demands of church leadership can lead to overwhelming stress and feelings of inadequacy when comparing themselves to others.

These factors highlight the urgent need for better mental health support in religious communities.

Measures Being Taken to Prevent Future Pastor Suicides

To prevent future pastor suicides, several measures are being implemented:

- **Training Programmes:** Initiatives such as LivingWorks Faith and Soul Shop provide training for pastors on how to recognise warning signs of suicide and engage in meaningful conversations about mental health.

- **Community Support:** Emphasising the importance of community, churches are encouraged to create supportive environments that foster open discussions about mental health.

- **Mental Health Resources:** Access to mental health services is being promoted, with pastors being trained to connect individuals with professional help when needed.

- **National Strategies:** Government strategies include over 100 actions aimed at early intervention and improving mental health services across various sectors, including faith communities. These efforts aim to equip pastors and congregations to better support those in crisis.

Case Study

A 40-year-old Asian woman discovered her husband was having an affair with her cousin. One day, when her husband had gone to work, her children discovered her in her bedroom. She had hanged herself.

These tragic narratives intertwine issues of faith, mental health, and personal relationships, each carrying significant implications.

Faith Implications

1. **Crisis of Faith:** For religious individuals, such a traumatic event could trigger a crisis of faith. The discovery of

betrayal, particularly by trusted family members, may lead to questioning the justice or benevolence of a higher power.

2. **Community Support:** Faith communities often provide support during crises. Religious leaders and community members can offer comfort, counselling, and practical assistance to the bereaved and those dealing with betrayal and loss.

3. **Moral and Ethical Considerations:** Religious beliefs might influence how the family interprets the act of suicide. Some faiths view suicide as morally wrong, which can add to the survivor's emotional burden.

Mental Health Implications

1. **Betrayal Trauma:** The discovery of her husband's affair, especially with a cousin, could result in betrayal trauma, where trust and attachment are deeply shattered. This trauma can lead to anxiety, depression, and feelings of worthlessness.

2. **Depressive States:** Her act suggests a severe depressive state, likely compounded by isolation and overwhelming emotions. Feelings of shame, guilt, and hopelessness might have been prevalent.

3. **Warning Signs:** The narrative might indicate undetected or unaddressed mental health struggles. Often, individuals in severe distress might not overtly display symptoms or might mask them due to stigma, particularly in communities where mental health is less openly discussed.

4. **Impact on Children:** The children discovering their mother in such circumstances can have profound psychological effects, potentially leading to PTSD, severe anxiety, and trust issues. They require immediate psychological support to process trauma healthily.

Cultural Factors

1. **Stigma and Shame:** In some Asian cultures, family honour and reputation hold significant weight. The betrayal and subsequent suicide could be perceived as bringing shame upon the family, potentially influencing her actions due to societal pressures.

2. **Lack of Mental Health Resources:** Cultural barriers might prevent individuals from seeking mental health care, either due to stigma or lack of understanding about mental health issues and resources available.

3. **Family Dynamics:** The distress caused by familial betrayal can be magnified in closely-knit family structures. Coping with such a betrayal could be more challenging, affecting her decision to end her life.

Conclusion

This narrative underscores the urgent need for comprehensive support systems that integrate faith-based support, mental health care, and community awareness. Encouraging open dialogues about mental health and ensuring access to professional help can significantly impact individuals navigating similar crises. Supporting children and families in the aftermath is crucial for promoting healing and preventing long-term psychological effects.

PTSD in the Words of a Patient

Chapter: Trauma and PTSD – Understanding the impact of traumatic experiences and finding ways to heal is an important topic for some young people.

"Living with PTSD can feel overwhelming, like you are constantly battling memories and fears. It is as if your mind has been hijacked, reliving past traumatic events even when you want to forget them. Flashbacks might feel real, pulling you back into the moment, as though it is happening all over again. Anxiety can grip you unexpectedly, sometimes triggered by a sound, a place, or even a smell.

You might find yourself on edge, vigilant, and ready to act. Sleep can become elusive, invaded by nightmares that jolt you awake. Your body constantly churns out stress hormones, making relaxation seem impossible. Small irritations may cloud your day, turning everything into an ordeal. It can feel like you are carrying a hefty burden that never seems to lighten.

Sometimes, you may withdraw from the people you care about, feeling detached or disconnected. The world feels different, as if you are watching life unfold from afar. It is normal to question your reactions and wonder if anyone understands.

But you are not alone, and it is crucial to remember that healing is possible, with support, time, and patience. Reaching out for help, whether it is through therapy, medication, or support groups, can be a vital step in regaining control and finding peace amidst the chaos."

Faith and Coping with PTSD

Faith can be a powerful source of strength and comfort when coping with PTSD. It can provide a sense of hope and reassurance, acting as an anchor during turbulent times. Here is how faith might intersect with the journey of healing:

1. **Sense of Purpose:** Faith can help you find meaning in your experiences, offering a perspective that transcends immediate pain. It allows you to believe in a larger plan or purpose beyond the trauma.

2. **Community Support:** Being part of a faith community can provide a support network where you feel understood and accepted. Shared beliefs often foster strong networks that offer emotional and practical aid.

3. **Rituals and Practices:** Engaging in prayer, meditation, or other spiritual practices can be grounding and calming. These practices create moments of peace and reflection, helping to reduce stress and anxiety.

4. **Hope and Resilience:** Faith can instil hope, reinforcing the belief that healing is possible. It encourages resilience, helping you hold onto the light even during dark times.

5. **Forgiveness and Compassion:** Many faith traditions emphasise forgiveness for oneself and others. This can be a key to letting go of lingering resentment or self-blame, which often accompany PTSD.

6. **Guidance and Wisdom:** Spiritual texts and teachings can offer guidance, providing comforting words and insights that resonate deeply with your situation. They can be a source of wisdom when making decisions or facing challenges.

7. **Mindfulness and Presence:** Emphasising being present in the moment, faith can help you focus on the now, rather than becoming lost in past traumas or future worries.

Remember, integrating faith into PTSD coping strategies is a personal journey and might look different for everyone. It is about finding what resonates with you, respecting your beliefs and needs, and seeking support when needed.

Case 2

An African man suffering from related stress was brought in by four struggling nurses. The PICU was not responding. He kept asking for his pastor, who was 200 miles away. He was put on the phone, and a family member intimated that he had a favourite gospel song. The nurses were mostly not religious, which posed a dilemma. After one hour of physical, followed by chemical restraints, he was still fighting; a burly man 6'4" tall. Everyone was tiring. In desperation, a gospel song from his playlist was played on speaker. Within seconds to one minute his struggling became less, but his facial expression changed gradually, reminiscent of the Incredible Hulk. By the end of one week he was discharged on a small dose of medication. He was eventually able to return to work.

Faith, Mental Health and Intersectionality

The intersection of faith, mental health, and intersectionality highlights the complex and nuanced ways in which individuals navigate their identities and experiences. Here is a look into how these elements interact:

1. **Faith and Mental Health:**
    - *Supportive Communities:* Faith communities can provide emotional support, reducing feelings of isolation and creating safe spaces for individuals to express their struggles with mental health.
    - *Spiritual Practices:* Activities such as prayer, meditation, or attending services can be therapeutic, offering a sense of peace, routine, and mindfulness.
    - *Stigma and Misunderstandings:* In some cases, faith communities may have stigmatised views on mental health, leading to feelings of shame or discouragement in seeking professional help. However, progressive faith groups are increasingly addressing these issues with more empathy and understanding.

2. **Intersectionality:**
    - *Complex Identities:* Intersectionality acknowledges that individuals have multiple, overlapping identities (e.g., race, gender, sexual orientation) that affect their experiences with faith and mental health.

- *Systemic Barriers:* People of colour, LGBTQ+ individuals, and other marginalised groups often face additional barriers to mental health support, such as discrimination, lack of culturally competent care, and limited access to resources.
- *Unique Challenges:* The interplay of identities can affect how mental health issues are experienced and perceived. For example, cultural or religious stigma might be stronger in some communities, impacting the willingness to seek help.

3. **Navigating Faith and Mental Health Through an Intersectional Lens:**
   - *Inclusive Environments:* Creating inclusive faith communities that acknowledge and celebrate diverse identities encourages open conversations about mental health and reduces stigma.
   - *Culturally Competent Care:* Mental health professionals who are aware of and sensitive to their clients' cultural and religious contexts can provide more effective support.
   - *Advocacy and Education:* Promoting awareness about the importance of mental health within faith communities can help break down barriers and encourage people to seek help when needed.

By understanding the intersection of faith, mental health, and intersectionality, we can better support individuals in their journeys, respecting and honouring their unique identities and experiences.

Benefits of therapy for individuals with strong faith backgrounds

Therapy can offer numerous benefits for individuals with strong faith backgrounds, helping them to navigate their mental health whilst honouring their spiritual beliefs. Here are some key benefits:

1. **Holistic Healing:**
   - Integrating spiritual beliefs with therapeutic practices can foster holistic healing, simultaneously addressing mental and spiritual needs.

2. **Enhanced Coping Strategies:**
   - Therapists can help individuals incorporate faith-based coping mechanisms, such as prayer or meditation, into their treatment plans, which can be comforting and familiar.

3. **Conflict Resolution:**
   - Therapy can assist individuals in resolving conflicts that may arise between their faith and personal issues, promoting internal harmony.

4. **Community Support:**
   - Counsellors can guide individuals in leveraging their faith communities for support, enhancing their network of care and encouragement.

5. **Reduced Stigma:**
   - Therapy can help challenge and reduce stigma surrounding mental health within religious communities, promoting a more open dialogue about emotional well-being.

6. **Value Alignment:**
   - Faith-informed therapy respects and aligns with individuals' beliefs and values, making therapeutic processes feel more relevant and validating.

7. **Improved Relationships:**
   - By addressing personal and spiritual issues, individuals can improve relationships with family, friends, and their faith communities.

8. **Spiritual Growth:**
   - Therapy can be a catalyst for spiritual growth, helping individuals gain deeper insights into their beliefs and how they relate to their mental health.

Overall, therapy can provide individuals with strong faith backgrounds with a supportive environment to explore and enhance their mental well-being whilst remaining true to their spiritual convictions.

Faith-based coping strategies

Faith-based coping strategies can be powerful tools for individuals looking to integrate their spiritual beliefs into their mental health practices. Here are some examples:

1. **Prayer:**
   - Engaging in prayer can provide comfort, guidance, and a sense of connection to a higher power during challenging times.

2. **Meditation:**
   - Many faith traditions incorporate forms of meditation, which can help calm the mind and foster spiritual awareness.

3. **Scripture Reading:**
   - Reading and reflecting on sacred texts can offer solace and wisdom, providing insights and strength for dealing with life's struggles.

4. **Faith-Based Community Involvement:**
   - Participating in community worship, study groups, or volunteer activities can build a sense of belonging and support, reinforcing one's faith and coping capacity.

5. **Rituals and Sacraments:**
   - Engaging in regular religious rituals or sacraments (such as communion or fasting) can provide structure, meaning, and spiritual renewal.

6. **Gratitude Practices:**
   - Cultivating gratitude, often emphasised in spiritual teachings, can enhance positivity and resilience in facing adversity.

7. **Spiritual Journalling:**
   - Keeping a journal to explore one's spiritual journey and express feelings and thoughts can be therapeutic and enlightening.

8. **Mentorship and Guidance:**
   - Seeking counsel from religious leaders or spiritual mentors can provide personalised support and perspective rooted in shared beliefs.

9. **Service and Acts of Kindness:**
    - Engaging in acts of kindness and service to others can be a way to live out one's faith, promoting well-being and purpose.

10. **Music and Worship:**
    - Music and communal worship can uplift the spirit, create a sense of unity, and offer emotional release.

These strategies, rooted in faith, can help individuals navigate life's challenges whilst deepening their spiritual connection and personal well-being.

The role of gratitude in spiritual coping

Gratitude plays a significant role in spiritual coping by providing emotional, psychological, and spiritual benefits. Here is how it works:

1. **Perspective Shift:**
    - Practising gratitude helps individuals focus on positive aspects of life, shifting attention away from difficulties and fostering a more balanced perspective.

2. **Spiritual Awareness:**
    - Many spiritual traditions encourage gratitude as a way to recognise and appreciate the presence of the divine or the blessings bestowed. This awareness can deepen one's spiritual connection.

3. **Increased Positivity:**
    - Grateful individuals often experience higher levels of positive emotions such as joy and contentment, which can enhance overall well-being and resilience.

4. **Enhanced Relationships:**
    - Expressing gratitude strengthens relationships by fostering mutual appreciation and understanding, reinforcing crucial social support systems during difficult times.

5. **Stress Reduction:**
    - Focusing on what one is thankful for can reduce stress and anxiety, as it helps to alleviate feelings of scarcity and focus on abundance.

6. **Empowerment and Control:**
    - Gratitude reminds individuals of the good in their lives, which can instil a sense of control over one's emotional outlook and life's circumstances.

7. **Encouraging a Grateful Heart:**
    - Spiritually, gratitude is often seen as a virtuous quality that aligns with humility and acknowledgement of one's blessings, fostering a humble and thankful heart.

8. **Motivating Positive Action:**
    - Gratitude can motivate individuals to give back or engage in acts of kindness, thereby spreading positivity and deepening their spiritual practice.

Overall, gratitude in spiritual coping catalyses emotional well-being, spiritual growth, and resilience, helping individuals navigate challenges with a more open and appreciative heart.

Stories

Horatio Spafford

Horatio Gates Spafford (20 October 1828 – 25 September 1888) was an American lawyer, Presbyterian church elder, and hymn writer best known for penning the Christian hymn *"It Is Well With My Soul"*. Born in Troy, New York, Spafford later became a prominent figure in Chicago.

Spafford faced numerous personal tragedies:

1. In 1871, he lost a fortune in the Great Chicago Fire.
2. His four-year-old son died of scarlet fever around the same time.
3. In 1873, his four daughters perished in a shipwreck whilst crossing the Atlantic Ocean.

After these tragedies, Spafford wrote *"It Is Well With My Soul"* whilst sailing to meet his wife in England. The hymn, composed by Philip Bliss, was first published in 1876.

In 1881, Spafford and his wife Anna moved to Jerusalem with a group of like-minded Christians, establishing a commune known as the American Colony. There, they served the poor, cared for the sick, and helped those in need.

Spafford died in Jerusalem on 25 September 1888. His legacy lives on through his enduring hymn, which inspires and comforts people worldwide.

Fanny Crosby

Fanny J. Crosby, born Frances Jane Crosby on 24 March 1820 in Putnam County, New York, was a renowned American hymn writer and mission worker. Despite losing her sight at six weeks old due to a medical mishap, Crosby became one of the most prolific hymnists, composing over 8,000 hymns, including *"Blessed Assurance"* and *"To God Be the Glory"*. Known as the "Queen of Gospel Song Writers", her work significantly influenced American congregational singing. Crosby was also deeply involved in urban mission work, dedicating her life to helping the poor and needy in New York City.

Andraé Crouch – *Through It All*

"Through It All" was originally written by Andraé Crouch in 1971. Crouch was a gifted musician and songwriter who composed this personal testimony as a hymn after experiencing heartbreak and disappointment during a concert tour in California. The song reflects his journey of faith and his experiences of relying on God through various trials and challenges in his life.

The Story

Andraé Crouch (1942–2015) was a gifted musician who received many honours and successes in life, but he also endured many heartaches. In one church he sang at, the first four rows of people walked out when he walked onto the stage; they did not know the man they had invited to sing was an African-American. At another engagement, the church could not find accommodation for him because of his skin colour, and a church member volunteered a shed next to a chicken coop for him to stay in.

However, this song was not written as a result of those events. It was written after Andraé had purchased a ring for a young lady who often sang with his group. He said, "We were working for three days at a church in Northern California, and I had picked out that time to ask her to be my companion for life."

The first night his fiancée-to-be did not show up. She did not come the next night either. On the third night she arrived, gathered the group together, and announced she was in love and planning to get married. But she was not speaking about Andraé; she was going to marry someone else.

After the service that night, the heartbroken Andraé drove five hours back to his home. During that long drive he wept and prayed, reflecting on David in the Old Testament, and how he had been directed by God's rod and staff. When he arrived home, he sat down and wrote this personal testimony as a hymn.

What this song means to me

It reminds me of the good times but also the difficult times when I had to rely on God.

Hold the Fort

"Hold the Fort" was written by Philip P. Bliss in 1870 after he was inspired by a story from the American Civil War, specifically the Battle of Allatoona Pass. The hymn was inspired by Union Major General William T. Sherman's message to hold the fort until reinforcements arrived, which Bliss interpreted as a metaphor for Christians to remain steadfast in their faith until Christ's return. The hymn quickly became popular in Christian circles and was later adapted as a labour anthem by workers' movements in the United States and Great Britain.

"And, behold, I come quickly; and my reward is with me, to give every man according as his work shall be." – Revelation 22:12

We are thrilled to share a series of brief accounts of how some of the great hymns of our faith were written.

Recognised Therapies

Faith-based Mentalisation Behavioural Therapy

Faith-based Mentalisation-Based Therapy (FB-MBT) integrates spiritual or religious beliefs with the principles of Mentalisation-

Based Therapy. This approach can be particularly beneficial for individuals who find strength and guidance in their faith. Here is how FB-MBT might work:

1. **Integration of Faith and Mentalisation:**
   - Combines the traditional elements of MBT with an individual's spiritual or religious beliefs, offering a holistic approach to understanding mental states.

2. **Faith as a Resource:**
   - Utilises spiritual beliefs and practices as tools for enhancing mentalisation. Faith can provide a framework for understanding emotions, motivations, and interpersonal dynamics.

3. **Enhanced Empathy Through Spirituality:**
   - Encourages empathy and understanding by drawing on faith-based teachings on compassion, forgiveness, and love, helping individuals interpret and manage their emotional and social worlds.

4. **Spiritual Reflection:**
   - Incorporates spiritual reflection alongside traditional mentalisation techniques, allowing individuals to explore the interplay between their faith and psychological experiences.

5. **Respect for Individual Beliefs:**
   - Therapists acknowledge and respect personal beliefs, creating a safe environment for individuals to explore both psychological and spiritual dimensions of their experiences.

6. **Coping Mechanisms:**
   - Faith-based approaches may offer unique coping strategies, such as prayer, meditation, or reading spiritual texts, which can complement traditional emotional regulation techniques.

7. **Interpersonal Harmony:**
   - Encourages the application of spiritual principles to improve relationships, promoting harmony and understanding in social interactions.

8. **Supportive Community:**
   - Leveraging community support within faith groups can provide additional emotional and social support, reinforcing therapeutic goals.

Faith-based Mentalisation-Based Therapy can offer a personalised and meaningful way for individuals to connect their mental and spiritual health, fostering a comprehensive path to healing and growth.

Coping Strategies Related to Faith

Scripture to Combat Fear

- **2 Timothy 1:7** "For God did not give us a spirit of fear, but of power and of love and a sound mind."
- **Deuteronomy 31:8** "He will never leave you nor forsake you. Do not be afraid; do not be discouraged."
- **Isaiah 43:1** "Do not fear, for I have redeemed you; I have called you by name; you are Mine."

- **Isaiah 41:10** "Fear not, for I am with you; be not dismayed, for I am your God. I will strengthen you, yes, I will help you, I will uphold you with My righteous right hand."

Scripture to Combat Depression

- **Psalm 34:17** "The righteous cry out, and the LORD hears them; he delivers them from all their troubles."
- **Psalm 42:11** "Why, my soul, are you downcast? Why so disturbed within me? Put your hope in God, for I will yet praise him, my Saviour and my God."
- **2 Corinthians 1:3–4** "Praise be to the God and Father of our Lord Jesus Christ, the Father of compassion and the God of all comfort, who comforts us in all our troubles, so that we can comfort those in any trouble with the comfort we ourselves receive from God."
- **Psalm 40:1–3** "I waited patiently for the LORD; he turned to me and heard my cry. He lifted me out of the slimy pit, out of the mud and mire; he set my feet on a rock and gave me a firm place to stand. He put a new song in my mouth, a hymn of praise to our God. Many will see and fear the LORD and put their trust in him."

Scripture to Combat Anxiety

- **Philippians 4:6–7** "Be anxious for nothing, but in everything by prayer and supplication, with thanksgiving, let your requests be made known to God; and the peace of God, which surpasses all understanding, will guard your hearts and minds through Christ Jesus."
- **Jeremiah 29:11** "For I know the thoughts that I think toward you, says the LORD, thoughts of peace and not of evil, to give you a future and a hope."

- **John 14:27** "Peace is what I leave with you; it is my own peace that I give you. I do not give it as the world does. Do not be worried and upset; do not be afraid."

Scripture to Combat Perfectionism

- **Galatians 1:10** "Am I now trying to win the approval of men, or God? Or am I trying to please men? If I were still trying to please men, I would not be a servant of Christ."
- **Psalm 18:32** "It is God who arms me with strength and makes my way perfect."
- **1 John 1:9** "If we confess our sins, he is faithful and just to forgive us our sins and to cleanse us from all unrighteousness."

If you are struggling with any of these issues, we hope these mental health scriptures are useful.

The Meaning of Recovery

- Christian Mental Health Advocacy
- When Troubles Come
- You Are Not Alone
- Helping Yourself
- How to Get Help
- You Figure it Out
- Getting Help, Have Faith, So Far So Good
- Each Step You Take: Anxiety, Depression

Techniques Used in Faith-Based MBT

Faith-Based Mentalisation-Based Therapy (FB-MBT) employs a variety of techniques that integrate traditional MBT with spiritual or religious elements. Here are some techniques often used in FB-MBT:

1. **Mindful Prayer and Meditation**
    - Encourages individuals to engage in prayer or meditation to enhance awareness of their own thoughts and feelings, fostering a deeper understanding of their mental state.

2. **Scriptural Reflection**
    - Utilises religious or spiritual texts to draw parallels with personal experiences, promoting reflection on emotional and interpersonal situations through the lens of faith.

3. **Faith-Inspired Imagery**
    - Involves imagining biblical scenes or spiritual stories to facilitate understanding of emotional experiences, enhancing empathy and perspective-taking.

4. **Spiritual Dialogue**
    - Engages individuals in discussions about their spiritual beliefs and how these can inform their understanding of themselves and their relationships with others.

5. **Compassion Exercises**
    - Draws on religious teachings about compassion and forgiveness to encourage kindness towards oneself and others, aiding in conflict resolution and emotional healing.

6. **Community-Based Support**
    - Incorporates support from faith communities, encouraging participation in group activities or discussions that reinforce therapeutic themes and provide social support.

7. **Emotional Journaling**
    - Involves writing about experiences and emotions while reflecting on spiritual insights, helping individuals process their feelings in a faith-oriented way.

8. **Reflective Storytelling**
    - Encourages sharing personal or spiritual stories that illustrate emotional experiences or challenges, helping individuals connect these narratives to broader faith-based teachings.

9. **Values Clarification**
    - Helps individuals identify and clarify their core spiritual or religious values and how they can guide their everyday behaviour and emotional responses.

10. **Interfaith Perspectives**
    - For those open to it, explores interfaith teachings to broaden understanding of emotional and interpersonal dynamics, highlighting universal spiritual principles of love, peace, and acceptance.

These techniques aim to harness the supportive power of personal faith, providing a comprehensive and comforting framework for understanding emotions and relationships.

Benefits of FB-MBT

Faith-Based Mentalisation-Based Therapy (FB-MBT) offers several unique benefits by integrating spiritual elements with traditional therapeutic practices. Here are some key advantages:

1. **Enhanced Emotional Insight**
    - FB-MBT helps individuals gain deeper insights into their emotions and behaviours, enhancing self-awareness through a spiritual lens.

2. **Holistic Healing**
    - By combining mental health practices with spiritual teachings, clients often experience healing that addresses both psychological and spiritual needs.

3. **Improved Coping Mechanisms**
    - Spiritual practices such as prayer and meditation provide additional coping strategies, helping individuals manage stress and emotional challenges more effectively.

4. **Strengthened Faith**
    - Engaging with therapy through a spiritual framework can reinforce and deepen one's faith, providing a sense of purpose and meaning in life's challenges.

5. **Increased Compassion and Empathy**
    - FB-MBT encourages compassion and understanding towards oneself and others, fostering healthier relationships and interpersonal interactions.

6. **Supportive Community**
    - Integrating faith communities into therapy can offer individuals a robust support network, enhancing feelings of belonging and reducing isolation.

7. **Alignment with Personal Values**
    - This therapy aligns treatment with an individual's spiritual beliefs and values, ensuring a more personalised and meaningful therapeutic experience.

8. **Resilience Building**
    - Spiritual teachings often emphasise enduring hardships, enhancing an individual's resilience and ability to navigate life's difficulties.

9. **Reduced Stigma**
    - For some, integrating faith into therapy reduces the stigma associated with seeking mental health care, making it more accessible and acceptable.

10. **Facilitates Forgiveness and Closure**
    - Religious teachings about forgiveness can aid in resolving past conflicts, promoting emotional closure and peace.

11. **Encourages Personal Growth**
    - Through reflection on spiritual teachings, clients are encouraged to pursue personal growth and transformation, enhancing overall wellbeing.

FB-MBT provides a comprehensive approach that respects and incorporates a person's spiritual beliefs, aiding in emotional healing and personal development.

Perinatal Mental Health

Mother and Baby Units and the Role of Faith Communities

As of 2025, there are 22 Mother and Baby Units (MBUs) in the UK, with 151 beds in England, 12 beds in Scotland, and 6 beds in Wales. Northern Ireland currently has no MBU, but a business case is under development.

The prevalence of perinatal mental illness affects up to one in five new and expectant mothers in England. It is estimated that approximately 3–5% of pregnant women are referred to psychiatric services, with 1% of women in the perinatal period meeting the criteria for specialised care in MBUs.

The current provision of MBU beds is insufficient to meet demand. It is estimated that 0.25 MBU beds per 1,000 live births are required if specialised perinatal community mental health teams are available, or 0.5 per 1,000 if no specialised teams are provided. Based on these estimates and the number of live births in England, approximately 6,600 women with serious mental illness require prescribed perinatal mental health services each year.

To address this gap, the NHS Long Term Plan aims to increase access to specialist care for at least 66,000 women by 2023/24. This expansion is part of a broader initiative to improve perinatal mental health services across the UK.

Mother and Baby Units (MBUs) provide specialised support for new mothers experiencing mental health challenges. These units allow mothers and their babies to receive the necessary care and treatment without being separated. The role of faith communities in supporting these units and the families they serve can be quite significant, encompassing several key areas:

1. **Emotional and Spiritual Support**: Faith communities can offer emotional and spiritual support through pastoral care,

counselling, and prayer. This can be comforting for mothers experiencing stress, anxiety, or postnatal depression.

2. **Community Engagement**: Engaging with MBUs as part of a broader community initiative can help reduce stigma associated with mental health. By creating awareness and promoting understanding, faith communities can foster inclusive attitudes and acceptance.

3. **Volunteer Services**: Members of faith communities often volunteer their time and skills. This could include offering babysitting services, organising support groups, or providing companionship to mothers who may feel isolated.

4. **Material Assistance**: Many faith communities have resources to extend material assistance, such as donating baby clothes, toys, or other necessary supplies to mothers in need.

5. **Advocacy and Awareness**: By leveraging their networks, faith communities can advocate for better policies that support mental health and family wellbeing. They can also host events or workshops to raise awareness about the importance of mental health care for mothers and infants.

6. **Respite Care**: Some community members might offer respite care for mothers needing a break, reducing stress on the family unit and providing time for mothers to engage in self-care.

By integrating these supportive roles, faith communities can become valuable partners for Mother and Baby Units, enhancing the wellbeing and recovery of the families they serve. These partnerships also strengthen community ties and foster a nurturing environment for mothers and their babies.

How Faith Communities Can Support

Certainly! Here are a few examples of how faith communities have supported Mother and Baby Units:

1. **Church-Based Support Groups:** Some churches have established support groups specifically for mothers dealing with postnatal depression or other mental health issues. These groups offer a safe space for sharing experiences, receiving guidance, and offering mutual support.

2. **Interfaith Coalitions:** Various faith communities have come together to create coalitions that sponsor events, workshops, or seminars focused on maternal mental health. These events often include expert talks, practical advice, and spiritual reflections.

3. **Pastoral Care and Counselling:** Many faith leaders make themselves available for pastoral counselling, providing spiritual guidance and emotional support. This can be particularly comforting for mothers experiencing anxiety, depression, or feelings of isolation.

4. **Charity Drives:** Faith communities frequently organise donation drives to gather essential baby items—such as nappies, clothing, or toys—for mothers residing in MBUs. These drives provide material support to families in need.

5. **Volunteering Efforts:** In some regions, members of faith communities volunteer at MBUs, offering companionship and support to mothers. They might also organise craft sessions or storytelling activities for mothers and their babies.

6. **Respite Programmes:** Some faith organisations have developed respite care programmes, where trained volunteers provide temporary relief to parents in MBUs, allowing them some personal time to recharge.

7. **Prayer and Meditation Sessions:** Faith communities often offer sessions in prayer, meditation, or mindfulness, designed to help mothers in MBUs find peace and relaxation during challenging times.

These examples demonstrate how faith communities can play a vital role in supporting the unique needs of mothers and infants within Mother and Baby Units, creating a supportive and caring network that enhances healing and recovery.

Faith and Perinatal Mental Health

Faith can play a significant role in supporting perinatal mental health, offering both spiritual guidance and community support to mothers experiencing mental health challenges during and after pregnancy. Here are some ways faith intersects with perinatal mental health:

1. **Spiritual Comfort and Coping:** For many individuals, faith provides a source of comfort and strength during challenging times. Spiritual beliefs can offer a framework for understanding personal experiences and foster resilience in dealing with perinatal mental health issues.

2. **Community and Belonging:** Faith communities often provide a sense of belonging and support. Mothers can find solace and empathy within these communities, knowing they have a network of people who care and are willing to assist them emotionally and sometimes materially.

3. **Rituals and Practices:** Religious rituals and spiritual practices, such as prayer, meditation, or attending services, can offer a routine, reduce anxiety, and promote a sense of peace and stability for mothers experiencing mental health challenges.

4. **Pastoral Counselling:** Many faith leaders offer pastoral counselling, providing a listening ear and spiritual guidance

to mothers facing perinatal mental health issues. This can help mothers feel understood and supported in a non-judgemental space.

5. **Education and Awareness:** Faith-based organisations can help raise awareness about perinatal mental health, providing educational resources, workshops, and seminars that help destigmatise mental health concerns and promote understanding and compassion.

6. **Support Groups:** Some faith communities organise support groups specifically for new mothers. These groups offer a safe space to share experiences, receive emotional support, and connect with others who may be facing similar challenges.

7. **Holistic Approach to Healing:** Combining spiritual and mental health support, faith communities may promote a holistic approach to healing that respects both the spiritual and psychological aspects of perinatal mental health.

While faith can be a powerful ally in addressing perinatal mental health, it is important to recognise that it may not be the primary solution for everyone. Mental health professionals play a crucial role, and faith-based support can complement professional treatment. Respecting and integrating individual beliefs and needs into mental health care can enhance the overall well-being of mothers and families.

Some Scriptures That Offer Comfort During Perinatal Mental Health Struggles

Here are some scriptures from various religious traditions that can provide comfort and support during perinatal mental health struggles:

Christianity

1. Philippians 4:6-7: *"Do not be anxious about anything, but in every situation, by prayer and petition, with thanksgiving, present your requests to God. And the peace of God, which transcends all understanding, will guard your hearts and your minds in Christ Jesus."*

2. Psalm 34:17-18: *"The righteous cry out, and the Lord hears them; he delivers them from all their troubles. The Lord is close to the broken-hearted and saves those who are crushed in spirit."*

3. Isaiah 41:10: *"So do not fear, for I am with you; do not be dismayed, for I am your God. I will strengthen you and help you; I will uphold you with my righteous right hand."*

Knife Crime, Mental Health, and the Role of Faith Communities

There is a link between mental health and knife crime, though it is a complex relationship. Here are a few key points:

1. **Mental Health Issues:** Individuals with untreated or severe mental health issues may be more prone to engaging in or becoming victims of violence, although the majority of those with mental health conditions are not violent.

2. **Socioeconomic Factors:** Poor mental health can be influenced by socioeconomic factors that also contribute to crime, such as poverty, unemployment, lack of education, and social exclusion.

3. **Substance Misuse:** Substance misuse is often linked to both mental health problems and increased aggression, which can lead to knife-related incidents.

4. **Trauma and Violence:** Experiencing trauma or living in environments where violence is prevalent can lead to mental

health issues, such as PTSD or anxiety, which might contribute to aggressive behaviours.

5. **Intervention and Prevention:** Mental health support and community interventions can help mitigate the risk of knife crime by addressing underlying psychological issues and providing support to at-risk individuals.

Despite these connections, it is important to avoid stigmatising those with mental health issues, as they are more often victims rather than perpetrators of crime. Understanding these dynamics can help in creating informed policies for crime prevention and mental health support.

Substance Use and Mental Health

The link between substance use and mental health is a pressing concern, with interest in prevention and coping strategies.

Specific mental health issues linked to knife crime can include:

1. **Conduct Disorder:** This disorder in children and adolescents is characterised by aggressive behaviour that can lead to serious violations of rules, including carrying and using weapons such as knives.

2. **Antisocial Personality Disorder (ASPD):** Often associated with a disregard for others, individuals with ASPD may engage in criminal behaviour, including violent acts such as knife crime.

3. **Impulse Control Disorders:** Difficulties with controlling impulses can lead to aggressive and violent behaviours, potentially involving knives.

4. **Substance Use Disorders:** Substance misuse can result in impaired judgement and heightened aggression, increasing the likelihood of involvement in knife-related incidents.

5. **Post-Traumatic Stress Disorder (PTSD)**: Those who have experienced trauma might exhibit aggressive behaviour as a response to perceived threats, sometimes leading to knife crime.

6. **Severe Depression and Anxiety**: While generally not directly linked to violence, extreme cases can lead to desperate behaviours, particularly when combined with other risk factors.

7. **Psychosis**: In rare cases, individuals experiencing psychosis may become involved in violent acts, including those involving weapons, due to distorted perceptions of reality.

It is essential to note that most people with these disorders do not engage in violent behaviour and that the presence of mental health issues alone does not cause knife crime. Contextual factors such as environment, social influences, and personal experiences often play a significant role.

The link between substance misuse and knife crime

The connection between substance misuse and knife crime is multifaceted and involves several factors:

1. **Impaired Judgement**: Substance misuse often leads to impaired cognitive functions and decision-making abilities. This can result in individuals making poor choices, such as carrying or using a knife in a threatening or violent manner.

2. **Increased Aggression**: Many substances, particularly alcohol and certain stimulants, can increase aggressive behaviour. This heightened aggression can lead to confrontations and violent incidents involving knives.

3. **Social Environment**: Substance misuse often occurs in environments where illegal activities are more prevalent. These environments can have higher rates of violence,

including knife crime, due to competition and conflicts related to drug dealing and use.

4. **Desperation and Economic Need**: Individuals suffering from addiction may resort to crime, including knife crime, to support their habit. The need for money or drugs can lead to violent robberies or assaults.

5. **Mental Health Issues**: Substance misuse can exacerbate existing mental health issues, leading to irrational and violent behaviour. This dual diagnosis scenario can increase the risk of involvement in knife crime.

6. **Peer Influence**: Associating with others who carry weapons or engage in criminal activities, often under the influence, can lead to an increased likelihood of committing knife-related crimes.

Addressing substance misuse as a public health issue and providing support for those struggling with addiction can be a crucial part of preventing knife crime. Community programmes, rehabilitation services, and policies addressing drug-related crime can all contribute to reducing this link.

Substance misuse and knife crime: data trends

While I cannot provide real-time statistics, I can outline general data trends and findings from various studies:

1. **Alcohol Influence**: Studies have shown that a significant percentage of violent crimes, including knife crimes, are committed under the influence of alcohol. For example, the UK Office for National Statistics has reported that around 40% of victims of violent crime believed the offender to be under the influence of alcohol.

2. **Drug-Related Crime**: The relationship between drug use and knife crime is complex, but data often suggest a strong

connection. Offenders involved in drug-related activities may carry knives for protection or intimidation, resulting in higher incidence rates of knife-related offences in drug-affected areas.

3. **Young Offenders**: Research has indicated that young individuals involved in knife crime often have a history of substance misuse, specifically with drugs such as cannabis and cocaine, which are associated with delinquent behaviour and violence.

4. **Hospital Admissions**: Data from emergency departments often reveal that a considerable number of patients admitted for stab wounds have drugs or alcohol in their system at the time of the incident.

5. **Crime Surveys**: Surveys such as the Crime Survey for England and Wales frequently highlight the role of substances in violent crime offenders, citing a direct connection in a notable percentage of cases.

It is important to consult the latest governmental reports, law enforcement statistics, and academic research for current and localised data on this topic.

Specific drugs most commonly linked to knife crime

Several substances are frequently associated with knife crime, often due to their disinhibiting effects or their role in fuelling conflicts within the illegal drug trade. These include:

1. **Alcohol**: Although legal, alcohol is a significant contributor to violent crimes, including knife crimes. Its consumption often leads to reduced inhibitions and increased aggression.

2. **Cocaine**: This stimulant can cause heightened aggression and paranoia, making users more likely to become involved in violent altercations, including those involving knives.

3. **Cannabis**: While generally considered less likely to provoke violence than other substances, cannabis is linked to knife crime primarily through its illegal trade, where disputes can escalate to violence.

4. **Heroin**: Users and dealers of heroin may become involved in knife crime due to the drug's illegal nature and the violent contexts in which it is often distributed.

5. **Methamphetamine**: Known for its strong stimulant effects, methamphetamine can lead to aggressive and unpredictable behaviour, sometimes culminating in knife-related violence.

6. **Synthetic Drugs**: New psychoactive substances (sometimes referred to as "legal highs" prior to prohibition) can also be involved in knife crime, particularly when their effects lead to unpredictable and violent behaviour.

Tensions, territorial disputes, and robberies tied to the illegal drug trade also play a significant role in the association between these substances and knife crime.

The role of faith and churches in knife crime reduction

Faith communities and churches can play several important roles in reducing knife crime. These include:

1. **Community Building**: Churches often serve as community hubs, bringing people together and fostering a sense of belonging. This can help reduce feelings of isolation or alienation that might lead individuals to engage in crime.

2. **Youth Engagement Programmes**: Churches frequently run youth clubs, activities, and mentorship programmes that provide young people with positive role models and alternatives to crime.

3. **Conflict Resolution**: Faith communities can offer mediation and conflict resolution services, helping to address and resolve disputes before they escalate into violence.

4. **Educational Initiatives**: Churches can provide education on the consequences of knife crime and promote messages of peace and non-violence.

5. **Support Services**: Many churches offer support services such as counselling, which can assist individuals dealing with issues like substance misuse or trauma that may otherwise lead them towards crime.

6. **Partnerships with Authorities**: By collaborating with local law enforcement and other community organisations, churches can be part of a broader strategy to tackle knife crime.

7. **Advocacy and Awareness**: Churches can raise awareness and advocate for policies and programmes that address the root causes of knife crime, such as poverty, lack of education, and unemployment.

By leveraging their influence and resources, faith communities can be powerful allies in the effort to reduce knife crime and promote safer neighbourhoods.

Examples of Successful Faith-Based Initiatives Addressing Knife Crime

1. **The Word 4 Weapons Initiative (UK):** Founded by Pastor Desmond Jadoo, this initiative places knife surrender bins across cities in the UK, allowing individuals to anonymously dispose of knives. It also promotes educational programmes in schools to raise awareness about the dangers of knife crime.

2. **St Giles Trust – From Gangs to Employment (London, UK):** Although not exclusively faith-based, this programme often collaborates with churches to mentor and support young individuals involved in gangs. By offering job training and personal development, the programme helps reduce reliance on crime.

3. **Peace on the Streets (USA):** Many churches across the United States, particularly in urban areas, organise events and workshops under banners such as *Peace on the Streets*. These events often involve community leaders, law enforcement, and young people, encouraging discussions on peace and providing alternatives to crime.

4. **Street Pastors Initiative (UK):** Established in London, this initiative involves church volunteers patrolling the streets at night to engage with young people, offering support and guidance, and helping to diffuse potentially violent situations.

5. **The Cure Violence Programme (Global):** Although not purely faith-based, this initiative frequently partners with local faith communities. It treats violence as a public health issue, using faith leaders as "violence interrupters" to mediate conflicts and prevent escalation.

These initiatives demonstrate how faith communities can effectively engage with local populations and authorities to address and reduce knife crime through a combination of prevention, education, and direct intervention strategies.

Personal Stories and Testimonies

These cases underscore the importance of mental health awareness in religious communities.

The suicides of pastors such as Jarrid Wilson, Andrew Stoecklein, and Darrin Patrick can be attributed to several interconnected factors:

- **Mental Health Issues:** Many pastors struggle with depression, anxiety, and loneliness, often exacerbated by the pressures of ministry. The burden and pressures of leading a congregation and the reality of burnout cannot be overstated.

- **Isolation:** A significant number report feeling isolated, lacking close friendships, and facing burnout.

- **Stigma:** Within churches there is often a cultural stigma that discourages open discussions about mental health struggles.

- **Professional Pressure:** The demands of church leadership can lead to overwhelming stress and feelings of inadequacy when comparing themselves to others.

These factors highlight the urgent need for improved mental health support in religious communities.

Measures to Prevent Future Pastor Suicides

Several measures are being implemented:

- **Training Programmes:** Initiatives such as *LivingWorks Faith* and *Soul Shop* provide training for pastors on how to recognise warning signs of suicide and engage in meaningful conversations about mental health.

- **Community Support:** Churches are encouraged to foster supportive environments that promote open discussions about mental health.

- **Mental Health Resources:** Access to mental health services is being promoted, with pastors trained to connect individuals with professional help when needed.

- **National Strategies:** Government strategies include over 100 actions aimed at early intervention and improving mental health services across various sectors, including faith communities. These efforts aim to equip pastors and congregations to better support those in crisis.

Faith Implications

1. **Crisis of Faith:** For religious individuals, such a traumatic event could trigger a crisis of faith. The discovery of betrayal, particularly by trusted family members, may lead to questioning the justice or benevolence of a higher power.

2. **Community Support:** Faith communities often provide support during crises. Religious leaders and community members can offer comfort, counselling, and practical assistance to the bereaved.

3. **Moral and Ethical Considerations:** Religious beliefs may influence how the family interprets the act of suicide. Some faiths view suicide as morally wrong, which can add to the survivors' emotional burden.

Cultural Factors

1. **Stigma and Shame:** In some Asian cultures, family honour and reputation carry significant weight. The betrayal and subsequent suicide could be perceived as bringing shame upon the family, possibly influencing her decision due to societal pressures.

2. **Lack of Mental Health Resources:** Cultural barriers may prevent individuals from seeking mental health care, either due to stigma or lack of understanding about available resources.

3. **Family Dynamics:** Familial betrayal can be magnified in closely-knit family structures. Coping with such betrayal may be more challenging, contributing to her decision.

This narrative underscores the urgent need for comprehensive support systems that integrate faith-based support, mental health care, and community awareness. Encouraging open dialogues about mental health and ensuring access to professional help can significantly impact individuals navigating similar crises. Supporting children and families in the aftermath is crucial for promoting healing and preventing long-term psychological effects.

Case Example

A 30-year-old man from Sussex left a suicide note to his wife, filled with guilt after a serious row. His extremely worried partner alerted the police when she found the note. Police used ANPR to locate his car and intercepted him en route to a secluded location. He was brought into hospital but, despite close observation on the ward, he tied a ligature and strangled himself.

Psychiatric Analysis

This narrative touches on complex themes involving faith, mental health, and the profound impact they can have on individuals and their relationships.

Faith Context

1. **Spiritual Crisis:** The man's situation may evoke a spiritual crisis, where faith is challenged by emotional turmoil. In times of extreme guilt or desperation, individuals may feel distant from their beliefs or unable to reconcile actions with moral or religious values.

2. **Hope and Redemption:** Faith often provides hope and the possibility of redemption, which can be vital in preventing

self-destructive actions. His partner reaching out for help could be seen as an act of hope, driven by belief in reconciliation and healing.

3. **Community Support:** Faith communities often offer guidance and support in times of crisis, emphasising forgiveness, understanding, and communal care. This can be crucial for individuals struggling with guilt or depression.

Mental Health Implications

1. **Guilt and Depression:** Guilt in the aftermath of conflict can lead to severe depression. The man's note and subsequent actions indicate profound emotional distress, where guilt overwhelmed his ability to see any positive outcome.

2. **Crisis Intervention:** The police intervention highlights the importance of timely crisis intervention. When someone shows signs of suicidal ideation, immediate action is crucial. However, as this case tragically shows, even swift intervention may not always prevent a loss of life.

3. **Monitoring and Care:** Despite close observation, the man's death underscores the challenges in mental health care, particularly the need for continuous and sensitive support. Mental health crises can persist even when individuals appear stable.

4. **Impact on Loved Ones:** The tragedy has profound implications for his partner, who raised the alarm. Feelings of guilt, regret, and grief are likely to follow, underlining the need for support for both individuals in crisis and their loved ones.

Case of Dr Sridharan Suresh

Dr Sridharan Suresh was a 50-year-old consultant anaesthetist at North Tees and Hartlepool Hospitals NHS Foundation Trust. He had an exemplary work record but tragically took his own life on 2 May 2018.

The incident occurred after Dr Suresh received an email from the General Medical Council (GMC) informing him of an investigation and upcoming tribunal hearing. This was related to allegations of sexual touching made by a teenage patient undergoing sedation for dental extraction. However, the drugs used in the procedure are known to produce hallucinations, and the police later closed the case due to insufficient evidence.

Dr Suresh's death raised serious concerns about the GMC's investigative process and its impact on doctors' mental health. His widow, Viji Suresh, has since campaigned for more compassionate regulation of doctors and better support for those under investigation. The case has led to calls for reform in how healthcare professionals accused of misconduct are investigated.

Reflection and Lessons

- The narrative serves as a poignant reminder of the intricate connection between mental health and faith. It emphasises the need for compassionate support systems from mental health professionals and within faith communities to provide hope, healing, and resilience.

- It highlights the importance of addressing mental health stigma, encouraging open dialogue about emotional struggles, and equipping individuals with tools for coping in times of crisis.

- Lastly, it reinforces the necessity for ongoing mental health education and awareness, reminding us that mental health is a crucial component of overall well-being and requires collective effort and understanding.

Teen Suicide

Teen suicide rates are alarmingly high and increasing globally. Suicide is the second leading cause of death among young people aged 10–24, with boys more likely to die by suicide but girls attempting it more often.

Contributing factors include mental health disorders (e.g., depression, anxiety), family issues, academic pressures, bullying, social isolation, and access to lethal means such as firearms.

LGBTQ+ youth and marginalised groups face disproportionately higher risks.

Recent data show a 35% rise in suicides among 15–19-year-olds in England from 2020 to 2021, highlighting the urgent need for improved mental health support.

By Michael Buchanan

Social Affairs Correspondent, BBC News

Examination pressures and physical health problems, such as acne, are major contributory factors in the suicides of young people, according to research.

Experts at the University of Manchester also found bullying and family bereavement were linked to suicides.

They investigated the suicides of 130 people under the age of 20 in England between January 2014 and April 2015.

In February, figures published by the Office for National Statistics revealed an increase in youth suicides.

There were 201 people aged between 10 and 19 who took their own lives in 2014 in the UK – up from 179 in 2013.

This follows separate figures published by the Office for National Statistics this week, which suggested student suicides have risen to their highest level since at least 2007.

Contributory factors

Suicide is the leading cause of death among people under the age of 35 in the UK.

However, the research by the University of Manchester's National Confidential Inquiry into Suicide and Homicide by People with Mental Illness marks the first time experts have studied contributory factors on this scale.

Their findings showed:

- 36% had a physical health condition such as acne or asthma
- 29% were facing examinations or awaiting results; four died on an examination day or the day after
- 28% had experienced bereavement
- 22% had been bullied, mostly face-to-face

The study also found that 23% had used the internet in relation to suicide – including searching for methods or posting suicidal thoughts.

Case Study: *'Bullies broke my mind 100 times'*

Eleni Delacour says she was 10 when she first tried to end her life.

Eleni has depression and borderline personality disorder. However, she says the main reason she has attempted suicide on 14 occasions is bullying.

"I was bullied for as long as I can remember – both emotional and physical bullying," she says.

"I have had my tendon snapped, my nose broken twice, my mind broken a hundred times."

Her first suicide attempt was when she was 10. "When enough people tell you something about yourself that is bad, you start to believe it too," she says.

"You are told you are worthless to the point where you believe you are worthless. And then you do not want to feel it anymore, and the only way you can stop it is to end it all."

Speaking about the report's findings, lead researcher Professor Louis Appleby said:

"There are often family problems such as drug misuse or domestic violence, and more recent stresses such as bullying or bereavement, leading to a 'final straw' factor such as an examination or relationship breakdown."

"I think the numbers are the tip of the iceberg," says Ged Flynn, chief executive of Papyrus, an anti-suicide charity.

Its support service, Hopeline UK, has seen a large increase in contacts from young people and parents in recent years, quadrupling since 2013.

The charity says that most of the calls, texts and emails it receives relate to examination stress.

"I think the pressure on young people is increasing," says Mr Flynn. "Peer pressure – from family, teachers and friends – has always existed, but it does seem to be rising.

"And I think the need to be liked, the need to be popular, the need to be happy, is fairly universal. And it is unrealistic."

Case Study: 'A catastrophic decision'

Image source: Falconer family

Morgan Falconer was known as Tigger – a bright, enthusiastic, inquisitive, and tactile boy. Without any warning, however, the 15-year-old took his own life last May.

He had spoken to his friends about feeling pressure regarding his upcoming GCSE examinations, but his father, Stuart, says the family will never know what ultimately drove him to end his life.

"I cannot – hand on heart – say anything was a concern," says Stuart. "He should be here today, of that I have absolutely no doubt.

"It was a consequence of matters that built up in his mind, which led him to make a catastrophic decision that could not be reversed.

"If he had known what he had left behind, he would not have done it. If he had seen the outpouring of grief at his funeral, he would not have done it."

His father has now established a charity, The Ollie Foundation, to provide teachers with suicide awareness training.

Young People, Faith & Mental Challenges

Suicide Rate
Men

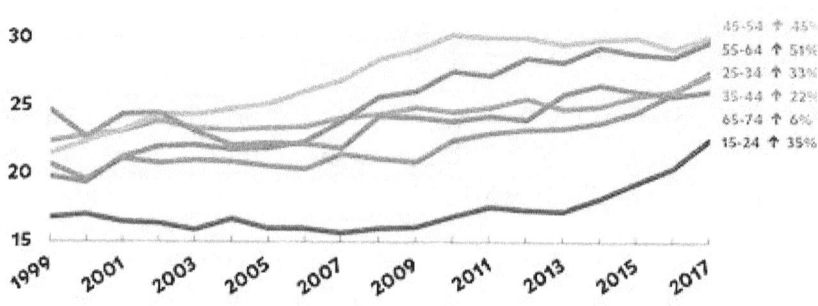

Source: Centers for Disease Control

Young People, Faith & Mental Challenges

The rise in teenage suicides is linked to multiple factors:

• Mental health disorders: Depression, anxiety, and other psychiatric conditions are significant contributors, with up to 90% of youth suicides associated with mental disorders.

• Family environment: A history of family mental illness, abuse, neglect, or unsupportive relationships increases risk.

• Stressors: Academic pressures, bullying (including cyberbullying), relationship difficulties, and bereavement are common triggers.

- Trauma and adverse experiences: Childhood abuse, neglect, or exposure to violence heightens vulnerability.

- Access to means: Availability of firearms or other lethal methods elevates the likelihood of suicide attempts.

Influence of Family Dynamics on Teenage Suicide Rates

Family dynamics significantly influence teenage suicide rates through several mechanisms:

1. **Family Functioning:** Dysfunctional families with low cohesion, poor communication, and high conflict are linked to higher suicidal ideation in teenagers. Balanced families with adaptability and emotional support act as protective factors.

2. **Parental Influence:** Parental psychopathology, neglect, or abusive behaviour increases suicide risk. Conversely, parental care and perceived love reduce it.

3. **Emotional Mediation:** Poor family relationships can exacerbate depression and anxiety in teenagers, which

mediate the link between family dysfunction and suicide risk.

4. **Social Support:** Lack of family support fosters isolation, worsening suicidal tendencies.

What Role Does Parental Monitoring Play in Preventing Teenage Suicide?

Parental monitoring plays a critical role in preventing teenage suicide by fostering protective behaviours and reducing risk factors:

- **Awareness and Communication:** Monitoring teenagers' activities, social circles, and emotional well-being helps parents identify warning signs of suicidal ideation early.

- **Setting Expectations:** Clear rules and consistent consequences reduce risky behaviours linked to suicide, such as substance misuse or isolation.

- **Supportive Relationships:** Open, trusting communication strengthens parent–teen relationships, making teenagers more likely to share struggles and seek help.

- **Intervention:** Active parental involvement in mental health care and problem-solving builds resilience and reduces maladjustment issues.

How Parents Can Improve Their Communication with Their Teenagers to Reduce Suicide Risk

Parents can improve communication with their teenagers to reduce suicide risk by:

- **Being Direct and Open:** Ask explicitly about suicidal thoughts without fear of "planting the idea." Teenagers often welcome the opportunity to share their feelings.

- **Listening Actively:** Provide undivided attention, validate emotions, and avoid judgement or dismissive remarks. Remain calm and empathetic.

- **Normalising Experiences:** Reassure teenagers that their feelings are not unusual or shameful, fostering openness.

- **Encouraging Emotional Expression:** Create a safe space for teenagers to discuss stress, fears, or confusion without fear of criticism.

- **Modelling Coping Skills:** Demonstrate healthy ways to manage stress and problem-solve collaboratively.

Common Regrets of People Who Survive a Suicide Attempt

These regrets underscore the importance of seeking help, maintaining open communication, and recognising that suicidal crises are often temporary, with many survivors gaining a renewed perspective on life after their attempt.

People who survive suicide attempts often experience a range of regrets:

1. **Immediate Regret:** Many survivors report feeling instant remorse for their actions, realising that their problems were temporary and that solutions existed.

2. **Missed Opportunities:** Survivors often regret potentially missing out on future experiences, relationships, and life events.

3. **Impact on Loved Ones:** Many survivors come to understand the profound effect their attempt had on family and friends, leading to feelings of guilt.

4. **Overlooking Support:** There is often regret for not reaching out to available support systems or professionals before attempting suicide.

5. **Impaired Decision-Making:** Survivors frequently recognise that their decision was made during a moment of acute distress, without fully considering alternatives or consequences.

6. **Misperception of Being a Burden:** Many regret believing that their loved ones would be better off without them, realising this thought was incorrect.

7. **Neglecting Self-Care:** Some survivors regret not taking better care of their physical and mental health prior to their attempt.

8. **Lack of Communication:** There is often remorse for not expressing their feelings and struggles to others who could potentially have helped.

Religious Faith and Its Influence on Self-Harm and Suicide

Religious faith can have complex effects on self-harm and suicide. While religious affiliation often protects against suicide attempts, it does not necessarily reduce suicidal ideation. Faith can provide a sense of purpose and hope, acting as a buffer against suicide by discouraging impulsive behaviour and promoting self-control.

However, some individuals struggle to reconcile their faith with mental health issues, feeling guilt or shame for self-harm and suicidal thoughts. Supportive faith communities that emphasise compassion rather than condemnation can help individuals navigate these challenges.

Christian Faith and the Experience of Self-Harm and Suicidal Thoughts

Christian faith can play a complex role in the experiences of self-harm and suicidal thoughts. Self-harm is often a coping mechanism for emotional pain, and while it is not necessarily linked to suicidal intent, it can be a cry for help.

Within the Christian context, self-harm is often viewed as a spiritual issue, where individuals may struggle with guilt and shame, feeling disconnected from their faith. Many Christians find hope and healing through their faith, emphasising the transformative power of Jesus Christ's sacrifice as a source of healing and redemption. Supportive faith communities can provide understanding and encouragement, helping individuals reconcile their struggles with their beliefs.

Churches can provide a safe space for individuals struggling with self-harm by implementing several key strategies:

Small group discussions play a crucial role in fostering a safe environment for mental health sharing by providing intimate settings where individuals feel more comfortable opening up about their struggles. These groups nurture trust and openness, allowing participants to feel seen and heard without fear of judgement.

Statistics on Suicide Among Psychiatrists

Psychiatrists have one of the highest suicide rates among medical professionals, estimated at 58–65 per 100,000, significantly higher than the general population rate of 11 per 100,000. Their risk is attributed to factors such as intense work conditions, perfectionism, the emotional toll from patient suicides, and access to lethal means. Studies also highlight a higher prevalence of depression, anxiety, and substance misuse among psychiatrists. Female psychiatrists face a particularly elevated risk compared to other women. This underscores the need for targeted mental health support and preventive strategies within the profession.

Impact of a Patient's Suicide on a Psychiatrist's Mental Health

The suicide of a patient profoundly impacts psychiatrists' mental health, often leading to emotional distress such as sadness, guilt, self-doubt, anxiety, and even post-traumatic stress disorder (PTSD). Up to 38% report severe distress, with some experiencing lasting effects for months or years. Common reactions include shock, grief, intrusive thoughts, and sleep disturbances. Professionally, it can result in increased caution, reluctance to treat high-risk patients, and career changes. Psychiatrists in training, or those with close therapeutic bonds with the patient, are particularly vulnerable.

Case of Dr Ikenna Erinne

A 36-year-old US-based Nigerian cardiologist, Dr Ikenna Erinne, reportedly died by suicide on 26 January 2025 after losing a child custody battle. The incident occurred following a prolonged divorce case with his ex-wife, which resulted in a court order for him to pay $15,000 monthly in child support. Dr Erinne allegedly shot himself after spending thousands of dollars in legal fees and losing his medical licence during the proceedings.

His father-in-law, Francis Van-Lare, claimed that before his death, Dr Erinne held his ex-wife and children at gunpoint for three hours, prompting police intervention. The tragic event has sparked discussions about the challenges faced by African men in the US legal system. Dr Erinne is survived by his two children, parents, and siblings.

Compelling Types of Personal Stories Related to Faith and Mental Health for Inclusion in a Book

1. **Recovery Through Prayer:** The story of someone who found solace and strength through daily prayer, helping them navigate depression or anxiety.
2. **Faith Overcoming Fear:** An individual who used their faith to overcome deep-seated fears or phobias, finding peace through spiritual teachings.
3. **Community Support:** A person whose mental health journey was significantly supported by a warm and accepting religious community.

4. **Spiritual Awakening:** A journey of someone who experienced a mental health crisis that led to a spiritual awakening, transforming their life perspective.

5. **Integration of Therapy and Faith:** The experience of someone who balanced therapy with faith-based practices, seeing a positive impact on their mental health.

6. **Crisis of Faith:** The story of an individual who went through a crisis of faith during a mental health struggle but emerged with renewed belief and understanding.

7. **Resilience Through Scripture:** The experience of a person who found encouragement and resilience in sacred scriptures during their mental health battles.

8. **Faith Leader's Perspective:** Insight from a religious leader who has personally dealt with mental health issues and used their experience to aid others.

9. **Cultural Impact:** The story of someone from a diverse cultural background who navigates mental health challenges while honouring their faith traditions.

10. **Transformational Retreat:** An experience where attending a faith-based retreat or workshop significantly improved someone's mental health.

11. **Finding Faith in Adversity:** How adversity strengthened a person's faith, leading to improved mental health and a robust support system.

12. **Mindfulness and Meditation:** The story of someone who incorporated faith-inspired mindfulness and meditation practices to manage stress and enhance well-being.

Into the Next Decade

DESTIGMATISING MENTAL HEALTH – LESSONS FROM THE TREATMENT OF FRANK BRUNO BY THE MEDIA

Looking back, Bruno tells *HuffPost UK*:

"The public now seem to have a better understanding. In my situation, it used to be the case where people would cross the road to avoid me, especially after my section in 2003."

It has been over 20 years since headlines like **'Bonkers Bruno Locked Up'** were plastered across *The Sun's* front page. It was 2003, and boxer Frank Bruno had just been sectioned under the Mental Health Act. He was there to receive help, but the tabloid showed little empathy or sensitivity in the way it covered the story. Bruno's journey is described later in the book.

Mental health charity SANE was one of the first to condemn the paper. Marjorie Wallace, the charity's chief executive, said it was an "insult" to Bruno and "damaging to the many thousands of people who endure mental illness". The backlash erupted so quickly that later editions of the paper carried the amended headline, **"Sad Bruno in Mental Home"**.

However, the damage had already been done. It was yet another blow for the sports star, who had retired from boxing in 1996 and was experiencing one of the most difficult periods of his life, navigating grief and divorce, alongside poor mental health.

"I used to hear people say: 'There goes that nutter.'"

The discourse surrounding mental health has changed significantly since then, with the new-found honesty of high-profile sports stars, including Bruno, playing a role.

Bruno began speaking to the media about his mental health issues after he was sectioned again in 2012, following his first admission around 2003. Unhappy with the way he was treated in hospital and the medication he was prescribed, he was persuaded by his agent, Dave Davies, to speak out "on behalf of the silent thousands who undergo the same treatments, but do not have a voice".

Bruno states that he was "wary" of opening up – understandably, given past press coverage – but he spoke to the *Mirror* in what he believes was a landmark moment for conversations and media coverage surrounding mental health.

Supplied by mental health charity SANE

The Sun's front pages when the paper reported on Frank Bruno being sectioned in 2003.

Since then, we have seen mental health become a priority for sports associations across the board – from the FA to Rugby League to the Professional Cricketers' Association – with understanding of mental health and mental illness growing both within the sports industry and among the wider public.

You only need to look at the thousands of people sharing their own experiences of poor mental health in blogs, tweets, social media posts and videos over the past decade to see how much the conversation has changed.

Today, *HuffPost UK* launches its mental health series, *Head In The Game*, in which athletes across a variety of disciplines speak candidly about their mental wellbeing – from occasional periods of poor mental health to ongoing, sometimes debilitating, struggles with mental illness. They also share coping mechanisms and the support they have turned to during their lowest points.

Their stories – and the emotions they have shared with us – will be relatable to many, whether or not you play or watch sport yourself.

Most interviewees touch on pressures particular to their disciplines, but there are factors at play – both personal and work-related – that build up in all our lives. It is a reminder that these people are human, like the rest of us – and nobody is unbreakable.

Getty Images / HuffPost UK

Head In The Game interviewees: (top, left to right) Frank Bruno, Jordanne Whiley, Becky Downie, Elise Christie, Andrew Strauss; (bottom, left to right) Rebecca Adlington, Liam Broady, Eniola Aluko, Marcus Trescothick, Jo Pavey.

Cast your mind back even a decade ago and it would have been difficult to find so many sports people willing to speak openly about their mental health in the press.

In 2008, Marcus Trescothick was the first high-profile active cricketer to go public with his depression and anxiety, an experience he discussed in his book *Coming Back To Me*.

And while the reaction to his honesty was positive – "we've had thousands of people say it's impactful," the retired cricketer tells *HuffPost UK* – the reason behind why he felt compelled to tell the truth is revealing of where the conversation around mental health stood at that time.

"I was constantly going around in circles, speaking to journalists and they were asking what was wrong"

– Marcus Trescothick

"There were a couple of parts to that," Trescothick says ahead of his *Head In The Game* interview. "I needed to tell people my own story. I needed to correct a few inaccuracies that had been written about me in various media outlets. I needed to tell the truth, and I needed to stop hiding away from it." Films often perpetuate several misconceptions about mental illness, creating stereotypes and myths that can affect public perception. Here are some common examples:

1. **Violence and Danger**: Films frequently portray individuals with mental illness as violent or dangerous. However, the majority of people with mental illnesses are not violent and are more likely to be victims rather than perpetrators of violence.

2. **Over-simplification**: Films often reduce mental illness to quirks or singular traits, which does not reflect the complexity of these conditions. This can lead to misunderstandings about the nature and challenges of living with a mental disorder.

3. **Instant Cures**: Many films depict characters overcoming mental illness quickly or through a singular event, such as finding love. In reality, treatment is usually a long-term process that may include therapy, medication, and lifestyle changes.

4. **Heroic Suffering**: Some narratives glorify the suffering associated with mental illness as artistic or essential for genius, which can romanticise genuine and painful experiences.

5. **Stereotypical Characters**: Characters with mental illness in films are often presented as eccentrics, outcasts, or geniuses. This stereotyping marginalises individuals and ignores the diversity of experiences among those with mental health conditions.

6. **Lack of Professional Help**: Films sometimes portray characters overcoming mental health issues without professional support, implying that therapy and medical treatment are unnecessary.

7. **Non-Recognition of Common Disorders**: Films tend to focus on dramatic disorders such as schizophrenia or dissociative identity disorder, while more common conditions such as anxiety or depression are underrepresented.

8. **Extreme Symptoms**: Symptoms of mental illness are often exaggerated for dramatic effect, making them appear more bizarre or severe than they typically are in real life.

9. **Mental Illness as a Plot Device**: Sometimes mental health issues are used merely as a convenient plot twist, rather than genuine aspects of a character's life. This trivialises the reality of living with such conditions.

10. **One-Type-Fits-All**: Legal dramas, thrillers, or horror films sometimes treat mental illness with a one-size-fits-all approach, disregarding the unique experiences and different manifestations of these conditions in reality.

These misconceptions contribute to stigma and misunderstanding, making it harder for those affected to seek help and for society to provide appropriate support and resources.

More accurate and empathetic portrayals can educate audiences and foster understanding.

How can films improve their representation of mental illness?

Improving the representation of mental illness in films requires several key steps:

1. **Research and Authenticity**: Filmmakers should conduct thorough research to ensure accuracy. This means consulting professionals such as psychologists, psychiatrists, and individuals with lived experience.

2. **Avoiding Stereotypes**: It is important to avoid damaging stereotypes, such as portraying individuals as dangerous or unpredictable. Instead, films should reflect a diverse range of experiences and symptoms.

3. **Complex Characters**: Characters with mental health issues should be portrayed as fully developed individuals, with personal stories and traits beyond their condition.

4. **Showing Recovery and Support**: Films should also show the recovery process and the value of support systems, including therapy, medication, and relationships.

5. **Diverse Representation**: Mental illness affects people across all demographics, so films should represent varied backgrounds and cultures. This helps to educate audiences on cultural attitudes towards mental health.

6. **Education Through Storytelling**: Films can be powerful tools for raising awareness, prompting conversations, and spreading accurate information. Including factual elements within the story or as supplementary material can be beneficial.

7. **Collaboration with Advocacy Groups**: Partnering with mental health organisations can ensure depictions are respectful and accurate, while also supporting advocacy and education.

By incorporating these elements, films can improve public understanding of mental illness, reduce stigma, and encourage empathy.

For a better depiction of Tyson Fury's mental health journey, the documentary *Tyson Fury: The Gypsy King* (2020) provides an in-depth look.

It covers his struggles with depression, anxiety, and suicidal thoughts, as well as his comeback in boxing.

The film highlights the support of his family and the importance of speaking openly about mental health challenges.

Additionally, Tyson Fury has been candid in interviews and in his autobiography *Behind the Mask*, detailing his experiences.

His openness helps to destigmatise mental health issues and provides encouragement for others facing similar struggles.

FROM A CAREGIVER MOTHER

The shock of watching your child change suddenly before your eyes and being sectioned is something that cannot be described. In those moments you have no words with which to pray; someone else has to do it for you. And there arises the issue: a diagnosis of mental health is like no other. The stigma attached to it, the shame you feel that you have somehow failed as a parent, prevents you from seeking help from family or friends.

In my case, I continued to work just a few yards away from where my son was sectioned. It was a bank holiday, and I felt I could not call in and ask for leave. Interestingly, no one relieved me of my shift and I continued right up to the point where he was sectioned. I will never forget the psychiatrist who took my hands in hers and reassured me after she had sectioned him.

Kindness that touches you sometimes comes from the most unexpected quarters.

In the ensuing days, witnessing his rage, tears, and vulnerability was different every day. We never knew what to expect. Then, you share small portions of what is happening with family, leaving aside the main story. You might say that your child is going through some difficulties without specifying what they are. People who love you will sustain you in their prayers without asking for details.

In my case, I could not find the words, but some dear friends supported and sustained me. My husband was a revelation—his stoic calmness as our child's mood fluctuated during every painful visit, his patience whilst watching his paranoid outbursts, the love for our child shown in so many ways, visiting him daily when I could not.

Life seemed suspended during those long days and painful nights as I continued to work. You believe that your child will get better, but every visit tests your faith. It is a dark place that I hope no parent ever has to visit. We had a wonderful psychiatrist who firmly believed in our child's recovery and went to great lengths to help him. In a way, his calm confidence helped us too.

In the ensuing months, life continued to fluctuate. There were good days and then very bad days. One day you would feel a glimmer of hope and the next there would be another violent outburst that left you frightened and helpless.

I prayed on some days; I could not on others.

When we thought we were finally getting somewhere, I lost my father—someone my child was very close to. We were back to square one as he suffered a relapse whilst we were thousands of miles away. It took several months for recovery.

In those dark days, what kept me functioning was the realisation that I needed to be there for my child more than ever; the calm patience and the love of my husband; the understanding of a few friends who listened to understand and not to reply.

We are in a better place now. There is always the watchful waiting, the realisation that life will never be the same again, the careful monitoring of his activities to prevent another crisis.

In faith, we walk and look forward to a new tomorrow where we will all be whole again—his father, his sister, and I.

No one goes untouched.

This book is for you if:

- You are exploring or dealing with mental health challenges and looking for guidance through faith.
- You are a member of a religious group interested in the intersection of faith with mental health issues.

- *You are a spiritual seeker, curious about how spirituality and mental well-being are interconnected.*

- *You are a mental health professional, counsellor, therapist, or social worker and you incorporate or integrate spirituality into your practice.*

- *You are clergy or a religious leader, providing spiritual guidance and seeking resources to support your community in dealing with mental health.*

- *You are supporting loved ones with mental health issues, seeking resources that particularly integrate faith-based approaches.*

- *You are a student or scholar researching the role of faith in psychological well-being, and may incorporate this into seminaries or religious studies programmes.*

- *You are interested in holistic care.*

- *You are simply curious.*

GLOSSARY

1. Anxiety: A feeling of worry or fear that can range from mild to severe.

2. Depression: A mood disorder characterised by persistent feelings of sadness and loss of interest.

3. Bipolar Disorder: A mental health condition that causes extreme mood swings, including emotional highs (mania) and lows (depression).

4. Obsessive-Compulsive Disorder (OCD): A disorder where individuals experience recurring, unwanted thoughts (obsessions) and behaviours (compulsions) that they feel compelled to repeat.

5. Post-Traumatic Stress Disorder (PTSD): A disorder that can develop after exposure to a traumatic event, characterised by flashbacks, nightmares, and severe anxiety.

6. Psychotherapy: Also known as talk therapy, this involves treating mental health conditions by engaging in conversation with a mental health professional.

7. Cognitive Behavioural Therapy (CBT): A form of psychotherapy that helps individuals change negative thought patterns and behaviours.

8. Schizophrenia: A severe mental disorder characterised by delusions, hallucinations, and disorganised thinking.

9. Mood Disorders: Psychological disorders characterised by the elevation or lowering of a person's mood, such as depression or bipolar disorder.

10. Personality Disorders: A group of mental health conditions characterised by unhealthy and inflexible personality traits.

11. ADHD (Attention-Deficit/Hyperactivity Disorder): A chronic condition involving attention difficulties, hyperactivity, and impulsiveness.

12. Eating Disorders: Disorders characterised by abnormal or disturbed eating habits, such as anorexia nervosa or bulimia.

13. Mental Health: An individual's condition in relation to their psychological and emotional well-being.

14. Stress: A physical, mental, or emotional factor that causes bodily or mental tension.

15. Resilience: The ability to recover quickly from difficulties or mental health challenges.

16. Self-Care: Activities and practices undertaken regularly to reduce stress and maintain or enhance health and well-being.

17. Stigma: Societal disapproval and discrimination against people with mental health disorders.

18. Mindfulness: A mental state achieved by focusing on the present moment while calmly acknowledging and accepting one's feelings and thoughts.

19. Psychiatrist: A medical doctor specialising in diagnosing and treating mental illness.

20. Therapist: A trained professional who helps individuals improve their mental health through counselling or therapy.

21. Mental Health Services: Professional support and treatment for individuals with mental health issues, such as therapy, counselling, and psychiatric care.

22. Coproduction: A collaborative process where service users (patients) and service providers (health professionals) work together to design, develop, and deliver mental health services. This approach values the input and experiences of users to improve service quality and effectiveness.

23. Colocation: The practice of situating different services or professionals in the same physical location to facilitate integrated care and improve accessibility for patients. In mental health, this might involve placing mental health specialists alongside primary care providers.

24. Integrated Care: A coordinated approach that combines mental health care with general health care services, ensuring comprehensive treatment of the patient's needs.

25. Therapy: A treatment method used by mental health professionals, including talk therapies such as cognitive behavioural therapy (CBT) and psychotherapy, to help individuals manage mental health conditions.

26. Counselling: A form of therapy focusing on providing guidance and support to individuals experiencing psychological challenges or life stresses.

27. Psychiatric Services: Medical treatments provided by licensed psychiatrists, including medication management and diagnosis of mental health disorders.

28. Case Management: A service that involves planning, coordinating, and managing a comprehensive treatment plan for individuals with mental health conditions to help them achieve health goals.

29. Crisis Intervention: Immediate and short-term assistance provided to individuals experiencing a mental health crisis, aiming to stabilise their condition and prevent harm.

30. Peer Support: Support provided by individuals who have personal experience with mental health conditions. Peers offer empathy, understanding, and guidance to others in similar situations.

31. Community Mental Health Services: Localised services offered within the community to support mental wellness and provide treatment outside of hospital settings.

32. Inpatient Care: Hospital-based services where individuals receive intensive mental health treatment and supervision for severe conditions.

33. Outpatient Care: Services provided to individuals who visit a mental health professional for treatment but do not stay overnight in a facility.

34. Residential Treatment: A live-in health care facility providing therapy and a structured environment for individuals with severe mental health issues.

35. Support Groups: Group meetings where individuals with similar mental health challenges come together to share experiences and offer support.

REFERENCES

1. Smokowski PR, Guo S, Rose R, Evans CB, Cotter KL, Bacallao M. Multilevel risk factors and developmental assets for internalizing symptoms and self-esteem in disadvantaged adolescents: modeling longitudinal trajectories from the Rural adaptation project. Dev Psychopathol. 2014;26(4pt2):1495–513. doi: 10.1017/S0954579414001163. [DOI] [PubMed] [Google Scholar]

2. Peterman JS, LaBelle DR, Steinberg L. Devoutly anxious: the relationship between anxiety and religiosity in adolescence. Psychol Relig Spiritual. 2014;6(2):113–122. [Google Scholar]

References

3. World Health Organization. Depression and other common mental disorders: global health estimates. World Health Organization; 2017. https://apps.who.int/iris/bitstream/handle/10665/254610/WHO-MSD-MER-2017.2-eng.pdf. Accessed 05 Nov 2018.

4. Bobinac AM. Comparative Analysis of Curricula for Religious Education: Examples of Four Catholic Countries; 2007. https://pdfs.semanticscholar.org/cd32/1d76ce93f52735b146d4840673ebf3ea6f68.pdf. Accessed 09 Oct 2018.

5. Coleman Elizabeth Burns, White Kevin., editors. Religious Tolerance, Education and the Curriculum. Rotterdam: SensePublishers; 2011. [Google Scholar]

6. Unknown Author. (2020, March 30). *Anxiety and Depression in Children.* Center for Disease Control and

Prevention. https://www.cdc.gov/childrensmentalhealth/depression.html

7. ORCID Dimitris I. Tsomokos http://orcid.org/0000-0002-9613-7823 s AbdAleati, N. S., Mohd Zaharim, N., & Mydin, Y. O. (2016). Religiousness and mental health: Systematic review study. Journal of Religion and Health, 55(6), 1929–1937. https://doi.org/10.1007/s10943-014-9896-1

8. Adedeji, A., Otto, C., Kaman, A., Reiss, F., Devine, J., & Ravens-Sieberer, U. (2022). Peer relationships and depressive symptoms among adolescents: Results from the German BELLA study. Frontiers in Psychology, 12, 767922. https:// doi.org/10.3389/fpsyg.2021.767922

9. https://doi.org/10.1016/j.eurpsy.2014.08.007 Sharpe, H., Fink, E., Duffy, F., & Patalay, P. (2022). Changes in peer and sibling victimization in early adolescence: Longitudinal associations with multiple indices of mental health in a prospective birth cohort study. European Child & Adolescent Psychiatry, 31(5), 737–746.

10. https://doi.org/10.1007/s00787-020-01708-z Singh, S. P., Winsper, C., Wolke, D., & Bryson, A. (2014). School mobility and prospective pathways to psychotic-like symptoms in early adolescence: A prospective birth cohort study. Journal of the American Academy of Child & Adolescent Psychiatry, 53(5), 518–527.e1.

11. https://doi.org/10.1016/j.jaac.2014.01.016 Slavich, G. M. (2020). Social safety theory: A biologically based evolutionary perspective on life stress, health, and behavior. Annual Review of Clinical Psychology, 16(1), 265–295.

12. https://doi.org/10.1146/annurev-clinpsy032816-045159 Slavich, G. M. (2022). Social Safety Theory: Understanding social stress, disease risk, resilience, and behaviour during the COVID-19 pandemic and beyond. Current Opinion in Psychology, 45, 101299.

13. https://doi.org/10.1016/j. copsyc.2022.101299 Slavich, G. M., O'Donovan, A., Epel, E. S., & Kemeny, M. E. (2010). Black sheep get the blues: A psychobiological model of social rejection and depression. Neuroscience & Biobehavioral Reviews, 35(1), 39–45.

14. https://doi.org/ 10.1016/j.neubiorev.2010.01.003 Slavich, G. M., Roos, L. G., Mengelkoch, S., Webb, C. A., Shattuck, E. C., Moriarity, D. P., & Alley, J. C. (2023). Social Safety Theory: Conceptual foundation, underlying mechanisms, and future directions. Health Psychology Review, 17(1), 5–59.

15. https://doi.org/10.1080/17437199.2023.2171900 Smart, N. (1996). Dimensions of the sacred: An anatomy of the world's beliefs. Univ of California Press. Smith, S. L., Ramey, E., Sisson, S. B., Richardson, S., & DeGrace, B. W. (2020). The family meal model: Influences on family mealtime participation. OTJR: Occupation, Participation and Health, 40(2), 138–146.

16. https://doi.org/10. 1177/1539449219876878 SOM. (2023). Religious faith, trust, and depression: Supplemental Online Material. Retrieved June 20, 2023, from

17. https://doi.org/10.17605/OSF.IO/M9EKJ Sosis, R. (2005). Does religion promote trust?: The role of signaling, reputation, and punishment. Interdisciplinary Journal of Research on Religion, 1, 1–30. Sosis, R., & Alcorta, C. (2003). Signaling, solidarity, and the sacred: The evolution

of religious behavior. Evolutionary Anthropology: Issues, News, and Reviews, 12(6), 264–274.

18. https://doi.org/10.1002/evan.10120 Steger, M. F., & Frazier, P. (2005). Meaning in life: One link in the chain from religiousness to well-being. Journal of Counseling Psychology, 52(4), 574–582. https://doi.org/10.1037/0022-0167.52.4.574 Tabak, B. A., Leng, G., Szeto, A., Parker, K. J., Verbalis, J. G., Ziegler, T. E., Lee, M. R., Neumann, I. D., & Mendez, A. J. (2023). Advances in human oxytocin measurement: Challenges and proposed solutions. Molecular Psychiatry, 28(1), 127–140.

19. https://doi.org/10.1038/s41380-022-01719-z Thapar, A., Collishaw, S., Pine, D. S., & Thapar, A. K. (2012). Depression in adolescence. The Lancet, 379(9820), 1056–1067.

20. https://doi.org/10.1016/S0140-6736(11)60871-4 Therriault, D., Lemelin, J.-P., Toupin, J., & Déry, M. (2021). Factors associated with parent-adolescent attachment relationship quality: A longitudinal study. Adolescents, 1(2), 159–174.

21. https://doi.org/10.3390/adolescents1020013 Tiliouine, H., Cummins, R. A., & Davern, M. (2009). Islamic religiosity, subjective well-being, and health. Mental Health, Religion & Culture, 12(1), 55–74.

22. https://doi.org/10.1080/13674670802118099 RELIGION, BRAIN & BEHAVIOR 17 Tomova, L., Andrews, J. L., & Blakemore, S.-J. (2021). The importance of belonging and the avoidance of social risk taking in adolescence. Developmental Review, 61, 100981.

23. https://doi.org/10.1016/j.dr.2021.100981 Tsomokos, D. I., & Flouri, E. (2023). Superior social cognitive abilities in childhood are associated with better reward seeking

strategies in adolescence: Evidence for a social-motivational flexibility model. Advances.in/Psychology, 01, 1–19.

24. Koenig, H. G., & Larson, D. B. (2001): This study reviewed the effects of religion and spirituality on mental health, finding that religious involvement is associated with better outcomes in various mental health conditions, including depression and anxiety.

25. Ano, G. G., & Vasconcelles, E. B. (2005): A meta-analytic investigation that confirmed the positive correlation between religious coping and psychological

26. Bilsen J. Suicide and Youth: Risk Factors. Front Psychiatry. 2018 Oct 30;9:540. doi: 10.3389/fpsyt.2018.00540. PMID: 30425663; PMCID: PMC6218408.

27. References

28. Turecki G, Brent D. Suicide and suicidal behaviouir. Lancet (2016) 387:1227–39. 10.1016/S0140-6736(15)00234-2 [DOI] [PMC free article] [PubMed] [Google Scholar]

29. WHO Preventing Suicide: A Global Imperative Geneva: World Health Organisation; (2014). Available online at: http://www.who.int/mental_health/suicide-prevention/world_report_2014/en/ [Google Scholar]

30. WHO Global Health Observatory. Geneva: World Health Organisation; (2017). Available online at: http://www.who.int/gho [Google Scholar]

31. Hawton K, Van Heeringen K. Suicide. Lancet (2009) 373:1372–81. 10.1016/S0140-6736(09)60372-X [DOI] [PubMed] [Google Scholar]

32. De Leo D. Can we rely on suicide morality data? Crisis (2015) 36:1–3. 10.1027/0227-5910/a000315 [DOI] [PubMed] [Google Scholar]

33. .Borges G, Nock MK, Haro Abad JM, Hwang I, Sampson NA, Alonso J, et al. Twelve-month prevalence of and risk factors for suicide attempts in the World Health Organization World Mental Health Surveys. J Clin Psychiatry (2010) 71:1617–28. 10.4088/JCP.08m04967blu [DOI] [PMC free article] [PubMed] [Google Scholar]

34. Nock MK, Borges G, Bromet EJ, Alonso J, Angermeyer M, Beautrais A, et al. Cross-national prevalence and risk factors for suicidal ideation, plans and attempts. Br J Psychiatry (2008) 192:98–105. 10.1192/bjp.bp.107.040113 [DOI] [PMC free article] [PubMed] [Google Scholar]

35. WHO Mental Health Geneva: World Health Organisation; (2018). Available online at: http://www.who.int/mental_health/en/ [Google Scholar]

36. Värnik P. Suicide in the World. Int J Environ Res Public Health (2012) 9:760–71. 10.3390/ijerph9030760 [DOI] [PMC free article] [PubMed] [Google Scholar]

37. WHO Global Health Observatory Adolescent Health. Geneva: Word Health Organisation; (2017). Available online at: http://apps.who.int/gho/data/view.wrapper.MortAdov?lang=en [Google Scholar]

38. Eurostat Satistics Explained. Being Young in Europe today. European Union (2017). Available online at: http://ec.europa.eu/eurostat/statistics-

explained/index.php/Being_young_in_Europe_today_-_healthMain_tables

39. Furlong A. Youth Studies: An Introduction. New York, NY: Routledge; (2013). [Google Scholar]

40. Orbach I. Suicide prevention for adolescents. In: King R, Apter A. editors. Suicide in Children and Adolescents. Cambridge: Cambridge University Press; (2006), pp.1–40. [Google Scholar]

41. Patton GC, Sawyer SM, Santelli JS, Ross DA, Afifi R, Allen NB, et al. Our future: a Lancet commission on adolescent health and wellbeing. Lancet (2016) 387:2423–78. 10.1016/S0140-6736(16)00579-1 [DOI] [PMC free article] [PubMed] [Google Scholar]

42. Hawton K, Appleby L, Platt S, Foster T, Cooper J, Malmberg A, et al. The psychological autopsy approach to studying suicide: a review of methodological issues. J Affect Disord (1998) 50:269–76. [DOI] [PubMed] [Google Scholar]

43. Van Heeringen K. The suicidal process and related concepts. In: van Heeringen K. editor. Understanding Suicidal Behaviour. Chichester: John Wiley & Sons Ltd; (2001). pp. 136–59. [Google Scholar]

44. Bridge JA, Goldstein TR, Brent DA. Adolescent suicide and suicidal behavior. J Child Psychol Psychiatry (2006) 47:372–94. 10.1111/j.1469-7610.2006.01615.x [DOI] [PubMed] [Google Scholar]

45. Pelkonen M, Marttunen M. Child and adolescent suicide: epidemiology, risk factors, and approaches to prevention. Paediatr Drugs (2003) 5:243–65. 10.2165/00128072-200305040-00004 [DOI] [PubMed] [Google Scholar]

46. Gould MS. Suicide and the media. Ann N Y Acad Sci. (2001) 932:200–21. discussion 21–4. 10.1111/j.1749-6632.2001.tb05807.x [DOI] [PubMed] [Google Scholar]

47. Palmer BA, Pankratz VS, Bostwick JM. The lifetime risk of suicide in schizophrenia—a reexamination. Arch Gen Psychiatry (2005) 62:247–53. 10.1001/archpsyc.62.3.247 [DOI] [PubMed] [Google Scholar]

48. Cooper J, Kapur N, Webb R, Lawlor M, Guthrie E, Mackway-Jones K, et al. Suicide after deliberate self-harm: a 4-year cohort study. Am J Psychiatry (2005) 162:297–303. 10.1176/appi.ajp.162.2.297 [DOI] [PubMed] [Google Scholar]

49. Apter A, Wasserman D. Adolescent attempted suicide. In: King R, Apter A. editors. Suicide in Children and Adolescents. Cambridge: Cambridge University Press; (2006). pp. 63–85. [Google Scholar]

50. Gould M, Shaffer D, Greenberg T. The epidemiology of youth suicide. In: King R, Apter A. editors. Suicide in Children and Adolescents. Cambridge: Cambridge University Press; (2006). pp. 1–40. [Google Scholar]

51. Brent D, Mann J. Familial factors in adolescent suicidal behaviour. In: King R, Apter A. editors. Suicide in Children and Adolescents. Cambridge: Cambridge University Press; (2006). pp. 86–117. [Google Scholar]

52. Portzky G, Audenaert K, van Heeringen K. Suicide among adolescents. A psychological autopsy study of psychiatric, psychosocial and personality-related risk factors. Soc Psychiatry Psychiatr Epidemiol. (2005) 40:922–30. 10.1007/s00127-005-0977-x [DOI] [PubMed] [Google Scholar]

53. Bondy B, Buettner A, Zill P. Genetics of suicide. Mol Psychiatry (2006) 11:336–51. 10.1038/sj.mp.4001803 [DOI] [PubMed] [Google Scholar]

54. Agerbo E, Nordentoft M, Mortensen PB. Familial, psychiatric, and socioeconomic risk factors for suicide in young people: nested case-control study. BMJ (2002) 325:74–77. 10.1136/bmj.325.7355.74 [DOI] [PMC free article] [PubMed] [Google Scholar]

55. Gould M, Fisher P, Parides M, Flory M, Shaffer D. Psychosocial risk factors of child and adolescent completed suicide. Arch Gen Psychiatry (1996) 53:1155–62. [DOI] [PubMed] [Google Scholar]

56. .Im Y, Oh WO, Suk M. Risk Factors for suicide ideation among adolescents: five-year national data analysis. Arch Psychiatr Nurs. (2017) 31:282–6. 10.1016/j.apnu.2017.01.001 [DOI] [PubMed] [Google Scholar]

57. Spirito A, Esposito-Smythers C. Attempted and completed suicide in adolescence. Ann Rev Clin Psychol (2006) 2: 237–66. 10.1146/annurev.clinpsy.2.022305.095323 [DOI] [PubMed] [Google Scholar]

58. Amitai M, Apter A. Social aspects of suicidal behavior and prevention in early life: a review. Int J Environ Res Public Healt. (2012) 9:985–94. 10.3390/ijerph9030985 [DOI] [PMC free article] [PubMed] [Google Scholar]

59. Soole R, Kõlves K, De Leo D. Suicide in children: a systematic review. Arch Suicide Res. (2015) 19:285–304. 10.1080/13811118.2014.996694 [DOI] [PubMed] [Google Scholar]

60. Cheng A, Chen T, Chen C, Jenkins R. Psychosocial and psychiatric risk factors for suicide. Br J Psychiatry (2000)

177:360–5. 10.1192/bjp.177.4.360 [DOI] [PubMed] [Google Scholar]

61. Klomek AB, Sourander A, Niemela S, Kumpulainen K, Piha J, Tamminen T, et al. Childhood bullying behaviors as a risk for suicide attempts and completed suicides: A population-based birth cohort study. J Am Acad Child Adolesc Psychiatry (2009) 48:254–61. 10.1097/CHI.0b013e318196b91f [DOI] [PubMed] [Google Scholar]

62. Pirkis J, Mok K, Robinson J, Nordentoft M. Media influences on suicidal thouthts and behaviors. In: O'Connor RC, Perkis J. editors. International Handbook of Suicide Prevention, 2nd Edn, Chichester: John Wiley & Sons; (2016). pp. 745–58. [Google Scholar]

63. O'Connor R, Pirkis J. Suicide clusters. In: O'Connor RC, Perkis J. editors. International Handbook of Suicide Prevention, 2nd Edn. Chichester: John Wiley & Sons; (2016). pp. 758–74. [Google Scholar]

64. Yip PSF, Caine E, Yousuf S, Chang SS, Wu KC, Chen YY. Means restriction for suicide prevention. Lancet (2012) 379:2393–9. 10.1016/S0140-6736(12)60521-2 [DOI] [PMC free article] [PubMed] [Google Scholar]

65. Florentine JB, Crane C. Suicide prevention by limiting access to methods: a review of theory and practice. Soc Sci Med. (2010) 70:1626–32. 10.1016/j.socscimed.2010.01.029 [DOI] [PubMed] [Google Scholar]

66. Biddle L, Donovan J, Hawton K, Kapur N, Gunnell D. Suicide and the internet. BMJ (2008) 336:800–2. 10.1136/bmj.39525.442674.A [DOI] [PMC free article] [PubMed] [Google Scholar]

67. Dunlop SM, More E, Romer D. Where do youth learn about suicides on the Internet, and what influence does this have on suicidal ideation? J Child Psychol Psychiatry (2011) 52:1073–80. 10.1111/j.1469-7610.2011.02416.x [DOI] [PubMed] [Google Scholar]

68. .Calear AL, Christensen H, Freeman A, Fenton K, Busby Grant J, van Spijker B, et al. A systematic review of psychosocial suicide prevention interventions for youth. Eur Child Adolesc Psychiatry (2016) 25:467–82. 10.1007/s00787-015-0783-4 [DOI] [PubMed] [Google Scholar]

www.ingramcontent.com/pod-product-compliance
Lightning Source LLC
Chambersburg PA
CBHW060048230426
43661CB00004B/706